9-22-99

GLORIA STUART

GLORIA STUART

I just kept hoping

GLORIA STUART

with SYLVIA THOMPSON

LITTLE, BROWN AND COMPANY

BOSTON NEW YORK LONDON

Copyright © 1999 by Gloria Stuart Sheekman and Sylvia Thompson

FIRST EDITION

Robert Benchley's recipes for New England Boiled Dressing for
Boiled New Englanders, Moulded Salmon, and Cucumber Sauce
used by permission of Peter Benchley.

"Résumé," copyright 1926, 1928, renewed 1954, © 1956 by Dorothy
Parker, from THE PORTABLE DOROTHY PARKER by Dorothy
Parker. Used by permission of Viking Penguin, a division of Penguin
Putnam Inc.

Ward Ritchie's poems and his letter to Gloria Stuart used by
permission of Jonathan B. Ritchie, Duncan W. Ritchie, and
Mark Detrick.

Ward Ritchie's poem "The World began . . ." and Lawrence Clark
Powell's note to Gloria Stuart used by permission of Lawrence
Clark Powell.

Library of Congress Cataloging-in-Publication Data
Stuart, Gloria.
    Gloria Stuart : I just kept hoping / Gloria Stuart with
Sylvia Thompson. — 1st ed.
       p.   cm.
    ISBN 0-316-81571-3
       1. Stuart, Gloria.   2. Motion picture actors and actresses —
United States Biography.   I. Thompson, Sylvia Vaughn Sheekman.
II. Title.
PN2287.S789A3   1999
791.43'028'092 — dc21
[B]   99-24234

10 9 8 7 6 5 4 3 2 1

MV-NY

Printed in the United States of America

For my beloved daughter and son-in-law,

Sylvia and Gene Thompson,

all my devoted thanks

Gloria Stuart

1

According to legend, my seaside hometown was named Santa Monica because its streams were so sparkling and full it reminded the Spanish fathers of Saint Monica's tears for her son's salvation. Santa Monica was put on the map by the explorer-soldier Portolá. Santa Monica Bay is a crescent, with Point Dume to the west and Palos Verdes to the south. It was called the Bay of a Thousand Candles by Cabrillo and other Spanish explorers, because the Indians built their campfires on top of the Palisades. These bluffs run between 50 and 250 feet high, then slope gently down to the beach. Palm trees along the top of the Palisades were not very high when I was not very high. Looking at them now, they're very, very tall. The Palisades palms fill me with nostalgia and a sense of growing old.

In the sea, when I was a child, there were seals and dolphins very close to shore, and the whales were very evident going south. There were acres and acres of rosy seaweed above the water, and we were always warned never to swim into a bed of it, that we would be caught and entangled and probably drown. That seaweed disappeared during the First World War, because it was harvested for medicines. Mama said iodine. And it has never reappeared. There are very few seals anymore, or sea lions, or dolphins. I don't remember sharks ever being spoken of. But certainly over a period of years we have had sharks in the Santa Monica Bay.

And every once in a while way offshore you can see a few whales going south. But today, Heal the Bay is the new ploy. Against pollution, you know, chum.

There were pelicans and gulls over the ocean — still are, but cranes in the wetlands around Venice are rare. Tiny blue butterflies, once in the thousands, are now nearly extinct.

When we stood on the Palisades, we looked across to China. Behind us were the San Gabriel Mountains, snow-covered in winter. There were no houses on the beach. The Santa Monica Pier was there, and way in the distance, to the south, a Pier off Ocean Park, now gone. Then way, way in the distance we saw the Venice Pier — until it burned. My brother came home after dark one night from his newspaper bike route with the news the Pier was burning. Daddy bundled us up into the car — an early open Studebaker — and drove down to the Venice beach.

It was a Fire! The beach was crowded with people, and, as the great dome over the ballroom at the end of the Pier collapsed into the sea, we all ooh ohh ohhed sadly, secretly thrilled at witnessing something so spectacular.

The aquarium went, too. I remember Mama saying she hoped "the poor things" made it into the ocean.

We agreed.

Skies were clear blue always — no smog. In the spring, from Sixth Street, where we lived, as far as we could see, fields of poppies, Indian paintbrush, johnny-jump-ups, wild iris, monkey faces, clover, and great patches of lupine and mustard gently rolled up toward the hills to the east. Today they're called the Hollywood Hills, but in those days, they were just The Mountains.

And off to our right, to the north, the Santa Monica Mountains, far enough away to silhouette darkly against the horizon. There are still deer in those mountains, coyote, rabbits, squirrels, possums. There were mountain lions, rattlesnakes, king snakes, garter snakes. On the road along the Pacific Ocean, up to Topanga Canyon, I remember hundreds and hundreds of what we called

Our Lord's Candles. Yucca, very tall with white blossoms. Picture ten-to-fifteen-feet-high bare stalks covered with dozens of lily-shaped waxy flowers. They dotted the hillsides singly up and down the slopes. Today, one or two to a hillside. Maybe. We used to dig one up after a weekend in my family's cabin in Topanga, and plant it on the front lawn at home. Eventually it was against the law to remove yucca from the mountains — which it should have been in the beginning.

Once, our father was driving us up the narrow road toward Topanga Canyon to watch one of our almost yearly brushfires, when we were stopped and he was commandeered to help fight that fire. Taken right out of the car that minute by two forest rangers! We didn't see him for several days, and I remember Mama driving us back up to find out about him, and the forest ranger saying he didn't know where Daddy was, but no one had been killed. My father didn't do that again. He decided the fires looked even more spectacular from what is now known as Pacific Palisades.

An orphan at fifteen, Mama went to work in the Ocean Park post office three years later. She became a clerk for the postmaster, Mr. Stilson. He and his wife befriended her. Around that time, my aunt Nellie Deidrick was listed in the Ocean Park telephone directory as a "seamstress." Uncle Jesse Deidrick was a "grocery clerk."

Then Frank Stewart, a law student moonlighting as a postal inspector, walked into Mama's life. He was a stern and handsome Scot born in The Dalles, Oregon — The Dalles is perched on the great Columbia River, and was the end of the Oregon Trail. Frank Stewart's family were farmers (related, Mama said, to Mary, Queen of Scots), but he went to San Francisco to study law, then came down to Los Angeles. In time, he proposed marriage to Alice Deidrick. Mama proudly told how her friends Colonel and Mrs. Scofield gave her a first-class wedding, complete with a silver flatware service, a huge brass samovar, cut-glass crystal bowls, china, even monogrammed linens — all for a nobody postal clerk!

My dear father booked a drawing room on the Southern Pacific Railroad train for San Francisco for their wedding night. It's not my idea of "thoughtfulness." All those whistles and tunnels.

In nine months, me.

(When I was in my twenties, Mama confided that on her wedding night and for almost a week after, she was so terrified at the prospect of intercourse she cried most of the time and couldn't cooperate!)

I was born around eleven o'clock at night on the Fourth of July, 1910. My mother said, "Honey, it was getting so close to midnight, the midwife kept saying, 'Push harder, harder' — I *had* to have you on the Fourth of July!" I was delivered on the dining room table (it seems a curious place, now that I think of it). Years later, I had my tonsils removed on that same table.

Eleven months after me came Boy. Boy's real name was Frank. Two years later came another baby boy, Thomas, named after both Mama's and Daddy's fathers. When I was three, suddenly Boy and I couldn't leave the house to play with our neighborhood friends. Our tiny brother was very sick and we were quarantined — it was spinal meningitis. Tommy died, but all it meant to me was that we could go out and play again.

In those days, women wore lockets holding a lock of hair. Years later, I realized that the blond curl in Mama's locket was from Tommy.

The attention my looks received probably affected the filial relationship between my brother and me.

I vividly remember sitting next to him on a bench in Palisades Park complete with an enormous stand-up, six-inch-wide pink-striped silk hair ribbon clamped to my blond Dutch cut — we were six and five — with passersby admiring me, and Boy loudly piping up, "Look at *me!* Look at *me!*" And he *was* a handsome little boy. But nobody noticed.

Despite this, I confess I was jealous of my brother when I was little. That's because Mama spent most of her time with him, driving him around to confer with doctors and charlatans, faith healers, and orthopedic specialists. She was searching for a way to heal Boy's leg. He had suffered an attack of infantile paralysis at the age of eleven months. It was misdiagnosed as a broken leg and put in a plaster cast, where it withered.

My father had been determined that Boy not use his paralysis negatively. But the methods Daddy used seem to me today very unwise — certainly unhappy. He devised games for the two of us after dinner. In one, we stood together, Daddy threw a beanbag across the room, and we scrambled for it. I always won. I was taller and almost a year older than Boy and not handicapped. Sometimes, Daddy threw pennies. I got those first, too.

Daddy also took Boy to the Ocean Park Plunge, a bathhouse where Boy learned to dive from a very high springboard — one small withered leg clinging in midair against his good one. The ocean waves were too strong for him, though he could wade out in calm water and dive over a wave, then swim in deeper water. But I was the original seal, riding the waves, diving under the big ones fearlessly. If I believed in such things, it's not surprising that I was born under a water sign.

Once, as a child, I asked my mother why I wasn't a princess. Her answer, "Because you have to be born a princess."

And I asked, "How do I do that?"

It has occurred to me that everything that I have wanted to do, to excel in, has had to do with theatrics. Starting with wanting to be an actress to display myself. For applause.

For me, giving parties, for example, is almost the same as going on stage. The door opens, the audience arrives, the curtain goes up, you walk out of the kitchen, and you have lines. In both cases, if you're good, there *is* applause, a feeling of great satisfaction, involvement, happiness, and recognition.

One of my favorite entertainments was a dinner party I gave in the 1930s for a Major Grey — but not *the* Major Grey of chutney fame — when he visited from England. He was a friend of a friend of ours, and I thought it would be very amusing to have a curry dinner, and to serve the other Major Grey's famous chutney.

Back in those prewar days, when we entertained, my friends and I outdid each other with finger bowls. Beautiful French or English or Irish crystal finger bowls set on flowery plates. Flowers floated in the bowls — sometimes, in green- or blue-colored water. Plus exquisitely fine linen doilies, probably four inches across, with beautiful lace edges and embroidery.

For Major Grey's dinner, it occurred to me it might be fun to have a duck with the finger bowls — a live duck, because ducks eat, then sip water in between nibbles.

So the finger bowls were finally served, naturally with little flowers. And then the lovely fat mallard duckling was let loose on the table. I put some duck food in my finger bowl, and "it" — I don't know whether it was a she or a he — ducked in and out, other guests followed, sprinkling duck food into their finger bowls. Major Grey loved the party. "This is *really* Hollywood!" he said.

Once, an interviewer asked me the inspiration of my frequent party-giving, especially my holiday celebrations. I suddenly knew it was because, when I was a child, Mama celebrated everything.

On May Day, we painted berry baskets and filled them with flowers from our garden, then left them early in the morning on neighbors' porches. For Decoration Day, we made wreaths of greens and took them down to the Santa Monica Pier to toss into the ocean in memory of "the brave men who gave their lives for our country," as Mama put it. April Fools' Day meant salt in our father's sugar bowl, a full purse on the sidewalk attached to an invisible thread attached to a lamppost — Mama! Lincoln's Birthday we reread the Gettysburg Address at dinner. Washington's Birthday fresh cherry pie and the retelling of the story about the tree — "I cannot tell a lie."

And, of course, for my Fourth of July birthday, Mama always made me a three-story red, white, and blue cake topped with candles and sparklers. My lawyer father had many Chinese clients and friends who sent me wonderful fireworks, which we set up in the backyard. One year, one set, lighted on the end, spelled out letter by letter, "Happy Birthday Gloria!"

Mama was a wonderful cook. When I was growing up, Sunday dinner would be a roast of chicken, lamb, pork, or beef. Mashed potatoes with creamy gravy made with chicken or beef fat, fresh green peas, hot biscuits with butter and jam or honey. In spring, there would be wild mustard greens gathered from the vacant lot next door. (Boy and I hated vegetables — I still do.) For dessert would come Mama's fresh devil's food cake, or a fresh lemon cream pie, or, if we were really lucky, her superb fresh coconut cake. It took six hours to make that cake, because she started by grating fresh coconuts.

To help her prepare these dinners, Mama usually had Indian help, girls from the reservation near Riverside who also helped keep our house clean. For some reason, they always seemed to be named Penny.

Even though Mama gave our family a lovely calendar of celebratory days — and there was always room for spontaneous excitement — strange to say, I have no memory of my mother's laughter. But I do recall the first time she was in tears. We were eating dinner around our dining table, Mama said something, and my father said, "Alice, shut up!" We three burst into tears. That, then, was the equivalent of today's "Alice, fuck off!"

There were more tears after my father had been diagnosed with tuberculosis, and Mama had to take Daddy to a sanitarium. For over a year we drove up to see him every Sunday, an hour's ride or so. Daddy was considered contagious, so Boy and I had to stay outside the screened porch while Mama went in and sat with him. We played jacks and marbles and read our children's books, and munched Cracker Jack or Animal Crackers.

When Daddy finally came home, he spent most of the day in a darkened living room, sitting in a fat brown leather upholstered chair. Even before his illness, my father was close to being a dour Scot, and he'd spent most of the time he was home in his study, reading his big law books. But he had never sat in a chair for so many hours before and I wondered about it. I know now that he must have been depressed.

When I was nine, my father was nominated to be a judge. I don't remember which court it was, but Boy and I understood that this was something exciting for our family. For Mama, it meant a secure future for the first time in her life, a position in Santa Monica social circles, a rainbow arching the blue sky.

As it was and still is in small, closely knit communities, an important part of Mama's social life was going to church. Her family had, for generations, belonged to the Christian Church. Boy and I went to Sunday school at Santa Monica's First Christian Church for a while with Mama. Then, when I kicked my third-grade teacher at Roosevelt School in her behind and was expelled, Mama put me into Catholic school for the fourth grade. But I didn't have to go to church, just morning prayer. Daddy had been a Presbyterian, but left that essentially Scottish church to become a Christian Scientist. Eventually, my father took Boy and me to Christian Science Sunday school. Mama was taking from the Episcopalians by then, but she didn't object to our going off in another direction. So my religious education was a patchwork.

Daddy believed Christian Science had helped cure him of tuberculosis. One evening not long after his appointment to the bench, as he was coming home from a Christian Science church meeting, a car backed into him and severely injured his leg. There were no antibiotics then, and nothing stopped the spread of infection. My father died two weeks later, leaving Mama with two children, no savings, and no means of support. I was nine, and Boy eight. Mama was thirty-five.

Mama rented out our house. We never saw the inside again, or our yard that had been teeming with animals — rabbits in a hutch, chickens in their coop, a goat, pigeons, our dogs and cats, peanut-eating blue jay "Charlie," and frisky gray squirrels. We also had a swing and a teeter-totter, and I had a little electric stove in a playhouse my father had built for me — I baked all sorts of cookies and made wonderful little doughnuts (interesting that Mama let me cook with hot oil, but she did). There was a peach tree I grew from a kernel — by then, it was five or six feet high. And the Rain Barrel. It furnished Mama and me soft water to wash our hair with occasionally (shampoo was unknown).

We moved across the alley into a cottage on a friend's back lot. It had a small kitchen and bedroom, and a very small bathroom. I slept with Mama and Boy slept on a cot.

That Christmas an Elks club basket was delivered to us in the little cottage. Mama cried all day. My father had been an Exalted Ruler at the Elks club, and she must have felt complete humiliation.

Mama went back to work in the post office — in Sawtelle this time, part of West Los Angeles. In a year or so, one of her customers began to court her. Fred J. Finch was a large, gruff man, lacking my father's refinement. But he wasn't as dour, either. He was a successful businessman, owning a large funeral parlor in Sawtelle, and had interests in a Santa Monica bank. He loved taking Mama on trips in his showy Pierce-Arrow.

Mama accepted Mr. Finch's proposal and they were married.

I was "in summer exile" at my aunt Nellie's home in Dinuba and met my stepfather weeks later.

He was initially kind to Boy and me, and, after several years, Mama and he had a baby girl, Patricia Marie.

I was so introspective that period, so self-preoccupied, I don't remember the pregnancy, the birth, Patsy's existence.

I always hated being "ordinary," which was reflected in the fact that I had the highest demerit record of any student in the history of Santa Monica High School up until that time! One reason was because I kept breaking the dress code. I just simply couldn't stand navy blue middies and skirts. I wanted to wear my own things. So I did. And I would be given a demerit or sent home to change. I was in revolt. So what else is new?

In those days — the days of flappers! — my high school friends and I were trying very hard to be very sophisticated like Clara Bow, the "It" girl (from the 1927 film of that name). We formed a sorority in school, which was not allowed, but we had one anyway. We were the (to us) top thirteen girls at school, and we called ourselves the "Damma Goto Helltas."

To date a boy with a red Stutz Bear Cat was the number one priority. Four of my friends had roadsters. After school, we'd drive up the Pacific Coast Highway to a hot dog stand. Around four-thirty we'd have hot dogs, then we'd drive back to an ice cream parlor and have a triple triple chocolate soda. Then we'd go home and have dinner, and then every so often, after dinner, we'd have a secret meeting with snacks. And, if possible, go outdoors and smoke cigarettes — Milo Violets, purple-paper-wrapped cigarettes with gold foil tips! I soaked blotters with Coty's Emeraude and layered non–Milo Violets in between. Emeraude cigarettes! We were intent on being wild! On weekends, we and our dates snuck into speakeasies, lying about our age. We read George Jean Nathan and H. L. Mencken, and pretended we believed in nothing; prattled as often as anyone would listen to us about nihilism. There's no point in anything. Live for the moment, enjoy! enjoy! Hedonistic notions. Quite childish, quite immature, but very compelling for us. We wanted to be terribly intellectual, to be connoisseurs — critics of the novelist, critics of the artist, critics of the composer, critics of the whole scene.

I wanted to be a writer, so the summer of my high school junior year, 1926, I signed up for classes in short story and poetry writing.

And asked to be a "girl reporter" at the *Santa Monica Outlook*. Hired, but no salary. Did high school and church news.

I also enrolled in an acting class where I met my first lover, Carl Meyer.

What a summer! I was on my way.

I wanted desperately to go to college. Translation: Leave Home.

Mama was agreeable, actually eager for me to go to college. But there wasn't money for it. My stepfather, who had been a thorn in my side from Day One, had a suggestion, which he made often enough — "You want to do something big and great, I'll get you a job in a circus washing elephants."

Yes, I did want to do "something big and great." I'd wanted to as long as I could remember.

In spite of Fred J. Finch, I made it to college. Mama secretly borrowed two hundred dollars from an old friend of my father's, Dr. Howard Levengood in Santa Monica, and made me promise not to tell my stepfather. It was enough to cover two semesters of the University of California at Berkeley (tuition: $25, room and board: $75). Books would be extra, of course, but not fatally so. My brother became Frank Finch, finished college, and became a top sports writer for the *Los Angeles Times*.

As for doing "something big and great," well maybe all the things I've done haven't wound up being great, but I've tried my damnedest. And I've never stopped hoping — as an actress, an artist, a printer, even as a writer — for great roles, great adventures, great things.

I became a movie star — capital M, capital S — by the time I was in my twenties! Then, sixty years later, I landed a role in the most successful film in history and was nominated by several groups of film aficionados as Best Supporting Actress.

And still nary an elephant in sight!

2

I guess you could say I really *was* a dish.

"Gloria's a legendary beauty," Groucho Marx once told my son-in-law, Gene Thompson. I was surprised to hear it because Groucho was always wary of me. But he once did say to my face, "You're a beautiful broad." I suppose that did seem to be the general Hollywood consensus.

A typical list of beauties in the thirties — the years I was in film — reads as follows (from the magazine *Screen Play*, October 1932):

Marlene Dietrich	Tallulah Bankhead
Greta Garbo	Gloria Stuart
Jean Harlow	Kay Francis
Joan Crawford	Janet Gaynor
Norma Shearer	Virginia Bruce

It's not my fault! Blame my mudder and my fadder!

I would rather have been listed as one of the ten most talented, but that was not to be. The roles the studios gave me resulted in only casual-to-satisfactory mention. Still, I confess that I had so much attention, from the press, the movie studio, the public, certainly my family and friends, that I felt like a movie star. Or should I say, I felt like a movie star should feel!

When I began in film, I was twenty-one, fresh from a wonderfully bohemian life in an artists' colony in Northern California.

I was married to my college sweetheart, a handsome young sculptor, Gordon Newell.

When studio publicists learned I advocated what was then termed "free love," they had a heyday, and suddenly articles about me started popping up in fan magazines. The articles provoked a lot of interest, positive and negative, but I stood my ground — or rather, made my bed — and experimented a bit. Gordon and I had an agreement that either of us could have an affair — but we would first tell the other person that we were going to.

I had had a yen for many many many years for someone I had gone to school with. Since kindergarten, actually. He had come back into my life after I'd returned to Southern California. I was playing at the Pasadena Playhouse in the balcony scene from *Romeo and Juliet* as a curtain-raiser with Douglass Montgomery. Gordon was still at our home in Carmel. I was living with Morrie Ankrum, one of the directors at Pasadena Playhouse, and his wife, Betty.

So I invited my friend to come over and see me and the show and spend the weekend. He did come, and he was very shy, very shy, and very uncertain of what was hopefully going to happen. After the theater, we came back to the Ankrum home. I was smoking in those days, and at some point after we'd gone to bed, we smelled smoke. The bedclothes were sort of smoldering. I had dropped my cigarette. We never got around to consummating our togetherness. So there went that affair. I didn't see him for another twenty years.

Now, all my lovers have been handsome and amusing. My first lover, Carl Meyer, had a wonderfully delicious sense of humor. Ari Chronus, whom I fell in love with my first semester at Berkeley, was *very* handsome. When I first saw him, he was holding a spear in the Greek chorus at the UC Berkeley Greek theater. And he was Greek. We became lovers, he thinking I was a virgin. In those days you didn't spread the good news around — or the bad news or any news. So most weekends we would hop in his coupe, a Ford two-seater, and go to a shabby hotel somewhere in the Emoryville district that took in college students without any explanation, and we'd spend the whole weekend making love! I remember one weekend there was so much activity I could hardly get out of bed. We didn't get up to go out and get food — so we didn't eat much either. There was no liquor, there were no drugs. Cigarettes, yes! My favorite then was Camels.

By my junior year, Ari had become very possessive. He didn't want me to *be,* to *do, act, say,* anything that he didn't want me to be, do, act, say. I was writing a great deal at the time, and working in the Thalians, a small theatrical group on campus, and he wasn't crazy about that because it took me away from him. The writing that I was doing was usually in his Ford coupe, because he had a job as an all-night attendant at a gas station. So for many evenings, when Ari was on, I would sit all night in the coupe writing poetry and short stories. What else was there to do?

Because I hated my stepfather, I stayed in Berkeley all year ex cept for Christmas, signing up for intersessions and summer sessions and taking off-the-wall subjects like History of the Hittites and Semites before 2000 B.C., the Hyksos Dynasty, Plumbing (truly!), Beginning German (yech!), Celtic Runes, Shakespeare vs. Marlowe — anything for an excuse not to go home. "I need the credits, Mama."

Then, during the six-week intersession before my junior year in 1929, I met another handsome young man. I was sharing an apartment with two friends. Someone knocked on our door and I answered it. A tall, blond young man was looking for a girl who didn't live there. I told him so, then we just stood and looked at each other. He asked my name, I asked his, one of my friends called out, "Ask him in!" So I asked Gordon Newell in.

Bingo!

That weekend he asked me to a dance at his fraternity, Phi Gamma Delta, a fraternity with a rowdy reputation. On that first date, in a borrowed car, I found out he'd left school to become a sculptor's apprentice working for Ralph Stackpole on the San Francisco Stock Exchange Building. Before that, he'd gone to Occidental College, and had been a runner in the international Olympic trials, where he had lost a shoe, and that was it! He was living with Stackpole's other apprentice, David Park, in a two-room walk-up in an old building on Telegraph Hill in San Francisco.

Gordon and I saw each other almost every night from then on. He'd come over from the city after work and I'd cook dinner for him and my roommates, such as it was. It was the first time I'd cooked since my little electric stove in the backyard. With expenses shared with my roommates and Gordon, I specialized in hamburgers and hot dogs with lots of mustard and pickle relish.

I told Ari our love affair was over, but being passionate and possessive, he was still hanging around all the time. I had to get rid of him. He was interfering with my affair with Gordon, and I was afraid that he might be, not violent, I don't think I thought in those terms, but that he might make a lot of trouble. Scary! I didn't want any trouble and I didn't want *him* anymore.

I dreamed up a meeting between my first lover, Carl, Ari, and Gordon. I called Carl at Stanford. "I'm having a big problem, Carl, with Ari Chronus — because I want to break off with him. I have a fiancé that I'm going to marry [I made that up] and I just want you to come up here and tell Ari that I was not a virgin when we met, and that I'm engaged. I think that will finish him off, and convince him I'm not the nice girl he thought I was, and that I'm not going to see him ever again!"

Carl came up one Sunday afternoon, Gordon was there in the living room, and Ari came in. For some reason or other I started the conversation by saying, "Ari, Carl was my first lover." Ari went absolutely white. He didn't have anything to say. He kind of looked at his feet, then at his hands, then stroked his brow.

Carl said, "Ari, you know Gloria really didn't want to hurt you or anything, but she and I were lovers for several years."

Ari was speechless, and then I remember saying to Gordon, "Gordon, please — tell Ari that you and I are lovers now, and we're going to get married!" But Gordon didn't say anything. Ari looked as though I'd hit him across the face on each cheek.

Then Gordon said, very quietly, "It's true."

And I said, "Ari, you have to accept it. It's over. I told you that weeks ago and you didn't believe me, but it's over. And I just want you to know that I have lied to you, but now I'm telling you the truth. I was not a virgin, and I love Gordon, and I really don't want to see you anymore."

How could I have done such a thing? I suppose I was excited by the possibility of melodramatic confrontation. I would be the center of it. But, most of all, I figured that if Ari got a double whammy, he would no longer bother me. And he didn't.

When I was widowed almost fifty years later, and was feeling bereft, I was in San Francisco, visiting, and thought to myself, "Why don't you call Ari and see if he's still breathing?" I knew he had changed his name — for some reason or other he had felt that a Greek name was a disadvantage. So I looked him up, and there he was. I was a little high, I must admit, and I called the number. I think he answered. I started to say, "Ari, this is Gloria . . ." But I didn't. When I was in film, I'd learned that he had been so deeply wounded and unhappy for so many years, I couldn't do it.

Unfortunately, I can't find Carl Meyer. Many years later, when I was married and living in Hollywood, he came visiting, still dear and loving, having followed my film career, according to him, with true love. I don't know that Carl would like to see me again, but I would love to see him. He was a dear sweet boy, but I'm now eighty-nine and he was about five years older, so even-steven, he's probably not available.

One weekend, soon after the high drama, a friend loaned Gordon a cabin across the bay in Marin County. It was isolated in a redwood grove by a running brook and had a fireplace. There was a phonograph, too. Gordon played Debussy's "Girl with the Flaxen Hair" and "The Engulfed Cathedral," then, the "Moonlight Sonata."

Need I say more?

I could *respond* to music — but I can't say I knew much about it. Mama had tried to give me a musical education. She had bought me a harp when I was young, because "You're so blond and beautiful, you look like an angel with the harp against your shoulder." I didn't feel like an angel or want to be angelic, the fingering was just too much of a challenge and hurt besides, so I gave up very soon and she had to take the harp back. Next she bought me a guitar. I couldn't do a guitar. She'd given up on my taking piano lessons, because I wouldn't practice. I did take ukulele lessons from various boyfriends. I wasn't great at them, either. So musically I was really not only inept but ignorant.

When I was a reporter for the *Santa Monica Outlook* that summer before Berkeley, its music critic, a man in his thirties, invited me to several concerts at the Hollywood Bowl. There were never any sexual advances. I mean, I was jailbait, for heaven's sake.

So, the music critic said to me the first evening, "You know you really don't have to bother about the three B's because today's music is so much more exciting, so much more in-depth, more interesting, and you really can enjoy it." I said I wasn't sure who the three B's were. "Oh," he said, "Bach, Beethoven, and Brahms."

*   *   *

One evening, Gordon phoned that he had met a most exciting person — a visiting professor at UC Berkeley — and that we had been invited to a curry dinner at his house! Wow! A professor? A curry dinner at his house? How exciting can life get? We arrived, and the professor — with a stupendous head of black hair — greeted us. The perfume of curry filled the room, and, at first swallow, fire engines clanged through my palate!

He was on sabbatical leave to lecture on The Physics of Metaphysics. The fact that I didn't have any idea of what that meant had nothing to do with the fact that I found this man with the wild, curly six-inch-long halo of black hair fascinating, worth making an effort to know. I must have somehow communicated this to him, because shortly after, he asked me to have dinner and go to a concert in the city. I accepted.

So all right, Gordon and I were pledged. Big deal. This was, he was, a happening! Not to be passed up!

We drove in a very large, open six-passenger car out to the ferry slip for San Francisco. There were no bridges then — the bay was inhabited only by ships. I was so impressed that I was with a professor, but I'm sure I was not the intoxicating young female he may have been envisioning before this date! Sort of a tongue-tied, laid-back flapper better describes me.

At the first interval between compositions — whatever they were — I remember saying to him, "One really doesn't have to bother about the three B's."

And he said, "What do you mean, 'doesn't have to bother'?"

I said, "Well, you know. Modern music, it's so much more interesting. . . ."

He replied, "Gloria, these three composers are the cornerstones of music, and paying attention to them will give you an idea of what the other composers in the world, before and after, are about."

I murmured, "Oh."

He continued, "You really *must* pay attention to them, because their music is so pure. . . ."

The professor and I dated a couple of times more, but then he kind of dissolved away.

I took a course in Music Appreciation the next semester.

Decades later, I bought a copy of *Time* magazine that featured J. Robert Oppenheimer, father of the atomic bomb — bald as a billiard ball — on its cover. I read with great interest about this extraordinary genius. It wasn't until I reached the paragraph describing his stint at UC Berkeley in 1929 as a physics professor lecturing about metaphysics that I recognized the bushy-haired, fascinating man I had dated. The man who had put me right about the three B's!

I spent weekends with Gordon at his and David's flat. The flat was the perfect setting for us — three would-be bohemians. Outside the windows — San Francisco Bay! Alcatraz, Angel, and Goat Islands, the white spire of UC Berkeley's Campanile against the Berkeley Hills, Mount Tamalpais, the ships and gulls, the foggy mists and foghorns. It was intoxicating — especially at night, warm in the embrace of my lover. Hallelujah!

David Park was a pink-cheeked young man, a year younger than I, full of smiles and good humor, Boston-born and mannered. (He later became one of our finest painters and central to the Bay Area Figurative movement.)

Gordon's young sister, Elizabeth, came to visit her brother, met David, and moved in. She and David slept in "the other room," actually a curtained-off double bed.

In time, the atmosphere chez Telegraph Hill became a little thick, so my darling left David and Elizabeth and moved into the historic Montgomery Building on the "Monkey Block." It was the home of many poor artists, writers, ne'er-do-wells. Enormous, with long smelly, dank, dark hallways, each "studio" furnished with a wood-burning fireplace measuring twenty-four by thirty-six inches, a zinc sink, and breadboard-sized counter. The johns and, ha! ha!, showers — behind doors without locks and with slatted wood floors — were down the hall. The halls were wide and uninhabited and, to me, Miss Fraidy Cat, dangerous (rapists) and scary. Gordon had to escort me to the john and shower on his floor, and Wait for Me!

Breakfast was rolls and coffee made on our one-burner electric plate, and otherwise, we ate Chinese down the street. A big bowl of rice, broth over it, with lovely slices of mushrooms and water chestnuts, bean sprouts, cost fifteen cents a bowl. Of course, there were no hamburger stops; those chains arrived many years later. We also ate fruit, loaves of bread, whatever!

We survived.

One of Gordon's best friends, Ward Ritchie, spent a weekend in San Francisco, and we "entertained" him in this flat. He was consulting the brothers Grabhorn re becoming a fine printer.

When he and I met again in 1983, forty-six years later, and shacked up together, he recalled, "I really envied Gordon you — you were so beautiful and fly!"

Meanwhile, weekdays in Berkeley, I finished my junior year but flunked drama and all my other subjects because I didn't bother to take any midterm or final exams. Gordon and I were going to be married in June!

Once when Gordon had to go out of town for ten days, I wrote him this poem.

> *You Are Gone Now*
> (CHANT)
>
> You are gone now. But I am here.
> Saying good-bye you caressed my face
> That I should feel the warm strength
> Of your hands, trembling wonder of them.
>
> Saying good-bye, they covered my ears
> That I should not hear the slow moan
> In your throat, throbbing stillness of it.

Saying good-bye, they blinded my eyes
That I should not see the dark deeps
In your eyes, haunting shadows of them.

Saying good-bye, you kissed me close
That I should know the near truth
Of your lips, trembling wonder of them.
You are gone now. But I am here.

Many years later, the great German tenor Richard Tauber set my poem to music. It was published (although I've never received a penny's royalty), and Mr. Tauber sang it at the Philharmonic Auditorium in Los Angeles in 1934.

One of Gordon's friends had a beautiful old house in the Berkeley Hills. Just before I didn't take my finals, a girlfriend from the boardinghouse and I were spending the night together there with her boyfriend, my Gordon, and another chick-less boy. I was awakened about four in the morning by the Berkeley police pounding on the door. I threw my package of condoms out the bathroom window and joined the four others downstairs. Told to get dressed, we were taken to the police station, fingerprinted, and made to sit down in a booking area. After about an hour, two of the police gave us a talking to, telling us they had not found us in bed, and believed we just were staying in the house on a friendly basis. But it would have to be reported to the university — the neighbors had complained about the parties and all-night student traffic — very suspicious.

My girlfriend had called her mother. Her mother arrived and really wrassled her daughter out of the station — she was livid. My girlfriend never came back to the boardinghouse. I was returned there by the police with a warning that this behavior could get me into trouble. Now my name was on the Berkeley police blotter. Mama never knew. So I've just realized, I have a record in Berkeley — on campus and off!

*   *   *

One Saturday night in a sketch class with Gordon and David, it occurred to me I could do that, too!

Be an artist's model, and earn a little eating money besides. Fifty cents an hour — several dollars for the weekend's meals, and ferry fare.

What a daring thing to do! Gloria Stuart, posing naked in a San Francisco artist's studio — me, a member of the Santa Monica haute bourgeoisie! I luxuriated in the idea. Shocking! Really shocking!

It was fun. Designing the poses, difficult perspectives, a simple stance, or a scatty one, challenging (it wasn't hard for me to hold a pose for a long time), with murmurs of approval, or small groans of frustration from the artists.

Ah! *La vie bohème!*

3

*M*y one and only one-night stand was when I was first in film. Playing opposite me was a very charismatic actor. I wanted very much to go to bed with him. And so, after the picture was finished, that night after the cast party, we went back to his apartment, and I spent the night. The next day I sent him a dozen roses. Two or three days later, I read in the *Hollywood Reporter* that he was engaged to a very famous comedienne who was coming out from New York to marry him. He called and asked, "Please don't send me any more flowers." And that was the end of that.

When I started, I had to sign a seven-year contract at Universal Studios. How that happened is a lesson in not doing your homework — assuming you know there *is* homework, and what the assignment should be.

I was making my debut at Gilmor Brown's Band Box as Masha in Chekhov's *The Seagull*. Gilmor was the regisseur of the Pasadena Playhouse, and the Band Box was his private forty-six-seat theater.

I had been promised a Paramount Pictures talent agent would be in the audience opening night. It had never been my goal to be in the movies. That was slumming. I was a theater actress. The "legitimate" theater. But Gordon and I were hungry. Very hungry.

Sure enough, Fred Datig of Paramount was there — but so was the casting director for Universal Studios! They both came backstage after the play and made dates with me for screen tests.

And who was my agent? they asked.

What was an "agent"?

Onslow Stevens was playing my suitor in the play and was also a movie actor, so I asked him. He told me agents represented one as to salary, contract, et cetera. And that he had one, and would speak to her. Jessie Wadsworth. She was Arthur Unger's sister. He was editor of *Variety*, very powerful.

The next morning, Jessie met me at Universal and kibitzed with several executives that came on the set. A makeup man was unavailable, so it was just a token test. No lines. No scenes. Just film of me from the front, back, left, and right sides. But everyone was agreeable, and Jessie seemed euphoric!

The next day I went to Paramount. I had makeup, wardrobe, lots of cosseting. Oh! I felt so important! I played the opening scene from *The Seagull* by myself, performed all the moves required, front view, right and left profiles, back view, smile, frown — could I weep?

No, I couldn't. I didn't master the art of sudden tears till I was in my sixties, and by that time, it was (almost) too late!

I didn't know one studio from another. I didn't know about "major" and "B" studios or what their components were, their directors, stars, writers, producers, and movie theaters (in those days studios owned their own theaters as outlets for their productions).

I didn't know that Universal was a family operation. It had been founded by Carl Laemmle in 1912 and handed on to his son, Carl Laemmle Jr., when Junior turned my age, twenty-one. The only actors of note the studio had under contract were Boris Karloff and Mae Clark. For directors, they had James Whale, John Stahl, and Karl Freund (also a cinematographer). Carl and Junior had won an Oscar for *All Quiet on the Western Front* two years before, and *Frankenstein* and *Dracula* had made big splashes the previous year, but . . .

Paramount was also founded in 1912, as the Famous Players Film Company. In the years since, it had absorbed an enormous amount of talent in the form of other production companies. When I came on the scene, Paramount had Marlene Dietrich, Maurice Chevalier, Claudette Colbert, Herbert Marshall, Cary Grant, Alan Ladd, Miriam Hopkins, and George Raft under contract — and they had just signed Mae West. As for directors, they had Ernst Lubitsch, George Cukor, Cecil B. DeMille, Josef von Sternberg, Rouben Mamoulian, and Mitchell Leisen. Second in rank only to Metro-Goldwyn-Mayer, Paramount movies had freshness and panache as their hallmarks.

So Jessie called me at noon the next day, saying Paramount wanted me on a standard contract, $75 a week, with singing lessons, acting lessons, and one tooth straightened (I wondered which one!) thrown in. Starting immediately.

But Universal would pay me $125 to start with, singing and acting lessons included. (Apparently they missed that one errant tooth.)

Jessie urged me to sign with Universal.

Since both studios claimed me, the argument received a lot of press. I didn't have to submit to arbitration. I didn't have to stay with Jessie. I was a free agent. But *nobody* told me so.

The studios flipped a coin. Universal won and there I went.

But I didn't have to!

Plucked.

Mama was beside herself with joy. Gordon was ambivalent, but he came to join me.

I'm sure Mama was deeply disappointed in my choice of a husband — all the more because I was marrying my way out of college. I'm sure she had hoped that I would marry a son of a
prominent Southern California family. While Mama and Fred J.
Finch were Santa Monica society Republicans, Gordon's parents
were public school teachers, living in McFarland in the San
Joaquin Valley. Social success meant a great deal to Mama. She
certainly had all the talents for it. A wonderful sense of beauty as
far as her personal appearance went. As far as her home went. As
far as her garden went. She aspired to the very best in everyday
living.

And here was Gordon Newell. His parents in modest circumstances, and he, a sculptor's ex-apprentice, the Stock Exchange
Building being finished, his only job that of caretaker of a miniature golf course in Carmel! And penniless.

But to us, I was a beautiful actress and artist's model who was
marrying a man who was going to be a famous American sculptor!
And it all came true!

Mama decided to put a really important face on the situation
for the sake of her friends. She paid dearly for it later, my stepfather truly beating up on her mentally, if not physically. She had
contracted to spend a great deal of *his* money. Still, I know now
she must have been very happy to see me getting married finally,
because she was very concerned about my "reputation."

The engagement announcement party was to be at the Uplifters, a beautiful old club in Santa Monica Canyon where Fred
Finch kept his horse and my parents entertained occasionally.

My engagement ring was also a disappointment for Mama. No
platinum and diamonds but a circle of carnelian around a gold-
washed silver-petalled rose — Gordon and I had found it in an arts
and crafts store.

But she delighted in the teas and showers that were given me.
Many! Linens, china, crystal, silver, although, to her despair, I had

requested pewter and pottery — she begged me to indicate the conventional choices, but I was living in an artist's world and wouldn't. (There was one set of goblets in Lalique, the very fine French glass, the stems were nudes — and a dozen salad plates with the nude figures underneath. They were much too fancy for my taste at that time. I asked Mama to keep the wedding presents and a lot of my clothes for me after the wedding because I didn't know where I was going to live or under what circumstances. She stored them for several years because we never really had a place for them. I have no idea what happened to them, but today, as the saying goes, I would give my eyeteeth for them!)

The wedding was at the Episcopal church in Santa Monica, and Mama really produced an exceptional wedding. I had six brides-maids — all high school chums — Damma Goto Helltas — Gordon's sister, Elizabeth, as maid of honor, and Gordon had an equal number of groomsmen, my brother, Boy, his best man. My half sis-ter, Patsy, thirteen years my junior, was flower girl. My wedding dress was custom-made of white satin, appliquéd lace, and a tulle cap with a long, long train. The bridesmaids were in delphinium blue taffeta.

There were just two flaws that I can remember. Mama couldn't find white gloves to fit the brilliant ceramist Jock Stevens's huge hands — he was instructed to keep them out of sight. The second flaw happened as Gordon and I turned to leave the altar. His col-lege buddy, now the prestigious man of letters Dr. Lawrence Clark Powell (a library at UCLA is named after him), was at the organ. Powell broke into Chopin's "Funeral March"!

Mama never forgave him.

After the ceremony there was a wonderful wedding supper at the Uplifters Club. Then we all went home, I changed, and threw the bouquet as I came down the stairs to my friends. My mother had somehow managed to get my stepfather to buy us an Essex two-seater as a wedding present, and off we drove to the Beverly Hills Hotel for our honeymoon night. It was June 21, 1930, and to the amusement of my friends always, the longest day and the shortest night of the year! Did we care?

Arriving in the small, pristine, and beautiful Carmel-by-the-Sea, Gordon carried me over the threshold into a two-room nest in the basement of an old residence. The front room had a double bed, bureau, and chair, and the back room, a john, shower, two-burner electric plate, table, and sink.

It was heaven!

We hung some clothes on the dividing rod between the two rooms and left the others in stacked suitcases.

We found the miniature golf course completely neglected, no owner to be found, and no customers. Gordon and I cleaned it up, raked, swept, picked up, painted peeling stakes, washed balls, tried to pull the whole schmeer together.

To no avail. The miniature golf course craze had evidently had its day. No customers.

I went to work at the local paper, the *Carmelite,* which was published once a week by Joseph Coughlin, a newspaperman from Shanghai. I was to do all the billing, all the writing, interviewing, learn to run the linotype machine, and so forth. Our deal was that after all the expenses were paid for the week — after the paper and the linotype and rent and lights — he and I would divide what was left, seventy–thirty. Sometimes I took home five dollars, and sometimes it was ten dollars, but it helped. And I loved everything I was learning and doing on the paper! Gordon began to teach sculpture, and also earned some money laying brick and stone, and doing carpentry, painting, all manner of house building. We were on our uppers but didn't know it.

I immediately showed up for tryouts at the Theater of the Golden Bough, one of the country's leading amateur little theaters. Ted Kuster was the owner-producer and Galt Bell the director at that time. Galt was very meticulous, very knowledgeable, soft-spoken, amusing, sharp-witted, sharp-tongued, and he had educated taste in set design and costume. I appeared in several plays — I particularly loved the comedy *See Naples and Die,* and the drama *Karl and Anna,* a German play that had a huge success abroad and in New York. Once a month, I directed and acted in the Drama Guild's one-act plays. I was also a monthly contributor to a New York City magazine, *The Fortnighter,* sharing space with the famous journalist and social reformer Lincoln Steffens, man-about-the-arts Merle Armitage, the poet Robinson Jeffers, the composer Henry Dixon Cowell — local boys! It seemed important, but it wasn't acting. Was I going to be a writer, after all? No curtain going up — applause at my entrance — or going down to applause?

Not long after we arrived in Carmel, I heard that the ex-mayor John Catlin needed a watchman to live in a shack in the middle of his block-square wood yard. Gordon and I dashed over there, and Catlin hired us, $25 a month. The shack was two rooms on stilts with an empty storeroom in back — Gordon's studio! The living room/kitchen and bathroom were on one level. And up a ladder, in a loft above the living room, was our bedroom — a mattress on the floor.

Gordon helped stack the logs as they came into the wood yard — which was often. Wood was in demand. Carmel has fogs galore — most all year round — cold, damp fogs. Nearly everybody heated their houses with fireplaces and heated their water through pipes in their fireplaces. Our shack didn't have a fireplace, so we had no heat and took ice-cold showers.

Mayor Catlin suggested we get a dog for nighttime patrol. We found two — a small German shepherd, "Black Bart," named after the famous California highwayman, and a half cocker spaniel, half something else, Luke — short for my favorite philosopher, Lucretius.

We charged groceries and paid for them when we could. We were under the aegis of Dr. Hal Bieler, of Pasadena — then Gloria Swanson's diet mentor, as well as Larry Powell's — who believed that one should not eat much meat at all, which was fine with us because we couldn't afford it anyway. Eating didn't really cost us very much. Our breakfast was homemade bran muffins, sweet butter, raw milk, and a head of lettuce. The lettuce was very filling — it was one of the major crops in the nearby Salinas Valley, a nickel a head. And, furnishing our own five-gallon can, milk was about twenty-five cents at the Carmel Valley Dairy. We also surf-fished, not too successfully. Our staple meals were macaroni and cheese, brown rice, lots of potatoes, and yams. Artichokes from a Valley farm, a nickel apiece.

Our dogs ate table scraps, with bones from the butcher shop. The dogs were our delight. They walked with us everywhere, patrolled whenever we surf-fished — no one swam, the sea was too cold and treacherous. The only problem was, if there was any carrion, any dead seal or any sea animal on the beach, Bart and Luke would usually lie down and ecstatically roll all over in it. And then we would have to get them in the ocean and wash them off. They loved that!

Gordon and I were blessed with the Henry Dickinsons. Henry owned a bank. Almost every Sunday morning, they entertained Carmel artists, writers, and musicians for an elaborate brunch. The conversation was so lively and joyous, every one of us delighted to be there. And to eat good!

We didn't have a radio or a telephone, and, of course, there was no television. The local movie house had films on weekends, but we never had any money to go. We offered to act as ushers, but there were so many volunteers that we were way down on the list. Most of the music available to us was our own phonograph and records. There was no local orchestra, no blue-ribbon lady's group sponsoring concerts. Every once in a while we would have a recital by a local musician or songster. Violin, piano, cello — even a whistler of birdcalls. So it was a great treat to go to San Francisco to the opera or symphony or an art show opening or the ballet or the theater. But we always had to hitch a ride, especially because our car was being repossessed. We had borrowed on it — that was what we were living on — and we were always afraid that the agent would follow us to where we had it hidden and take it away.

Which finally he did!

Robinson Jeffers was the most important celebrity in Carmel. His poem *The Roan Stallion* had been published to splendid notices. Gordon went over to Tor House one morning — the stone house Jeffers built — talked with the great poet, and offered to give his and Una's twin sons, Garth and Donen, wood-carving lessons. Then he asked permission to return with both me and his best friend, Ward Ritchie, fresh from Paris, where he had been an apprentice to France's greatest book artist and printer, François Louis-Schmied. Robin reluctantly agreed.

Jeffers was extremely reclusive, but when Ritchie drove up from Pasadena to interview him — Ward wanted to print and publish some of Robin's poems — Una invited the three of us over for tea. What a thrill! I was only able to visit them that once, but Gordon continued the friendship, and several of his monumental sculptures of Jeffers are now at Tor House and other venues.

Wherever you were in Carmel, you could hear the all-embracing sea. We walked along its beach almost every evening — exploring the tide pools, or along the lonely beach fronting a nunnery. Standing on its shores, the rocks, the cliffs — it gave you its power. You felt invincible. But there were also times when it made you feel vulnerable.

The mesmerizing rhythm of a tide coming in or going out — of its climax — was best described late one afternoon by Ann Harding, a famous actress from New York, then in film. We met in the Dickinsons' parlor. She looked slightly distraught, and, at Mrs. Dickinson's question, replied, "I felt a death pull. Out on Point Sur. Looking down at the water — no sound, no sound but in and out in and out — I wanted to throw myself in — it was a death pull!"

How right she was. The silent surging tides on Point Sur invite you into the water almost irresistibly.

Whenever a would-be suicide walked into the sea and was drowning, the siren would go off and everybody would run down to the beach to see the person lifted out of the water. Hopefully.

About a year after Gordon and I got married, as the result of a botched abortion, I developed a very dangerous leg infection, was hospitalized, and Mama was sent for. She had no idea of where we lived, so when Gordon, in a borrowed car, took her down from the hospital to our shack on stilts, she became hysterical, abusive, and accusatory. The latter because, when she climbed the rickety stairs and entered the "living room," there was a big hole in its wall. Gordon had started to build a fireplace several months before and then never got around to finishing it. But with Mama there for several weeks, The General, as he called her behind her back, saw that he finished it pronto! so her Gloria would be kept warm during her convalescence.

Just before she left, Mama asked what was that stuff on the ceiling. I had to admit that during one of our really broke times, we just ate cornmeal mush. And after a week of it, when Gordon asked, "What's for dinner?" and was given my answer, "What do you think we're having? We're having cornmeal mush," he made a rude noise, so I threw the pot of mush up to the ceiling.

A lot of it was still stuck up there when we moved out of the wood yard a year later to a two-story house where we took in roomers. I couldn't handle boarders, because of my work all-day all-night at the *Carmelite* and the Golden Bough.

Part of our wonderful life there was our unique friends — aplenty. Squiggs — she professed no first name — a would-be entrepreneur, opened a swap shop, Squiggs' Attic, off the main street in an attic. The idea was to bring in articles of clothing, foods (preferably homemade goodies), art objects, anything, and "make a swap." Or donate something for a pack of cigarettes, which was fifteen cents then.

I paid for many packages of Camels with small squares of needlepoint, beanbags, dried flower bouquets, fresh flowers (courtesy of unknowing neighbors). I sewed and embroidered a great deal then. I designed and created patchwork pillows, tea table linens, kitchen towels, and aprons for a tea and gift shop where I waited on tables when needed.

Two older lady friends of ours owned an art gallery, the Denny-Watrous Gallery. The most serendipitous purchase I've ever made was from them. For the *Carmelite,* I reviewed a photographic show they gave of Carmel's finest photographer, Edward Weston. There were two photographs in the show I wanted desperately, one of tiny delicate sea things on rocks at Point Sur, one an extraordinarily sensual image of a wide-open seashell nestled in a black rock's hollow. I asked the ladies if I could buy the photographs, more or less on time. They were five dollars each, and I did buy them, a dollar at a time.

Many, many years later, a friend said to me, "Gloria, those photographs hanging in your bathroom are Westons. They're very valuable."

I said, "Really? I've had them for years. I knew him," and I pooh-poohed it, but she insisted I find out just how valuable they were.

Eventually, I called Parke-Bernet's and Christie's offices in Beverly Hills. They came, and I signed with Christie's for a New York City auction. The photographs' estimate being around $5,000 each, I went to New York to witness the sale. And that's just about what they went for!

My bathroom and I miss them.

Moira Wallace was my best friend when I lived in Carmel and for years later. She was the first white child born there (until then, Carmel-by-the-Sea had been largely Indian and Mexican). Her father had been a bon vivant journalist with Jack London and other newspapermen in San Francisco at the turn of the century. Moira was a very beautiful brunette, and a very gifted artist. When

Gordon and I arrived and met her at the Dickinsons', she had just completed two murals at the Del Monte Hotel. She married one of the local boys, and soon divorced him, marrying Guthrie Courvoisier, from the French family of distillers. He and Moira created the wonderful Couroc trays that are still being sold all over the world, with Moira designing the patterns for them for many years.

I think that one of the defining moments of my life was when I went back to Carmel in the late forties — when I thought I was at the end of my career as a motion picture actress. I telephoned Moira. Visiting with her, it was apparent that she was tiddly and wobbly. She was chain-smoking. Guthrie had died and left her well-off. She wasn't really with it that day. She wasn't drunk, but she didn't seem sober, just very pleasant and smiling and vague. She was so beautiful, and so talented, and had had such a brilliant career ahead of her as an artist. As I sat there that morning and watched her, unkempt, and listened to her, a little tuned out, I think I subconsciously said to myself, "Gloria, you were one of two beautiful young friends in Carmel. And this is what's happened to the other. Don't let it happen to you."

I also had met another wonderful person, the muckraker of the thirties, Lincoln Steffens. He had an honorary place on the masthead of the *Carmelite* and wrote an article for us once in a while. His wife, Ella Winter, had gone to Russia, and left their little boy, Peter, with him. Lincoln had a beautiful house at the beach, and he used to come in to the *Carmelite* every so often and schmooze. He was a big figure in Carmel and very complimentary to me about my published poems and feature stories. He told Joe and me Ella was joining the Communist Party. This was 1930. The fact that his wife was a Communist sympathizer fascinated me.

Later, in 1939, my mother asked me, "Are you a Communist, Gloria? Some people in Santa Monica say you are a Communist." She said it in such a disapproving manner I almost said, "Yes, I am." Of course, I wasn't, but a part of me always wanted to shock her. For example, I had started smoking because she said, "You can't smoke. No lady smokes." So who wants to be a lady?

In college, when I was seventeen, I had wanted to join the Young Communist League. I was told it was for the poor and the oppressed. That appealed to me. But membership wasn't open to anyone under eighteen, so I couldn't join. Now my friendship with Steffens gave me much deeper insight into the abuses of laborers and blue-collar workers and made me ready to work for liberal causes when I got to Hollywood a few years later.

I met my lifelong friend, the fine writer Catherine Turney — also a fighter for liberal causes in Hollywood — in Carmel in 1931. She was in a traveling theatrical company, an offshoot of the Pasadena Playhouse, and came to the *Carmelite* to place an advertisement for a performance. It was to be in some very rich person's living room in Pebble Beach. The contact was fortuitous. Cathy's patrons were the first of a number of very rich people whose houses Gordon and I babysat in Pebble Beach. With their pets. Once, a parrot got away. (Well, how long can you listen to a strident "Hello! Hello! Hello! Hello! Hello!" twenty-four hours a day?)

Cathy and I went through several marriages, divorces, career swings together. She wrote for Bette Davis at Warner Brothers, and in 1940, with Jerry Horwin, wrote John Barrymore's last play, *My Dear Children.* Then, working at her desk at the Huntington Library in San Marino, she wrote a fictionalized biography, *Byron's Daughter,* and a couple of fascinating historical novels. Cathy left us for good just recently.

It was because I was very active in Carmel theatricals (more roles! more! more!) that I met the gifted and important actor-director Morris Ankrum, when he came to the village in October of '31. A friend of Galt Bell's, Morris was looking for an actress to play Olivia in the *Twelfth Night* he was directing for a December engagement at the Pasadena Playhouse.

Already in his cast were John Craig, a fairly famous old Shakespearean actor-manager, and Betty Bronson, a noted Peter Pan
person.

Galt asked me if I'd like to do it, or could. Of course, I'd love it
and could.

I gave Gordon a good-bye kiss and drove down south with Morrie Ankrum. You will understand my total passion to be a stage actress when I tell you it never occurred to me to try and use this
appearance to get into the movies.

Opening night, Mr. Craig had an entrance, and I was onstage
alone. My line was, "What ho, Malvolio!" And he was to come on.
No Malvolio. So I walked over the center of the stage, "What ho,
Malvolio!" a little more urgency in the voice, a little louder. Nothing. I walked over to the wings, looked at the prompter, who was
waving his arms, gesturing with one hand pointing over his shoulder to the dressing rooms. The audience by this time had begun
to titter. There was so much brouhaha going on backstage, they
could hear it. I walked back to the center of the stage, because it's
impossible to improvise in Shakespeare, or at least it was impossible for me. I looked at the audience, shrugged, and walked back to
my first position. Finally, I waited in the wings, because you can't
stand there shrugging and smirking at the audience when they are
laughing at you.

What happened was that the old man had gone down to the
greenroom, which is a room below the stage where actors relax between scenes. He had forgotten about his next entrance and taken
his symmetricals off. Symmetricals were worn by actors with less
than handsome legs who were playing Shakespeare in doublets.
They are worn from above the knee to the ankle to give a dashing
calf line. Mr. Craig was sitting there with his symmetricals off
when I started with my "What ho, Malvolio!" Someone finally got
them back on. At last Craig ran onto the stage, and I followed him
with only "Malvolio!!" The audience applauded lightly.

But! The next year, when I was twenty-one, Morrie Ankrum returned to Carmel and presented *The Seagull*. I played Masha. When he left, he asked if I would be interested in playing the role again in Pasadena. Of course I would!

And I had a change of heart about the movies — a defining moment!

At this point, Gordon and I were stony broke, living hand to mouth. I now hoped for an opportunity to be in the movies and make us some money.

I called Mama and she phoned Robert Holliday. He had been the editor of the *Santa Monica Outlook* when I worked on it. Now he was managing editor at the *San Francisco Call-Bulletin* and a good friend of William Randolph Hearst's. He was also a very close friend of my parents and had always said to me, "Gloria, you ought to be in pictures." But, seeing as how I wanted only to be in the New York theater, I had paid no attention to the idea.

Holliday promised Mama he would call the Paramount casting director and ask him to go see me.

Ward Ritchie happened to be up in Carmel visiting us, and he drove me down to Pasadena. I never returned to my cherished life in Carmel.

4

I bought Gordon a bucket-seated open racing car, a Mercer, painted yellow, from one of my high school beaux. I also rented a studio for him near his chums, Ward and Larry, and bought the materials — wood and stone — and new tools, everything that he needed for his sculpture.

I worked like a crazy lady that first year, yo-yoing from set to set to wardrobe fitting to makeup to hair and back again. When I wasn't filming, I was doing publicity — interviews, fashion spreads, head portraits, being dolled up for a premiere, everything from soup to nuts. (I had shortened "Stewart" to "Stuart" because I thought — and still do — its six letters balanced perfectly on a theater's marquee with the six letters in "Gloria.") The first year of my contract with Universal Studios, 1932, I made four films. Later, this would seem like child's play.

For my first movie, Universal loaned me to Warner Brothers for *Street of Women*. It was a story of the fashion business in New York — the star, beautiful Kay Francis, was in real life and in this movie a glamorous clotheshorse. She was one of the highest-paid stars of the time.

Even though my entire experience with film was acting in one test, I was playing the ingenue to Kay Francis's lead and I felt so superior because I was a stage actress and she was — well, *you* know!

Coming onto the set my first morning, I saw this very heavy man seated in a director's chair with a big triple-decker sandwich in one hand. The assistant director said to me, "That's the director, Archie Mayo."

He guided me over and I said, "Good morning, Mr. Mayo."

He answered, "Oh, good morning, nice to have you aboard."

I said, "Thank you very much."

He didn't say anything more, took a big bite of his sandwich, so I turned away. Suddenly, I was goosed — hard and deep with a buzzer! I jumped, and when I turned, I saw the finger, and the buzzer, and the sandwich, and the fat man, and heard the laughter. It was shocking to me, but everybody thought it was hilarious. That was my first five minutes on a Hollywood set. It substantiated my feeling about Hollywood that I was slumming and doing it a big favor.

But Archie Mayo wasn't a bumpkin. Four years later, he did a fine job of directing Leslie Howard, Bette Davis, and Humphrey Bogart in *The Petrified Forest*. It was Bogey's breakthrough movie. The story goes that the producer, Jack Warner, wanted Edward G. Robinson to play Duke Mantee. Even though Bogart had created the role on Broadway, he had only appeared in B movies. When Leslie Howard, who had also been in the play with Bogart and was a big star, heard this, he went to Warner. He told him that if Bogey didn't do it, he wouldn't do it. Howard was a generous man in addition to being a gorgeous actor. In 1943, while he was flying from England to Lisbon for the war effort, his plane was shot down by the Luftwaffe, who thought that Prime Minister Winston Churchill was aboard. After the war, British Intelligence acknowledged that Howard's plane had been a decoy.

My second movie was for Universal. *Variety* called it "a pleaser for all audiences." It was about the life after college of a football star — handsome Richard Arlen. I was the love interest. Crinkly-voiced Andy Devine and laconic James Gleason (who came from a theatrical family and was an equally gifted playwright and screenwriter) were also in it, but you probably won't find *The All-American* in their filmographies.

The best thing that happened to me during my seven years' bondage was being directed by James Whale three times at Universal. James was the first — what I call — "Renaissance" director I worked for. A professional artist, actor, director, with great credits. James had made the incomparable *Frankenstein* the year before.

The first film I did with him was *The Old Dark House*, a superb script adapted from the novel *Benighted*, by J. B. Priestley. It is in that rare delicious genre, horror comedy. One film book calls *The Old Dark House* "a stylist's and connoisseur's treat."

The cast was superb. Charles Laughton, Melvyn Douglas, Raymond Massey, Boris Karloff (of course he was the centerpiece of *Frankenstein*), Ernest Thesiger, Eva Moore (mother of Jill Esmond, Laurence Olivier's first wife, and rumored to have been a once-ravishing mistress of King Edward VII), plus perky Lilian Bond — also a leading lady in the film — Brember Wills, and Elspeth Dudgeon. Melvyn and I were the only Americans, the others were English imports.

The cameraman was one of Whale's favorites, Arthur Edeson. His credits were prodigious. He had shot *All Quiet on the Western Front* and *Frankenstein*, then would do *The Invisible Man, Mutiny on the Bounty, Casablanca,* and many others.

I am happy to report that the reviews for my work in this film were gratifying. (But has any performer ever received accolades he/she felt were enough?)

James Whale was very kind to me, and besides taking me down to the theater in Los Angeles to see Jane Cowl, Katharine Cornell, and Lunt and Fontanne, I treasure a note that he wrote me the first day that I shot *The Old Dark House*. At luncheon in the studio commissary, he sent a menu over from his table. On the back it said, "Miss Stuart, Question number one. Who is your favorite director?" And I wrote back, "James Whale." And he crossed off

James Whale and wrote back, "My *next!*" He was wrong. I've never been one to suck up.

I was very innocent about gays in those days. I thought that the reason James Whale and his friend, the producer David Lewis, took me to the theater, and the reason that James came over to see me in Pasadena when I played *Peer Gynt* (I managed to find time to do this, the stage being so dear to my heart) was because he found *me* fascinating. However, I think I was their — what we used to, and probably still do, call — "beard." I recall that in my innocence and uninformed judgmental approach I mentioned the fact to James that backstage after a performance of Katharine Cornell in *The Green Hat* there were a great many fairies flying around! I shudder today to think that I said it. But the dear man surely forgave me. He was always kind and considerate and knew I adored him.

Now one of the things that used to annoy Melvyn Douglas and me on the set was that every morning and every afternoon all the Brits stopped to have their "elevenses" and "foursies" — tea and cakes. We were not invited to join them. So Melvyn and I chatted, passed the time, talking about the theater. One day, he said a magic word to me: "Union."

"What's that?" I asked.

Melvyn had come from the New York theater and told me about the vicious Actors' Equity strike of 1919, in which actors struck their managers and theater owners. The actors suffered dreadfully, but their union prevailed. Actors' Equity was a very strong union in New York. But I had no idea that it had been trying to organize screen actors in Hollywood since 1924. Around the time when the Academy of Motion Picture Arts and Sciences was formed, 1927, Equity called for an eight-hour workday. Nothing. Then in 1929, they asked producers for rehearsal and overtime pay. Forget it! They next asked members not to work in film for producers who hired actors outside their union. No way. Actors worked unconscionable hours — especially females, because every morning our needs included a great deal of time in hairdressing and makeup. Meals were served at the convenience of the production staff. There was no allotment for travel time, no standard hours between work calls, no pay for overtime or double overtime — what we call golden time. And if an actor under contract refused a role the studio had chosen, he/she was suspended without pay — and the time was added on to the contract!

So naturally when Melvyn explained the concept of a union to me, I was eager to join and instantly became very active collecting members for the Screen Actors Guild — ever since called SAG.

The time to organize was right. In 1933 producers cut salaries of actors, working six days a week, by 50 percent! Of course there was resistance to the guild by the studios. But we had all the ammunition we needed. We had Marie Dressler, Will Rogers, Janet Gaynor, Eddie Cantor, Wallace Beery, Jean Harlow, Clark Gable, Mae West, and Joan Crawford — top stars at the box office that year.

One fine day, a number of such actors told their studios that they wouldn't be coming to work the next day, or the next, or the next unless . . .

We had been organizing less than a year, and we had our contract overnight! When I say "we," I mean Melvyn Douglas and his wife, Helen Gahagan, Franchot Tone, James Gleason and his wife, Lucille, Edward G. Robinson, Jimmy Cagney, Ralph and Frank Morgan, and Humphrey Bogart. All were New York theater actors, who knew the value of a union.

On June 30, 1933, SAG was formed, with Ralph Morgan as president. Boris Karloff was also on the Guild's founding board of directors.

But we still were part of Actors' Equity. By October, we broke away, establishing a sister union — one exclusively for screen actors. Eddie Cantor was elected president, Jimmy Cagney was vice president, and Groucho Marx (fox in the henhouse!) was treasurer.

I found I took to politics like a duck to water. In June 1936, I was involved in forming the Hollywood Anti-Nazi League with other actors Paul Muni and Franchot Tone, directors Lewis Milestone and Ernst Lubitsch, screenwriter Donald Ogden Stewart, and lyricist Oscar Hammerstein II. That year, Dorothy Parker and I helped form the League to Support the Spanish Civil War Orphans. In 1938, as a member of the Hollywood Democratic Committee, I was on the Executive Board of the California State Democratic Committee. And so forth and so on.

The fourth movie I made in 1932 was *Air Mail*. Our director, John Ford, had directed over sixty movies and nearly a dozen shorts since his start in silents in 1917. This was an action movie, with Pat O'Brien, Ralph Bellamy (I played his apple-pie-perfect sweetheart), and Lilian Bond, a lovely bitch in her naughty-girl role (a part I would much rather have had!). I enjoyed. This time, all American actors. I was at a John Ford festival last year. Although his greatest work was later in reflective films like *The Grapes of Wrath, How Green Was My Valley,* and *The Quiet Man,* they ran *Air Mail*.

Unbelievable. Our brave airmail pilot stepped into his United States Air Mail plane from an apple box on the snowy ground. And flew through blinding snowstorms in open cockpits. True!

I was afraid of flying for many years, a state of mind not helped by my first cross-country trip. As a publicity stunt for *Air Mail* the studio mailed me from Universal City to New York City.

I boarded by stepping into the plane from a twelve-inch-high footstool. Then the pilot and I, just the two of us, flew from Burbank Airport to Newark. It took us four days and four nights, because we came down in Prescott, Arizona, on account of a storm. We came down in Cincinnati because of a storm. We came down in Albany, New York, because of a storm. And then the fourth day we flew out of Albany in very dark weather to Newark.

I moved from the back of the plane up to right outside the pilot's compartment. I heard someone say, "You're over the right end of the field . . . *tick tick tick tick* . . . You're over the left end of the field. . . ." We couldn't see anything. Visibility was zero. But they finally talked the pilot down.

We got out of the plane, me shaking with fear. I said something like, "Thank heaven! You were wonderful. I never thought we'd make it!"

And he said, "Well, I had such a terrible hangover from last night, I didn't think we'd make it either."

As part of the publicity for the movie, I was going to appear at New York's glorious and venerable Palace Theatre. Only the top top top vaudevillians played the Palace. In my appearance there, I was just taking a bow, as an "airmailed" movie star — not a "legitimate" Palace Theatre performer. But who's counting?

I went back to Hollywood by train!

For some time, Gordon had been growing unhappy, restless.

Looking back, I still am not sure why he felt displaced. True, Carmel and our life there was wonderfully quiet and happy. Its magnificent sea and shore, its mountains and hidden valleys, fogs — silent, embracing, impenetrable — the artists, poets, writers, just plain characters we knew, leaving them *was* wrenching. But we were eating — and our dogs were on dog food. In fact, suddenly there was lots of money.

But I'm afraid I didn't have the time or energy to witness his work, his progression, new ideas, techniques, and he certainly couldn't mine. In time, I began to realize that Gordon was not working — surely not as hard as I was, all hours of the day and night. Without a union, I could work ten, twelve, fourteen hours a day, seven days a week, and be called back without eight hours' rest. Oftentimes I'd come home exhausted, and the dear lad would be entertaining friends. He professed to hate Hollywood, but we just gradually weren't happy together.

We decided to separate. It was a fairly fond farewell.

I paid for the Mexican divorce.

The studio publicity director, Johnny Johnson, came up with a great deal of ballyhoo about our "trial separation." Newspapers ran the stories above the fold, as they say! *Big* headlines — this was hot news! The press had a field day with that term, "trial separation" — also "companionate divorce." Companionate marriages were a big subject then (today, it's called living together). But we may have been the first — and last — "companionate" divorce.

I began dating. One of my beaux was Harry Ruby, of the popular songwriting team of Kalmar and Ruby — Harry was the lyricist. Harry and Bert had written the score for the Marx Brothers' *Animal Crackers* and *Horse Feathers* — and they worked on the script of *Horse Feathers* as well. When Harry and I were dating, he and Bert were doing the same thing on *Duck Soup.* Did he ever mention the names of the other writers he was working with, for example, Groucho's friend Arthur Sheekman, and his collaborator, Nat Perrin? Who knows. They wouldn't have meant anything to me if he did.

Harry sent me two dozen red roses the morning after our first date. I had never received flowers before, other than the corsages my escorts always sent me for special dances in high school. Harry was a darling and a very gentle man. He was almost as crazy about music as he was about baseball. In fact, he had hoped to play ball professionally but couldn't make a living at it. He never learned to drive a car. And during his life he picked up several hundred dollars in coins on the streets of Beverly Hills when he walked to the market or walked to the drugstore or walked to the library or just took a walk. He had the coins all mounted on fancy cardboard. He was very proud of his collection.

Another beau was George Oppenheimer. He was a writer-producer for Samuel Goldwyn. Goldwyn was one of the top

Hollywood producers at that time — Louis B. Mayer and Irving Thalberg were the others.

George took me to parties with the crème de la crème of Hollywood society. The screenwriter Donald Ogden Stewart and his wife once gave a great costume party at the Trocadero nightclub on Sunset Boulevard. (Don's stock-in-trade was sophistication — he later won an Academy Award for his screenplay adaptation of Philip Barry's *The Philadelphia Story*.) There was a slide from the entrance of the club down to the party in the basement! George came as Maurice Chevalier. My costume consisted of red satin shorts, red satin bra, and a long red satin forked tail. We were quite spectacular — for the early thirties!

George was a favorite beau because he never made a pass at me, and it was refreshing not to have a wrestling match in the back of a limousine or a grabbing at my front door!

However, I really didn't have or see anyone else that interested me enough to have an affair. I was making too many movies too fast, even for my formidable energy! So much for that free love the fan magazines were so titillated by!

P. S. Gordon and I remained dear friends. He became one of our finest sculptors — a wonderful fountain in Washington DC, and monumental sculptures in Scottsdale, Monterey, the Priory in Vallyermo, the Carmel Highlands, the sculpture garden at UCLA, Rockefeller Center in New York City. On our last meeting, in 1997, he observed, "You're still beautiful, and I'm very happy with your *Titanic* trip!"

5

*M*aybe the films were forgettable, but myohmyohmy! being a "movie star" could be such fun! I enjoyed — and so did Mama — going to the great department stores of the day like Bullock's Wilshire and J. W. Robinson and buying a whole "personal appearance" wardrobe at one time. The shopping girl would bring us suits or dresses, then hats, shoes, handbags, gloves, lingerie — all coordinated for the occasion.

I had a lovely and extensive wardrobe, ever donated to Salvation Army, ever replenished!

The one activity I really disliked about being a movie star was the photo sessions. Although "leg art" then was quite modest and seemly, fashion stills, soap commercials, cigarette "plugs," and cosmetic endorsements really interfered with the few hours I had just to relax.

I can't believe the leg art photographs that I'm seeing in my scrapbook of 1932–33. In one, I'm wearing a black-spangled triangular neck handkerchief. The tip of the triangle is at my throat, suspended from a gold necklace, and then the rest of the triangle goes down under my armpits. In another photo, I am wrapped in lots of gold yardage, and the caption reads, "Mermaid." And then in another, I have on little shorts and a bra covered in black sequins, not doin' nuttin'. And in another, a three-quarter shot, I'm holding two large chrysanthemums against each tit. Sensational!

Lots of fan mail and requests for copies! These photographs were run in movie magazines opposite pictures of me in *Air Mail*, where I have on a housedress, or *The Old Dark House*, where I'm muddy and windblown, or *The All-American*, when I'm sitting in a grandstand. I'm not sure why.

And there were loads of pictures of me in slinky dresses. I find it interesting how fashion comes around. Not too long ago, one of the actresses at the Oscars announced that she was not wearing anything underneath her dress. And she emphasized, *"anything."* I remember when Jean Harlow announced that she was not wearing anything under her white satin, white fox–trimmed gown. Many people were scandalized. I thought it was rather daring and fun and admirable. Today, many fabrics are stretch-something — plastic — chemical. Then, it was the silkworm's delight — soft, silky, clingy — like us, warm and sensuous.

The fabric of these gowns had to be cut on the bias, otherwise the gowns wouldn't cling. And clinging was the objective. I had a dressmaker that I kept busy. Mrs. Rhea was a master cutter. All I had to do was bring her an illustration of a gown/coat/suit from *Vogue* or *Harper's Bazaar* and she would go over it very carefully, then put it together, adding my own fillip that made it uniquely my style. She had a beader who worked for Adrian, the fabulous dress designer at Metro who married Janet Gaynor. Perhaps my most treasured gown from Mrs. Rhea was a copy of a Schiaparelli: an unlined black silk bias-cut skintight evening dress with spaghetti straps. The front of the bodice is apron-shaped, solidly hand-beaded with black jet. (I still have it. Fifty years after I wore it, my daughter, Sylvia, wore it — after dieting like crazy, she says — to a black-tie New Year's Eve party.)

Another of my favorites — I wore it to Grauman's Chinese Theatre at the premier of *The Story of Louis Pasteur*, starring Paul Muni — was a bias-cut black silk velvet evening dress with spaghetti straps and a cape edged with white fox.

I loved furs. I had a silver fox coat, a white fox jacket — plus a

Russian Persian lamb coat, hat, and muff, and for everyday, grey squirrel. I regret to this day that I bought leopard and monkey and a long scarf of six beautiful individual canary martens, complete with heads and eyes, each mouth snapping onto the tail ahead of it. Shame on me!

Fancy gloves were very "in" during the thirties. My favorite pair was French three-quarter-length paper-thin black suede — the fingernail areas were cut out and satin stitched in Schiaparelli pink. Made by Elsa Schiaparelli, who else?

I had fanciful garter belts — black silk for black panties, nude silk for nude panties, white lace — you get the idea! And I was always very careful to keep the seams in the back of my silk stockings straight. Actually two things that women always looked for in other women were straight seams and spanking clean gloves.

I also collected fine French silk underwear, exquisitely hand embroidered — teddies, panties, slips, petticoats, brassieres. Writing this now, when I think of the little girls I later saw in Saigon in dark sheds under a single bare electric bulb, embroidering all the kinds of underwear that we collected using the finest needles, I shudder.

I went to the beauty parlor once a week and had a manicure, shampoo, and finger wave. (Pedicures, facials, and electrolysis were not part of my routine — I just wasn't interested in giving time to all of that.) A so-called finger wave was done usually with a curling iron, and it was a deep wave rather than curls. At one time we all put our hair up on top of our heads with lovely combs to keep it there. Then spray came in.

Wearing silver and gold dust in your hair was very fashionable in the thirties. It came off on everything, but it was wonderful for a party. There's a story about Marlene Dietrich and Tallulah Bankhead when they were working at Paramount (I think *Shanghai Express* and *Devil and the Deep*, respectively). Both were bisexual. And both wore gold dust in their hair. Bankhead walked onto her set after lunch one day, her face smeared with gold dust, and said, "Guess where I've been and what I've been doing!"

I do miss the tiny star- or crescent-shaped black "beauty spots" we used to glue on our faces — or tummies or bottoms when feeling playful!

Hats! I wore hats always. To the movies, theater, restaurants, traveling, and just visiting. I still have some from that period.

Once I had a dreadful quarrel with my husband and decided to "get even" by buying some outrageously extravagant hats. Driving fast and recklessly to Sak's Fifth Avenue, I purchased two quite extraordinary hats — a pink French silk felt eighteen-inch cartwheel by the leading French milliner, Tatiana du Plessix, with divine fat pink silk roses and pink silk veiling for $125, and a stunning off-the-face-on-the-side-of-your-head blue silk felt festooned with feathery plumes in several rich shades of blue, $185. I think that's the equivalent of well over fifteen hundred dollars today. Well! I still have them, wear them at home on festive occasions, and wonder what the quarrel was about! But so happy we had it!

Looking at movie star's faces of the thirties and early forties, how could we arch our eyebrows so thinly and perfectly? Or "cupid's bow" our lips? Joan Crawford, at least, with her sudden, very defined mouth, helped bring back the natural look.

Crawford was the quintessential movie star. Limousines, fabulous furs, fabulous clothes. The first time I had ever heard of or seen a star sapphire, I saw one hanging around Joan Crawford's neck — a beautiful many-carated star sapphire as a pendant from a diamond necklace. (Otherwise, diamonds and pearls were the gems that my friends and I coveted and wore. But pearls only at night. Diamonds were OK for the day, but never pearls!)

When our dear friend Kyle Crichton came out from the East to write Crawford's biography, I remember he said about her, "She even makes an entrance to the bathroom."

Around the time I was dating Harry Ruby and George Oppenheimer, I was also dating Lynn Riggs. Lynn was Franchot Tone's best friend. He called one day and asked if I would like to go dancing at Ciro's with Joan Crawford and Franchot Tone. They were engaged, and I thought, Ooh, big thrill. I had what I call a Jean Harlow dress, long, bias-cut gold satin, diamanté straps, sexy and chic. We were to meet at Crawford's. Lynn picked me up and we drove over, and Franchot led us into the bar — a very narrow room facing the pool and garden. He said Joan was still dressing, and would be down in a minute, what would we like to drink?

So we're sitting at the bar, I'm perched on a stool, and Crawford came in, in a, well, it was a plain bouffant black tulle dress, sort of high school prom queen. I got up and walked toward her in my gold satin, no underwear thing.

She stopped cold, looked at me, and suddenly said, "Oh, I'm so sorry! I spilled perfume all over myself, I have to change." Then, retreating, "I just, I can't get near you, I just wanted you to know . . ."

Well, she finally came down in a clingy all-over crystal-beaded white thing. Gorgeous!

Lynn Riggs, by the way, was a poet and playwright from the Midwest. Can't remember how I met him, but the year before, his play, *Green Grow the Lilacs,* had an eight-week run on Broadway. Only a modest success — Robert Benchley wrote in *The New Yorker* that it seemed less like a play than a musical. Well, twelve years later, *Green Grow the Lilacs* became that, a turning point in American theater, as Rodgers and Hammerstein's *Oklahoma!*

Next, Lynn took me to meet Bette Davis.

Bette Davis was more my style. At the time — it was just before she filmed *Of Human Bondage* — she was married to Ham Nelson, a bandleader. That night, I was gussied up much more than Bette, and consequently very uncomfortable. She was formidable even in those days, and not happy with her soon-to-be-divorced husband, so the evening was not a pleasant one. Quite a few long pauses. Sorry Lynn had brought over a girl. I never met her again.

At that point, Joan and Bette were big stars. But I was getting my share of attention. Fan letters were a whole new world to me, and gifts arrived in the mail and at my door all the time. Garters were a favorite from men. Combs, barrettes, jewelry, bits and pieces, came from the ladies. But being a public person could also be scary. The worst letter I've ever received asked for a pair of my unwashed panties. (I wish I'd had the brains to write back, "Oh dear! I don't wear any!")

On a lighter note, publicity could be fun — and confusing. Once a studio publicist made up a story about my nearly stepping on a rattlesnake in my garden. The gossip columns gobbled it up. A couple of years later, looking over Hedda Hopper's column, I read that Joan Fontaine had had a near-fatal encounter with a rattlesnake in her garden. My instant reaction was "Poor Joan!" before I caught myself, laughing.

Those seven long years I was under contract, I was loaned to many other studios at a fancier salary than I got at Universal. Universal kept the difference!

One happy loan-out was to RKO, where in 1933 I had the honor and privilege of working with Lionel Barrymore in *Sweepings*. Mr. Barrymore played a feisty Chicago merchant. Mild stuff after his previous role, Rasputin in *Rasputin and the Empress*. (For those interested in movie trivia, that was, I think, the only film in which all three Barrymores appeared, and it was the reason you always see this disclaimer: "The events and characters in this film are fictional and any resemblance to characters living or dead is purely coincidental." One of the aristocrats who murdered Rasputin — his identity was barely disguised in the film — claimed the scene in which his wife was raped had never occurred. He sued MGM for libel and was awarded $1 million!)

Barrymore was not well, used a wheelchair to and from the set, but when the camera and sound were going, he rose to give a strong, persuasive performance. His male nurse evacuated him from the set to his trailer after each shot and none of us ever had a conversation with him. But with a life in the theater still deeply desired, for me to be in the presence of and working with a legendary Barrymore was heaven.

Then I lucked out again, and was cast as the leading lady in my second James Whale film: *The Invisible Man*. R. C. Sherriff and Philip Wylie wrote a fine adaptation of H. G. Wells's eccentric novel. Claude Rains had the title role, and among my fellow players were William Harrigan, Henry Travers, and Una O'Connor.

Claude Rains was what we call "an actor's actor" — and twenty-four hours a day, on a set, on a stage, in a bar, going to the loo, baking a cake, he was giving a performance.

Claude had been highly acclaimed in the New York theater, and this was only his second film — his first in America, and first with sound. But Claude knew where the money was. When he started to move me around during a scene so that the back of my neck was to the camera and he was full-face, I stopped him.

I said to the director, "James, look what he's doing. Upstaging me!"

James got up from his director's chair and said, "Now, Claude, this is film. This is not the stage. This is a two-shot, even-steven — two full profiles, not your profile and the back of Gloria's head, or Gloria's profile and the back of your head. And if we don't get it on the next shot, we can do it over and over again until we do!"

Apologies, apologies. "So sorry — forgive me — so sorry!" But he did try to do it again — the eternal ego at work — although on the third take, he got it right!

I had no way of knowing it, but that film gave me lasting recognition. A pet project of Junior Laemmle's, in most film books the movie gets four stars and lines like "a superb blend of eccentric character comedy." And *The Invisible Man* is in most worldwide museum film collections.

Next, lots of fun, I did a bit in a one-reeler, part of a series — *Hollywood on Parade No. 9* — with W. C. Fields, Buster Crabbe, and Chico Marx. At various points during this year, Universal stuck me in a string of forgettable films: *The Girl in 419* (a crime genre with David Manners), *Private Jones* (a war movie with Lee Tracy), *Laughter in Hell* (a story about a chain gang with Pat

O'Brien), and *It's Great to Be Alive* (a science fiction musical — my costar was a Brazilian tenor!).

My last with James Whale directing was *The Kiss Before the Mirror,* with Frank Morgan, Nancy Carroll, Paul Lukas, and Walter Pidgeon. It was from a play by Ladislas Fodor, a Hungarian playwright whose work had become fashionable. I opened my scenes walking down a path, sensually inhaling the perfume of magnolias. Of course James showed me how to cradle the flower, inhale the perfume, project passion, and look toward my lover's room, feeling the excitement of an illicit love affair! Running it on videotape today, the film seems overly melodramatic. Not *my* performance, you understand, just one or two of the others!

A bit of trivia. My friend Leonard Maltin tells me that the sets on *TKBTM* were recycled from Whale's *Frankenstein.* I must look closer next time to see if the garden and my bedroom look familiar. . . .

Also among my films released in 1933 was *Secret of the Blue Room,* about a mansion's haunted room. For the first time I was with Paul Lukas and Lionel Atwill — he seems to have specialized in scary movies (*Mystery of the Wax Museum, The Vampire Bat).* This was an American version of a UFA film. Universum Film Aktien Gesellschaft was Germany's semiofficial film studio — Dietrich's *The Blue Angel* was made there. Universal used all the great exterior shots from the German movie, then shot interiors with us English-speaking actors.

(I heard that once when UFA was shooting a war film with a huge number of extras, at lunch, those actors dressed as officers refused to sit with those actors dressed as enlisted men.)

One of Universal Studios' strengths was its liaison with UFA. Nearly all of filmdom's German greats who fled Hitler and settled here came from UFA. Max Reinhardt — internationally one of the most influential film directors of his day — his son Gottfried (writer, producer, director, and our good friend), Ernst Lubitsch, William Wyler, Otto Preminger . . .

Dear Lionel Atwill — a still handsome, late-fortyish ex-theater-matinee-idol-making-it-in-Hollywood! So! All of a sudden, one Saturday afternoon when our film was finished, I opened the front door. Lionel. I looked at him, he smiled at me, moments of silence, so I asked him to come in. We had never had more than lunch together in the Universal Studios commissary, in the company of various other actors. Why?

He was, as we used to say, put away in a smashing gray tweed jacket, with a smashing vest and smashing gray flannel trousers, an ascot, and — I couldn't believe my eyes — smashing gray felt spats. Yes, spats! In Southern California!

Into the living room. Sherry or port was the polite social drink then. Yes, he would have a sherry. The conversation was so hesitant, so stilted, so barren, I became impatient and lied, saying I had an appointment very soon with Percy Westmore for a makeup consultation.

As he rose, and I rose, he very clumsily put his arm around my waist, and I very quickly disengaged him. He burbled something, we walked toward the front door, I let him out, and that was that.

Spats?

Then also in 1933, I was loaned out to Goldwyn Studios. Mr. Goldwyn was a man of great taste. He wanted the best of everything, in his domestic life and his professional life. For each picture, he hired the best writers, the best director, the best composer, the best choreographer. But he was not knowledgeable in every artistic venue. George Oppenheimer told me that once when production had played the score of a movie for Mr. Goldwyn backward by mistake, he had loved it.

As a shrewd man who appreciated talent, however, he could be tough. Once, our friend Don Hartman — who later became head of production at Paramount Pictures — wanted Goldwyn to release him from his writing-producing contract. Goldwyn wouldn't. Again and again, Don pleaded with him. Wouldn't budge. A genial man, Don still gave Goldwyn occasional rides home after work.

One night, after Goldwyn got out of the car, Don backed up too soon and knocked him down. Of course Don was terribly upset and jumped out of the car to help Sam up. But Goldwyn said, "Don't worry, Don. I'm fine. I know you didn't mean it."

Don replied, "I know, I know, Sam, but who would believe me?"

The movie I made for Goldwyn was *Roman Scandals*. Eddie Cantor played a slave and I was the Princess Sylvia, captured and enslaved by an evil Emperor, played by the imposing character actor Edward Arnold.

The production was first class all the way — what a difference from second-class Universal! John Harkrider was the dress designer Goldwyn brought in from New York. Even the transparent silk brassieres on the chorus girls — called the Goldwyn Girls — had hand-beaded Roman chariots racing across their breasts. Although in one sequence choreographed by Busby Berkeley the girls were supposed to have nothing on except long blond wigs, it was wigs and nude body suits.

The only direction I can remember from the director, Frank Tuttle, was his saying, "Okay, kids, here we go, laughing and scratching. Roll 'em!" Incredible. A million-dollar production!

But this was fairly typical. In those days, many directors left the reading of the lines to the dialogue directors — the ones who technically were there to see if the actors *knew* their lines. Then the directors left the action — where people were going to be and how they were going to move — to the cameraman. Then they listened to what shots they should do from the cutter. Then, seated in front of the camera, they called, "Action!" and eventually, "Cut!"

For this they were paid tens of thousands of dollars.

Nice work if you can get it.

6

So Princess Sylvia was lying on a velvet chaise longue in between takes, reading a Chinese newspaper, when a deep voice behind her said, "You're holding that thing upside down."

Now, because of my looks, reputation, and rating as an actress, I often was approached by men hoping for an interlude!

Then: "Do you read Chinese?"

I didn't bother to look up, simply answered politely, "Fluently."

The voice said, "My name is Arthur Sheekman, and I'm one of the writers on the script."

Still not looking up, I asked, "So why didn't you write me a bigger part?"

The person then walked around so I could see him. He was very slender, "tall, dark, and handsome," as we used to say! A neat mustache, perfect aquiline nose, soulful hazel eyes, dark hair, high forehead, a quizzical half smile, rather teasing, equivocal.

My type.

He said, "I've wanted to meet you, but the producer won't introduce us." The producer on the picture was George Oppenheimer.

"So?" I answered.

Well, it went on like that. He asked me for a date.

I checked up on his reputation. He was given an OK by Arthur Unger, editor of *Variety,* and I finally agreed to have dinner with him.

Arthur and I were instantly attracted to each other. Our first date was dinner with him in his home. His Filipino houseboy served it, and it was delicious. Arthur was very witty, very touchy feely, and I felt like being touched and felt. We didn't make love that night, but we were very close to it. The next night we did make love. I remember he asked me to dance naked for him, and I was very happy to. It was a wonderful feeling of freedom, physicality (if there is such a word), involvement, pleasing someone, pleasing myself. And I'm sure he felt like a Middle Eastern sultan. As a matter of fact, Frances Goldwyn, Samuel Goldwyn's wife, according to Arthur once said to him, "You have an Oriental mind." What she meant by that we never discovered. Arthur was certainly laid-back, certainly subtle. Anyway, those were glorious nights together, and breakfast was always a large tray of fruit and hot coffee outside the bedroom door, carefully put down by his houseboy, who was always cheerful and gracious and sweet. Arthur and I showered together, which is lots of fun, very delicious, slippery. Especially when you're all soaped up. And drying each other off, briskly, tenderly. Embracing all the while. And then into the beautiful bed.

Arthur once said that he fell in love with me because I could eat peppermints while making love, chocolate peppermints. It's close to the truth. They were an addiction.

So was he.

I fell in love with Arthur because he made me laugh before and after and sometimes during sex.

Like his story about his interview as a cub reporter in Chicago with the great movie star Gloria Swanson during a train stopover. "Who are your favorite authors, Miss Swanson?"

Thoughtful moment. "Zane Grey and Sigmund Frood."

Or, knocking on Gilda Gray's dressing room door after a performance in Chicago. She was a super vaudeville dancer starring as the Queen of the Shimmy. (Shake it, Baby, shake it!)

"Come in," she said, and he did. She was stark naked. "Oh!" she said. "I thought you were the laundryman."

Part of Arthur's appeal for me was that — with the exception of Gino, my son-in-law — he was the most widely read person I've ever known. You name the author, he'd read all of him! (His friend Groucho tried to emulate him.)

We dated almost exclusively from then on — me working week in and week out, and he, too, with several trips to New York to see plays he would be turning into screenplays.

He told me that once in Tiffany's looking for a present for me, in answer to a clerk's question, "What does she look like?" he pointed to a silver frame on the counter with my photograph in it and answered, "Oh, like that."

Was that the time he bought me my beautiful silver hand mirror? Can't remember. It is still one of my favorite things.

A comment Arthur made about me some years later is right on target. "You never look in a mirror. You are either the vainest woman in the world or the least vain."

Well, maybe I'm both. Having Mama's friends exclaiming over me when I was growing up — being considered by my teenage friends as "so pretty" and by my boyfriends as "gorgeous" — gave me complete confidence as to my looks.

Arthur was very, very skittish about commitment or constancy. I was too much in love to worry, and I was sure he was mine.

Meanwhile, I was hearing about his Russian-Jewish family. They had come steerage class past our Lady of Liberty and settled in St. Paul, Minnesota. He was not raised — and his immediate family was not — religious.

Arthur described his childhood, and that of his older sister, Edith, and his younger brother, Harvey, as being very poor. They were neglected by their father, who had taken a mistress of Norwegian descent. Charlie Sheekman — a bright, inventive man who owned a bar and made a catch-as-catch-can living — seldom visited his family.

Evidently, his three children were very industrious. They sold newspapers, delivered groceries, baby-sat, ran errands, shined shoes, tried to wash cars — which were not plentiful in the 1910s — and at twelve, Arthur went to work in the St. Paul Library after school and on Saturdays sorting books.

I marveled at Arthur's lack of concern about money. Especially after he told me, our first Christmas together, that the present he remembered best from his childhood Christmases was an orange!

Most of Arthur's friends when I met him — the Marx Brothers, Milton Berle, George Jessel, George Burns — had been poor boys. They had no connections, no money — few of them ever finished grammar school — just their own gut feeling and talent that they were going to make it. Harpo played piano in a whorehouse as a teenager. All of them struggled to keep alive and viable. The dreadful thing is that we didn't have tape recorders. All these incomparable writers, comedians, and actors and their tales of childhood, early manhood, first professional breaks, the vaudeville scene on the road, the hand-to-mouth poverty, the prejudice against actors — escapades, shenanigans, unbelievably funny happenings — are gone, gone, gone! Forever! It's a crying shame!

Arthur introduced me to this comical scene, these inimitable clowns and usually beautiful wives, right away. I/we, our families and friends, laughed a lot.

For example, after dinner one evening in downtown Los Angeles — we loved going to a French restaurant that featured pressed duck — Helen and Nat Perrin (dear Nat was Arthur's collaborator on the Marx Brothers movies), Ruth and Groucho Marx, Ruth and Norman Krasna (playwright, screenwriter, producer, director, delightful man, very gung-ho), and Arthur and I went on to the Burbank Burlesque Theatre. We're sitting up in the balcony, away from the verrry relaxed gentlemen below who were noisily encouraging the strippers, when a truly fantastically endowed lady came on.

She took out one breast, and twirled it, then the other.

Applause. Short silence. Arthur, in a sweet, confidential tone, called down, "Don't wrap it up, I'll eat it here!"

Then one weekend, we went up to Vegas. We went out to see the construction on Hoover Dam. We joined a group of about fifty people. We're down at the bottom, looking up hundreds of feet at this tremendous concrete structure. The tour guide is giving us the tonnage of cement and the tonnage of dirt moved. The size of the lake behind the dam and the amount of water that was going to be coming through. The amount of electricity that would be generated and the places where everyone was going to benefit. It was a long half hour of all kinds of statistics, and as the guide paused, Arthur said in a very small voice, "It won't work."

The man turned and said indignantly, "What do you mean, it won't work?"

Arthur said, "It won't work."

He demanded, "What's your theory?"

Arthur and I just laughed. It was a wonderful moment.

And then there were stories about Georgie Jessel — singer, songwriter, storyteller, man of good works, later considered incomparable as a speaker at weddings, bar or bat mitzvahs, christenings, and memorializing a fallen friend. Jessel was regarded by his peers as one of the funniest of them all.

George once told us about when he and three other barely pubescent boys decided the time had come to "have a woman." They each contributed a quarter and engaged a lady. She was very fat. She was in a fleabag hotel and they drew straws for first dibs. Jessel won and went into her room and closed the door. The others climbed on each other's shoulders to take turns looking in over the transom. As Jessel caught sight of them, he looked up, grinned, and hollered, "Acres and acres of ass and it's all mine!"

Years later, Jessel married the silent screen star Norma Talmadge. He was mad about her. She was temperamental and he was difficult, too. One day, she threw him out. George called Harry Ruby from San Francisco and said, "Harry, Norma has thrown me out for the last time. I'm finished and I'm going to kill myself!"

And Harry said, "Please, Georgie, no woman is worth killing yourself over. Hold everything. Grouch and I will be right there!"

So Harry and Groucho took a plane up to San Francisco, taxied up to the hotel, dashed into the lobby, got Jessel's room number from the clerk, and called out, "We're coming, Georgie, hold it!"

They threw open the door. George was lying on a sofa, with a naked girl standing beside him playing the violin.

Another: When the Second World War started, he volunteered in the navy and was given the rank of captain. He told us that when he called his mother with the good news, she replied, "Georgie, by you you're a captain, by me you're a captain, but by a captain, you're no captain!"

With that crowd, I started to laugh really deeply for the first time in my life.

P.S. Arthur had discovered me on the set of *Roman Scandals,* and I had made a discovery of my own. There was a very amusing girl in the chorus. She was so funny in between takes, such a natural clown, and so pretty — what we used to call a "cut up." I said to Arthur, "There's a very funny girl in the chorus." Eventually he and his good friend William Perlberg, an agent, saw her and talked to her, and Perlberg got her a contract at Columbia. She bounced around in bit parts and from then on, Lucille Ball was on her way. It pleases me that Arthur had a hand in giving Lucy her start.

*   *   *

I made *Beloved* with the gifted composer-conductor-director Victor Schertzinger, and my costar, the tenor John Boles, in 1933, but it was released on New Year's Day, 1934. It consisted of me mainly listening to John with a rapt expression on my puss. Victor had directed the great American soprano Grace Moore in her one and only hit, *One Night of Love.* Opera stars are noted for their temperament. Victor told me that, from the beginning, the diva had warned him several times she was going to be temperamental. And she was. He advised me that such shenanigans worked against one 100 percent. The rest of the cast, the crew, the front office, everyone, resents it and becomes *molto molto furioso!* And not disposed to being accommodating or even simpatico.

It was the most useful advice I'd been given in film — and in my life. You don't make problems with people that can help you.

Opening 1934, I made *The Love Captive,* a drama with Nils Asther, and *I'll Tell the World,* a comedy with Lee Tracy. Fortunately, with titles like that, I have no memory of either!

But *Here Comes the Navy* — another loan-out to Warner Brothers — playing the love interest of James Cagney, was fun. Certainly, an "A" picture, with Pat O'Brien (crazy about that feisty Irishman) and Frank McHugh, locations with the U.S. Navy, and airplane flights with film's top stunt pilot, Paul Mantz. In fact, the movie was nominated for an Academy Award as Best Picture of 1934!

Paul Mantz had done the flying on *Air Mail* — and I hadn't been in a plane since I was mailed across the country for that movie. Paul offered to take me up, and I thought I should go, to get my courage back.

So I said, "I'll go up with you, Paul, but no loop-de-loops, or deep dives, or anything." He was a charming man, and promised none. But he did do a loop-de-loop. And I did not fly again for twenty years. Sad to say, Paul was later killed doing a stunt for a movie.

That year, two more dreadful musicals were forced on me. I costarred in *Gift of Gab,* with Edmund Lowe and Ruth Etting, the Ziegfeld and musical comedy star who had also been in *Roman Scandals.* The only good part was that Harpo's friend, *New Yorker* writer Alexander Woollcott, made a cameo appearance in that movie. So did my pal Béla Lugosi with my pal from *The Old Dark House,* Boris Karloff. The bad part was that I had to dance in chorus lines. Jitterbugging badly is my finest achievement in that art — and I really shouldn't sing at all.

And what can I say about *I Like It That Way?*

Yech!

Bette Davis and Loretta Young and Olivia de Havilland were getting wonderful *dramatic* parts.

Why not me?

What had I ever done to deserve all this dreck?

1

*W*ell, after about twenty-one movies and stardom and a gorgeous lover, all of a sudden I was possessed with an overwhelming desire for a child. I was twenty-four years old, and recalling my pervasive lack of motherliness, I wonder now at that all-compelling urge. I had never picked up a baby to coo over. I had never wanted to play with a child or rejoiced over a friend's pregnancy. Besides, it meant giving up almost a year's salary, being out of the scene, maybe losing The Great Role.

Still, I wanted a child. *Now!*

In those days, sixty-five years ago, a single female did not co-habit with a lover and have his child publicly. There were couples we knew who were having affairs, and once in a great while, a child sub rosa, but the newspapers never printed anything, the Hollywood reporters on radio kept their mouths shut, and although we all knew the scandals, I don't think I even talked about them to friends. None of us gossiped like that.

So, in 1934, I wasn't looking for scandal. I proposed to my darling Arthur Sheekman. He was thirty-three at the time. A dedicated bachelor. He thought about it for a few days, then decided he would get married.

Huzza! Huzza! Huzza!

Our friends rejoiced. My mother and stepfather rejoiced — Arthur was the only man I'd ever loved who could support me. The actress who had advocated free love rejoiced — about to abandon her stance and conform!

Arthur called his mother in Chicago and said, "I'm engaged to marry Gloria Stuart!"

His mother was very happy about that, and called her sister and said, "My boy Arthur is engaged to Gloria Stuart, the movie star."

Hoping he would marry a nice Jewish girl, the aunt asked, "Doesn't he know Sylvia Sidney?"

Off we went to Agua Caliente for a Mexican marriage — head-lines in the columns — Louella Parsons, Hedda Hopper, Jimmy Starr, the *Hollywood Reporter, Variety.* Gordon and I hadn't quite managed an American divorce by then, but we had a Mexican divorce, so all right, already!

Mama and Mr. Finch met us at the great hotel there — gambling, strolling ever-present mariachis, swimming pools. The mayor of Tijuana came to marry us.

We had the bridal suite — all red velvet, hovering golden cupids, and humming mosquitoes! Swarms, hordes, platoons of mosquitoes ganged up on us, half undressed. We called for help, and a pair of boys armed with flit guns arrived. By the time they emptied their weapons of insecticide, the suite was uninhabitable. And hot — the twenty-fifth of August. No air-conditioning then.

So we dressed and went into the casino, where my parents were watching at one of the crap tables. Jean Harlow was finishing thirteen passes! It was a record. Margaritas for everyone!

We moved to another suite and, I think, conceived Sylvia. Groucho had advised me to "get knocked up" instantly. He loved his children, and Arthur, and wished us his happinesses!

The next day, to the racetrack, then back to Tijuana to the Hotel Caesar for the new Caesar Salad, and to the jai alai games, where I was given a lifetime pass. Then the next day down the coast to Ensenada. The one street was barely paved, a few shops, tourist stalls, bars. There was just one great big beautiful hotel on the beach. Wonderful food. And two happy and eager orchestras playing Mexican music almost twenty-four hours a day. We went surf-fishing, and I caught what up until then was the largest corbina that had ever been caught on that beach! There was a great hullabaloo when the chef cooked it and presented it to us that evening.

Back to Hollywood, where we had rented a beautiful home in Beverly Hills, and bought two dogs — a German shepherd, Officer, and Schlemiel, a Saint Bernard.

While filming *Laddie* at RKO early in 1935, our fine director George Stevens took me aside one morning and asked, "Gloria, are you pregnant?"

Looking at the production stills today, he had good reason to wonder. Thick waist, full bosom.

What was there to say?

I lied.

Trouble is, my role was that of a rich young lady who was practically glued to horses. My doctor didn't want me galloping after four months of pregnancy — and I was in my fourth month!

George Stevens, tactful and considerate man that he was, didn't press me for the truth, but he clearly didn't believe me, either. No jumping on and off my horse, he decreed. No galloping!

John Beal was the leading man and Pandro S. Berman the producer. Stevens later won an Academy Award for *Alice Adams* with Katharine Hepburn — Pandro Berman was again producing. A first-class team — for a change.

After we finished shooting, I took a maternity leave of absence. Dear darling Universal lost one of their moneymakers for a while. What a blessing not to have to rise and shine at 5:30 A.M., drive to the studios, go into makeup, hair, wardrobe, act, come home, have dinner, learn lines for the next day, week in and week out in banal fillums!

I had a very happy pregnancy. I listened to music because I had been told that then the baby would have a musical ear, which the baby did.

I began to do some flower planting, weeding, learning how to prune, gardening things I'd watched Mama do over the years. Mama was so pleased!

As I observed the garden, it seemed to me that there must be a Great Force, a Great Intellect, a Great Power that says to a poppy, "You are going to be orange." That says to a tree, "You're going to have five-fingered leaves and grow to be very, very tall and have acorns that will contain seeds." And says to a ladybug, "You're going to have a lovely red jacket and be able to fly." Or says to a worm, "You're going to be blind, and you're going to be able to live away from light and sound and water and manure, and old food and coffee grounds are going to nurture you so you can make compost." And how does one tree grow crookedy? And how does another tree grow straight up, and each one of its kind, by the millions, can put out a different set of limbs, with the same set of leaves?

And! After years of dieting, I ate and I ate and I ate! I went up to one hundred and sixty some-odd pounds. What shall I say? I floated free!

To match my mood, my dressmaker made me wonderful tents of chiffon in jade, peach, Schiaparelli pink, sky blue, truly floaty floaty things. I didn't try to hide the pregnancy, as was the custom many women observed at the time.

I also decided to make a patchwork quilt robe for myself. I did not know about ultra ultra expensive silk tie makers. Lanvin, Charvet, Hermès, Sulka. So I went through Arthur's ties one morning and took a few out that I thought he didn't need, cut them into odd-shaped patches, and started sewing them together in a traditional crazy-quilt patchwork. Gorgeous colors and patterns!

One evening, me sewing, Arthur and I tête-à-têteing, he asked, "Where did you get that patch?"

I answered, "It was one of your ties."

He said, "That's a Sulka tie."

"So?"

Too late. Anyway, after I got all the patches put together by hand, I featherstitched the seams in various-colored silk threads. I faced the robe — it was empire style, almost a full circle in the skirt — in garnet velvet and lined it in hot pink silk. I wore it for quite a while, even though it stopped fitting me the last couple of months. (I kept it, and in the fifties I cut it apart and made a skirt of the bottom, and Sylvia later lined an evening cape with the top.)

In June, along came our beautiful baby. I opted for natural childbirth — I wanted to know how it felt. After all, millions of women had done it, why shouldn't I? I asked Arthur and my mother to be with me at the birth, but Arthur was squeamish.

Sylvia was a breech baby. I didn't know from breech babies (they come out feetfirst), so when I heard the nurse exclaim, "It's a breech baby," I called for an anesthetic — I was going to birth a monster! However, as I came to, the doctor showed me Sylvia, and, as our daughter looked at her mother, quietly, alert and smiling, Mama was crying, I was crying, and fairly soon Arthur came in with his secret smile and took Sylvia's tiny hand.

We named our darling Sylvia because I was playing the Princess Sylvia when Arthur introduced himself — and because it's a favored Jewish name for girls, and an Old English name from Latin — a woodland nymph, a warbler thrush!

After having the baby, of course, I was heavy. My contract said I was to go back on salary when I was willing and able. Two months after Sylvia's birth, I said I was ready. I made a test.

I was not svelte.

Junior Laemmle and the front office were not happy.

But I was. I had my sweet baby, I had my witty, talented husband, and I had my friends — whom I loved to entertain.

I absorbed a great deal about the art of entertaining those months of freedom. For example, at the table, I learned to put talkers next to nontalkers — the talkers love to talk and the nontalkers would rather listen. It's very seldom that I put talkers with talkers, or nontalkers with nontalkers, because it's either a dead spot around the table, or else no one else gets on. When they're balanced, *due a due,* or *uno a uno,* there's a nice balance all the way around.

I hadn't yet plunged into cooking. I left cooking — on this level — to the professionals.

But creating an exuberantly elegant table — *that* I loved to do!

Our linens were Irish linen, hand hemmed by nuns in a Hollywood nunnery. Our silver pattern was Georgian shell and gadroon (small curves and arcs along the border of the handle, scallop shell at the base). For place cards, I wrote out the name of each guest on a beautiful card — its color appropriate to the tablecloth — in my best rounded artist's script. Inserted them into silver clips on small crystal vases, set a tiny nosegay of flowers in each vase.

I think flowers are very important at a party, so let's have a frolic! One of my most successful centerpieces was dark purple eggplants, gardenias, white eggs, and dark purple begonia leaves.

Then there was my delightful collection of place plates. Those were set on the table before dinner and were china of many different patterns — no two the same — Wedgwood, Spode, Meissen, Dresden, Limoges — and large. We call them "chargers" today.

For the first course, the butler would come out and replace the plates with new pieces, then serve the soup or seafood cocktail, all the china now matching!

I also took great pains with the butter — curls, rounds, and stars, with sprigs of parsley or nasturtium petals. The rolls were always warmed, and cuddled in a napkin-lined silver basket.

I served a great deal of pork and beef and lamb in those days. Not so much poultry and fish — although even then duck and lobster were considered the tops on a restaurant or home menu.

Salads were always served after the main course, then along came the cheese platter, the subject of much gourmand discussion. Although I don't think any of us knew anything about cheeses, we pretended to know. Then when the salad and cheese plates were removed, the finger bowls came in on another plate!

Usually I served the dessert myself because usually my desserts were from a chafing dish — crêpes suzette, cherries jubilee, flaming rum apples. They were delicious and it was a *performance* to put these things together gracefully and elegantly and with bright remarks. I was on!

Serving wine was still rare — only on special occasions, and then we might have champagne. Beer, if the main course indicated it. Otherwise, we drank what is known today as branch water. Los Angeles aqueduct water.

Anyway, wines were just coming into fashion, and some friends were in the vanguard. Alfred Newman, one of Hollywood's most gifted composer/conductors, had decided that he really knew wines, and that to be in, one really should know something about them. He was carrying on and buying cases of this and cases of that something fierce. Like a true connoisseur! So Harry Ruby and some of his buddies bought a bottle of wine and had the studio prop man decorate it with cobwebs and old dust and a label dated in the early twenties. They presented it to Al. He opened it at a dinner party. He poured it out, and swirled it around the glass, and sniffed it, and sipped it, and sipped it again, eating a piece of toast in between. A big deal. All of us were dying. He finally announced that it was really very *very* fine. The truth is, it was an el cheapo jug red.

A prop man can do anything.

Our help was divided pretty equally between Negroes (the accepted word then), Filipinos, and Chinese. We usually had couples; very seldom could one person handle an elaborate household. Regulation days off were every Thursday and every other Sunday. We had substitutes come in for the days off.

All of us with children had governesses. We did not call them nannies. Maybe "nurse" sometimes. And we had seamstresses that came in every so often during the year and mended, let out, took in, whatever was needed. They usually came and stayed in the guest room for three or four days, then moved on. Who they were, where they went, what their fees were, I have no remembrance. But they always seemed to be very happy to be in our home.

Most of our servants were from agencies and not always trained terribly well. It was, of course, during the Great Depression, and those who had lost their jobs in one trade quickly took up anything available any way they could.

After the great stock market crash of '29, I was still living up north in Carmel. We had no inkling of depression. There were the very rich up the coast in Pebble Beach, and the artists and modest villagers in our colony. I have been told California suffered the least those years, and the Monterey Peninsula — our part of the world — the least in the state.

But when I moved to Hollywood, the steady procession of men coming to the back door for food and/or work, the unemployed on street corners with apples for sale, or holding out their caps for small change or bills, was shocking. Because many people would spend their last quarter to go to the movies and be able to forget their troubles for a few hours — those who had an extra quarter could shelter in a theater almost all day and all night — the Depression did not seriously affect the film industry.

We always opened our back or front door to these needy men — and they were always men — asking for work in exchange for a meal. We brought them into the kitchen for food, whether or not the yard or driveway needed sweeping, the cars washed, or other chores done. (Where, I wonder now, were the women and children?) Even more astonishing today, there never was an untoward scary episode ever. No, we never were afraid.

However, once, when I went back to work after Sylvia was born, I got a call at the studio from the police department that our cook had gone berserk and had holed up in the kitchen with a butcher knife. The governess and Sylvia were upstairs, safe. The police had somehow managed to get the knife away from the cook, and the cook away from our house. All was well! Big sigh of relief!

But we were giving a dinner party that night! So I called the employment agency and told them that I needed a couple immediately because I was expecting guests for dinner. When I got home around six o'clock, I started to put the whole party together. I think there were twelve of us. Linens, china, crystal, silver. Tonight, no centerpiece! The couple had arrived, with recommendations, and she started cooking, and he and I started to set the table.

I said to him, "After dinner, we will have brandies in the bar." I showed him the big bell snifters and a fresh case of brandy. I said, "Please bring the glasses in on a tray when I buzz for you." Agreed.

The guests came and it was a lively go around the table. After dinner, we went through the living room into the bar. The bar was a small room — I have always found that small rooms are cozier for dinner parties than large ones. We were sitting there when the butler staggered in with the twelve oversized snifters, each filled to the brim! Everyone got hysterical. The poor butler, not knowing that a snifter should contain no more than a slosh of brandy, was mystified by the laughter.

Probably the most memorable party we gave around that time was when we were living in a big house in Beverly Hills. Arthur and I gave a party at which Joel Sayre, New York newspaperman and novelist, a teddy bear of a man, brought along Mrs. Patrick Campbell. She was the English actress who created Eliza Doolittle in *Pygmalion* and many other George Bernard Shaw roles. Of course I was terribly impressed that Mrs. Campbell, Bernard Shaw's great love (but no sex), was my dinner guest.

Mrs. Campbell was a piece of work, as they say. Joel had mentioned that, in London a couple of years before, she'd made her entrance in Ivor Novello's spoof of a play, *A Party*, in a fabulous long black gown, a small white Pekinese dog under her arm, trailed by clouds of smoke from her cigar.

That night Joel also brought a man who was wildly popular on college campuses, the novelist Thomas Wolfe. *Look Homeward, Angel* had been published six years before to huge success. He would live but three years after we met him, dying at thirty-eight.

Sylvia was in her cradle upstairs in the nursery. I was charmed when Mr. Wolfe asked to see the baby, so we took him upstairs. He gently touched our daughter's forehead and said, "May the fairies bless you forever." Sylvia tells me that, indeed, they have.

At the end of the evening, as she was leaving, Mrs. Campbell asked for her black cape. I sent the maid upstairs to where we kept the coats, but she came back and said she couldn't find it.

I said, "That's nonsense. She had it on when she came in, it has to be someplace." So we started looking upstairs, downstairs, couldn't find the cape, and I was very worried because I didn't want to tell Mrs. Campbell I couldn't find her black cape. I really was very upset!

Finally I had to say, "Mrs. Campbell, I'm so embarrassed, we cannot find it. I don't know what could possibly have happened to your cape."

And Thomas Wolfe said, smiling, "Oh, Gloria, Mrs. Campbell didn't have a black cape at all."

Mrs. Campbell had a naughty look on her face.

I didn't get it.

Then Wolfe whispered that Mrs. Campbell was famous for asking hostesses for her black cape when she left — a cape that was nonexistent — and for discombobulating her hostesses.

I would love to know if she tried this bit on Mrs. Bernard Shaw!

8

There were about twelve couples at a wonderful party we gave one Easter. Bogey and Mayo were one of the couples. Arthur had met Bogart at Warner Brothers, and I had met him at Screen Actors Guild board meetings, probably early in 1934. Mayo Methot was Bogey's third wife. She had been a leading Broadway actress when the two of them worked in New York. The four of us were very good friends.

Everyone was into hats at that time, so I went down to the wholesale millinery district in Los Angeles and bought undecorated straw hats and a lot of flowers and ribbons and veils. And fruit. The idea was that the men were to make Easter Bonnets for their wives or girlfriends. For a prize.

The ladies and I retired into the playroom, where we could watch the men in the garden trying the hats on each other, pinning the flowers on, draping the veils, and making bows with the ribbons and so forth. They were very earnest about it. We ladies were drinking champagne and it was *très amusant!*

The prize was a jeroboam of champagne, which was all beribboned with Easter colors.

Bogart won it because he composed a darling hat with orange and green ribbons, and then had taken a flower with a long stem and woven it into the brim of the hat, and hung a carrot on the end of it, dangling in Mayo's face! Everybody voted him first prize. He was given the champagne, and of course the glasses were out and ready, but he tucked that big bottle under his arm and took it home — without opening it. Quite a shock.

Bogey and Arthur often played chess together (during the war, Bogey kept countless chess games going with boys overseas, playing by mail). Mayo and I played bridge together almost every week with Ruth Pidgeon (her Walter played my lover in *The Kiss Before the Mirror*) and Gertie Hatch (the wife of *New Yorker* writer Eric Hatch).

Sadly, Mayo usually had bruises on her face — left or right cheek, chin. It seems unconscionable today to remember that we used to remark, "They must get their jollies that way."

I'm with the French, who say that in most love affairs there is the one who loves and the one who is beloved. I think in Bogart's relationship with Mayo, she was the loving one. I'm sure that in his relationship with Betty (Lauren) Bacall, he was the loving one. I don't think he ever laid a hand on her. If he had, I would be very surprised, especially that he survived it.

One cook's night off when Arthur and I were at Chasen's (practically everyone ate there on Thursday nights), Mayo and Bogey were in the next booth. She had on a very décolleté dress. At some point during the evening — I guess I was tiddly — I lobbed a pat of butter over into their booth. I don't remember whether or not it hit Bogey or Mayo but she lobbed another pat of butter over to our table. End of that game.

Then came some general loud conversation, which led to Bogey saying to her, "That's too low, I don't like it."

Mayo was plain in a pretty kind of way. She was very quick and had a sharp tongue to match Bogart's. She said, "Well, up yours, Buster."

He grabbed both sides of the low-cut dress and tore it right down to as far as it would go. A very jolly evening.

Another night, Bogey and Mayo and Arthur and I went to Slapsie Maxie's. Slapsie Maxie Rosenbloom was a prizefighter who had opened a large nightclub in Hollywood. Bogey and Mayo were tipsy, and about whatever it was, he said to her, "You say that once more, Sluggy, and I'm really going to give it to you." So Sluggy said it once more, and Bogey reached across the table and pushed her into the next table along with the table that we were sitting at.

Mayo started screaming, and I got up and said, "My God, Bogey!" and went to pick her up.

Still seated, he turned to Arthur and said, "Well! Wouldn't you have hit her?"

And Arthur answered, "Not necessarily."

I helped her up and the whole room was completely silent, with Mayo crying and carrying on and calling Bogey names. I put my arms around her and the four of us left.

Yet another time, the Bogarts asked us over to dinner with Mary and Mel Baker. Mary was a successful writer's agent and Mel was a prominent screenwriter. After we'd been there awhile and Bogey was busy with the cocktails, I asked where Mayo was.

Bogey said, "She's upstairs and she's drunk. She has a gun."

I said, "She has a gun?"

He said, "Yeah, she's got a gun. She's gonna kill me."

I answered, "Oh, my God."

He grinned, and dinner was announced. There was spirited conversation — and an empty chair.

When we finished dinner, Bogey said to us, "I'll tell you what. Let's go upstairs. We really should flush her out."

I said to Arthur, "You've never handled a gun, don't go with him up there. It's suicide! And Mel, you shouldn't go either!"

Mary said, "Mel knows how to shoot!"

Bogey said, "Come on, Gloria, that's ridiculous. I have a gun, and I'll go first, and Mel and Arthur can back me up."

Needless to say we all were slightly inebriated.

Well! Mary and I stayed below and the three idiots went upstairs and I heard Bogey say, "Come on, Mayo, come on out, drop the gun, come on, Sluggy, don't shoot, come on, I love you. . . ."

I went to the top of the stairs and looked, and the three men were lined up flat against the wall of the hall, Bogey with a gun in his hand, Arthur and Mel behind him, with Mayo yelling and hollering inside the bedroom.

Well, she did come out. And he dropped the gun, and she dropped the gun. The four of them came downstairs and we split.

Arthur and I weren't happy playing Russian roulette with these gifted and temperamental actors. But we loved them. And they were bright and sassy and never boring.

The time we came close to lightsome trouble was when four couples — Bogey and Mayo, Mary and Mel Baker, Honey and Gil Gabriel (he was a New York City theater critic trying his hand at screenplays), and Arthur and I decided to spend Labor Day weekend yachting to Catalina Island, about thirty miles off the coast.

I was in charge of renting the yacht. I chose John Barrymore's old *Mariner,* a ninety-three-foot black-hulled schooner. Scruffy but romantic — it had been Barrymore's honeymoon boat with his ravishing bride Dolores Costello. It had belonged since then to several owners.

No one but Bogart knew anything about sailing, but we had rented a captain and one sailor with the boat and Bogey said that was enough. Everyone had also brought along their houseboys, for extra hands.

Loaded with food and liquor — passengers and crew wearing the yachting caps I'd bought — we put-putted out of San Pedro Harbor. Into the fog.

Bogey went up to check with our captain, came down, and mentioned casually that the foghorn wasn't working.

Dear! Dear! What did that mean?

Nothing more than that it should be working.

Mayo looked out the window and remarked that there was no running light portside. She checked the starboard side. No running light there, either.

Bogey grinned and assured us he could find Fourth of July Cove on Catalina Island blindfolded, hands tied behind his back. We were not to worry. By that time, none of us were in any shape to worry. Bogart was our leader, and we were having a wonderful time.

As he promised, we docked in the cove — all of us hungover — early the next morning.

When it came time to put up the sails — all forty-six hundred square feet of them on two huge masts — the men heave-ho'd, the sails barely got above the deck, their rotted ropes broke, and the sails collapsed onto the deck, the men barely escaping.

John Ford was anchored nearby and sent his motorboat over to take Bogey and Arthur off to phone for another yacht.

When it arrived, it took us hours to unload and load the two boats, but the next day we motored around the island, visiting other seagoing friends and a couple of bars on the island.

That night on our way back to San Pedro, while having post-prandial brandies, Mayo announced she wanted to steer the boat. "My father was a sea captain and I know how!"

Over our protests, Bogey said, "Ah, come on, kids, let her do it. What can happen?" Silence. Bogart: "OK, Sluggy, go to it!"

And off she swayed.

Shortly after, in the midst of our sort-of harmonizing, we realized that our yacht was making a full circle in the sea. The full moon in front of us was now at our backs! Bogey dashed up the stairs. Saved! We almost swamped a tiny becalmed sailboat, three souls aboard, but Heaven intervened, and we docked safe and sound.

In our crowd, in those years, drinking too much — getting high — was considered fairly amusing. Even driving while drunk was thought rather funny.

Extraordinary.

(I still remember the night Prohibition was declared. I was eight and a half. As we walked along the boardwalk in nearby Ocean Park, people were swooning or falling down, and bumping into each other with bottles in their hands. Saloon doors were open, and I could see the crush of people in there, all shouting and screaming and jostling each other. I thought of it later as being something to do with Liberty and Free Will, but I have no idea of where my parents stood on these principles, except that Mama kept a pint of Jack Daniel's under her pillow for as long as I can remember.)

Of course, dinner with friends could be amusing without one's getting drunk.

My old beau George Oppenheimer introduced us to Dorothy Parker and her husband, Alan Campbell. Dottie was George's shining star. When George and Arthur worked together, Arthur would take him home (George never learned to drive). On the way, George would always ask Arthur to go past the house where Dottie and Alan lived. When cars were parked in front, George would be very unhappy that they were giving a party that he was not asked to.

There was a curious social custom going around Hollywood then. "Please come in after dinner." And other guests were invited for dinner!

George did this to the Marxes and us. Never to be outwitted, Groucho suggested we take box lunches over and arrive early, in the middle of his dinner, and picnic in the living room. Which we did. It caused George some consternation and embarrassment — and the other guests, Dorothy and Alan among them, a great deal of laughter.

Groucho and Arthur showed me how ridiculous and pompous and dull people can be and certainly how most situations are not to be taken seriously. For this gift of laughter, I am eternally grateful!

After their first meeting, Arthur became Groucho's close, if not closest, friend. They met when the Marx Brothers came to Chicago late in 1928 touring with *Animal Crackers*. Arthur was a columnist for the *Chicago Sun Times* and interviewed Groucho backstage. When The Boys (which is what they called themselves) left town, Arthur was on the train with them — Groucho had asked him to come to Hollywood to write for them.

Arthur lived with Groucho and his wife, Ruth, the first year. That next year, Arthur ghostwrote Groucho's small amusing book, *Beds,* and contributed to the script of *Monkey Business.* And in 1930 he worked on *Duck Soup* with Bert Kalmar, Nat Perrin, and my then-beau, Harry Ruby.

The ancients had a saying: "No gift without a curse."

After Arthur and I married, Groucho took up a great deal of our spare time. Especially Arthur's. Although he didn't always earn a writing credit, Arthur was on each and every movie as Groucho's consultant and pal.

Grouch was not my favorite person. This made things difficult for me, to say the least, because he and my husband were best friends. The key to life with Groucho was that he had to respect you. Those whom he perceived vulnerable were in trouble. He was especially hard on women. Coincidence or not, nearly all the women in his life ended up drinking or on pills.

And he had, shall we say, a thrifty side.

In 1934, shortly after Arthur and I were married, the Screen Actors Guild voted that all actors should give one-half of one per-cent of their salaries to found and support the Motion Picture Home — the remarkable facility that took care of old or disabled down-on-their-luck members of our industry.

At Groucho's for dinner not long after, he announced he wasn't giving a dime to old actors, vaudevillians, prop boys, or — or — or.

I got up from the table, threw my napkin down, and said I couldn't eat dinner with him — then or ever again. Why did he have contempt for unlucky old actors, vaudevillians, performers?

And walked home. We lived near Groucho then, and as I entered our house, the phone was ringing. It was Arthur. He said, "Gloria, I order you to return."

I said, "You what?"

"I order you to return." This was a 180-degree turnabout of my husband's manners. He was never vocally contentious. His ploy was silence.

"There's no way in the world I'm going to return. I don't care if he is your best friend. He's a cheap, chintzy, unfeeling bastard."

"Come back, Gloria."

"Fuck off, Arthur. No!"

Thus began a long Arthurian silence. Sometimes Arthur didn't speak to me for days, once for several weeks!

At the time, my judgment of Grouch was not based on knowledge of his history. I didn't know he was one of five children (he was the middle child, after Chico, and Harpo) with very, very poor parents — so poor, the children had to sleep five in a bed. I didn't know how bleak his childhood had been, or that he and his brothers had lost their life savings in the stock market crash of 1929. That he had vowed never to be poor again. Certainly, with a family to support and the future of *any* movie being a BIG success an uncertainty, Groucho had a right to be careful.

So, OK, irritating as I found him, I must say life with Groucho was amusing.

Mama had taught me to play bridge when I was about fourteen. I played bridge all during high school and college — never for money, but I played a lot of cards. Then I didn't play for years. After I married Arthur, I urged him to learn to play because I missed it.

Groucho had never played cards, although Harpo, Chico, and Zeppo were brilliant card players. Actually they played for very high stakes, and in very heavy games.

So I hired a teacher for the three of us. It was when Culbertson (his bidding system) was just coming in, and the teacher brought duplicate boards. We sat playing with the teacher for about three lessons, but neither Arthur nor Groucho got it at all.

The lesson had moved from our house to Groucho's to our house. The fourth time she arrived at Groucho's with the boards, we were late.

Groucho said to her, to pass the time of day, "How do you like the Sheekmans?"

She said, "Oh, I like them very much."

And he said, "It is a shame, isn't it?"

And she said, "What do you mean, Mr. Marx?"

And he said, "Oh, I thought you knew."

And she said, "Knew what?"

"That they're brother and sister." He said, "It's a scandal in Hollywood."

She said, "Mr. Marx, they're brother and sister?"

He said, "Yes, and they're married, and they have a child."

She picked up her boards and left. We never saw or heard from her again. And that was the end of the bridge lessons.

The Boys had a lot of escapades. My favorite one was at lunchtime in the Empire State Building in New York City. They were invited to a large convention of studio executives on the umpteenth floor. They inveigled the elevator operator to halt it just short of their floor, took all their clothes off, and, as the elevator door opened, marched arm in arm into a luncheon for female employees of a telephone company.

Favorite Groucho story about Frenchy, his father, concerned a fancy party Groucho gave. Frenchy was, at that point, more than a little spacey, and wouldn't fit in. So Grouch suggested he eat in the kitchen with the children.

Halfway through dinner, the kitchen door opened, the old man poked his head through, and said, "More meat or I'll come out!"

(When Frenchy was dying, The Boys couldn't keep a nurse because he kept grabbing them.)

Groucho was mad about writers. His friends were almost all

writers, although he enjoyed the company of comedians and musicians. Groucho entertained several times a week, and Arthur and I were almost always invited.

At Groucho's, even though the menu was usually some version of pot roast and potatoes, the guest list never was dull.

One night, George and the Ira Gershwins were there, and after dinner, Groucho cautioned us not to ask George to play, so we didn't. Nor did anyone else. Finally, about ten o'clock — we always ate early at Mr. Marx's — George moved over to the piano and played, with our singing until midnight!

To be in the same room listening to Gershwin playing the piano, or Harry Ruby singing ("Show me a rose, and I'll show you a ship at sea, show me a rose, or leave me alone . . ."), or Groucho ("Hooray for Captain Spaulding . . ."), or listening to the incomparable riposters — Jack and Mary Benny, George Burns and Gracie Allen, Milton Berle, Georgie Jessel . . . ! Plus the conversation of George Kaufman, Moss Hart, Ben Hecht, Sinclair Lewis . . .

But such a life wasn't for Groucho's first wife, Ruth, a lovely blond Swede who had been a chorus girl. She was a devoted mother to her children, Arthur and Miriam, and certainly was a devoted wife, hostess, and chief appreciator to Himself. But Ruth was never greatly impressed by the extraordinary people Groucho gathered around him.

At one dinner, there was Charlie Chaplin and his wife, Oona, the fine English novelist G. B. Stern, the great Spanish guitarist Andrés Segovia, Norman Krasna, and us. I knew Groucho's marriage was in trouble when I was sitting next to Ruth and she whispered to me, "What am I doing here with all these jokers?"

I whispered back, "Ruth, there isn't a hostess in Hollywood who wouldn't give her eyeteeth to have these people at her table."

She shrugged and whispered, "I'd rather be at the tennis club," and returned to eating.

*   *   *

Often, during those seemingly dream-come-true years, I had night-mares. I was onstage and I forgot my lines . . . missed an en-trance . . . there was no audience in the theater . . . I was all alone.

Waking, I was still stuck in Universal's B unit. I was back to work, farmed out to Warner's for *Gold Diggers of 1935,* a Busby Berkeley — the Magician of Musicals — movie in a charming role, Dick Powell's romantic interest. But then I had to play the lead in a Warner's comedy, *Maybe It's Love.* I wanted desperately out of my contract.

Junior Laemmle called me into his office and enthusiastically informed me that the (birdbrained) front office was going to make me "a female Tarzan!"

I pounded his desk, stomped around it, and in his face screamed, "I won't! I won't! You can't make me!"

Then the "sons of bitches" and ruder epithets arrived.

For a wonder, Arthur and his good friend the producer Freddy Kohlmar managed a coup that took me to Twentieth Century–Fox, headed by the legendary Darryl F. Zanuck. The price was that I had to return to Universal for two or three pictures a year.

At Twentieth, I was given a beautiful suite in the female stars' building — Sonja Henie, Alice Faye, Loretta Young — and a thor-ough publicity go-round.

My first film for Twentieth was Zanuck's *Professional Soldier.* It was a family film with a story by Damon Runyon, and Freddie Bartholomew playing a young prince. The rest of the cast was Victor McLaglen, Constance Collier, and Michael Whalen.

Constance also was a product of the theater — London calling! She had been a distinguished star there, confidante of Bernard Shaw, Virginia Woolf, Sir Beerbohm Tree. I was thrilled! But she was reclusive, and protected by an ogress, so I never got to talk to her. Who could believe that years later in summer theater, I would have to support her onstage, feeding her her lines in an English comedy?

Next Zanuck cast me in one of my more interesting roles —

Peggy Mudd, wife of the doctor who treated Lincoln's assassin. Warner Baxter played Dr. Mudd and John Carradine the prison warden. The script of *The Prisoner of Shark Island* was by our dear friend Nunnally Johnson.

Again, I was privileged to work with the legendary John Ford. Although I must say, Ford never gave any noticeable direction to his actors — at least not in the two films I made for him. He would place the actors and their moves, with concurrence from his cameraman, then sit down, tie a white handkerchief around his left hand, and indicate a rehearsal take place. The most direction I ever had from him was during the scene where my husband, hooded and probably about to be hanged, is led in with the other suspected assassins.

I'm standing with my father (Claude Gillingwater), reacting to this horror, and after the first take, Mr. Ford came over and whispered, "I think a little more reaction. (Pause, pause, pause.) Maybe just a little!"

How much is "just a little"?

Why, I wonder, the white handkerchief?

Then I got a call from my agent, Phil Berg, saying that Mr. Zanuck wanted to see me.

I thought, "Gloria, here it comes! Here it is! You're on your way! Hi diddle diddle — the cat and the fiddle!"

I entered his office with all the smiling charm I could muster, ready to pay homage.

"Gloria," Zanuck said, "I've decided to put you in a Shirley Temple film. *Poor Little Rich Girl*. We want to build you up and you'll be playing her sister." He smiled his snaggletoothed smile.

I couldn't believe it. After a moment, I answered, "Mr. Zanuck, I'm a stage actress. I come from Molnár, Chekhov, Shakespeare. I'm a dramatic actress. Shirley Temple's *sister*?"

His reply, annoyed, was, "Gloria, in a Shirley Temple movie you'll be seen by millions — millions all over the world. The pictures you've made so far haven't been seen by many people. You do it."

He had a point. Even I can't remember a thing about many of the fillums I made that year. *Girl Overboard*? *The Girl on the Front Page*? *36 Hours to Kill*? *Wanted: Jane Turner*? Can't tell you about them. A movie text describes *The Crime of Dr. Forbes* as "a competently handled minor item." Sounds right.

I was sick to my stomach at the thought of doing a Shirley Temple movie — but I did it. And in 1938 — two years after *Poor Little Rich Girl* and doozers like *Life Begins in College*, *The Lady Escapes*, *Keep Smiling*, *The Lady Objects*, *Island in the Sky*, and *Change of Heart*— I was again called into Mr. Zanuck's office, and I ended up making another Shirley Temple film, *Rebecca of Sunnybrook Farm*. This also with Randolph Scott, Jack Haley, and Bill "Bojangles" Robinson. Of course, Zanuck was right. I still hear from friends and fans, "Saw you last night with Shirley Temple . . ."

Three more — a mystery, a comedy, and a drama — my last picture under contract was an action/adventure/singing/takeoff on *The Three Musketeers*. With Don Ameche, the Ritz Brothers, and Joseph Schildkraut, another ex–New York theater matinee idol. I played Queen Anne. The producer was Raymond Griffith — he had produced *Rebecca of Sunnybrook Farm* and also worked with Zanuck on *Les Miserables,* nominated for an Academy Award as Best Picture of 1935. Needless to say, *The Three Musketeers* wasn't nominated for anything.

Let's see. How many films had I made in seven years? According to the release dates, there were four in 1932, ten in 1933, six in 1934, three and a baby in 1935, eight in 1936, two in 1937 (odd!), six in 1938, and three in 1939. That makes forty-two, an average of six a year.

When I was finished, the studio made no signs of keeping me. Phew!

My agency, Berg-Allenberg, likewise.

For seven years your agents take 10 percent of your salary, and let the studio botch a career without a word of protest, and at the

Wasn't I a dish?
*(Courtesy of Marvin Paige's Motion Picture
& T.V. Research Service)*

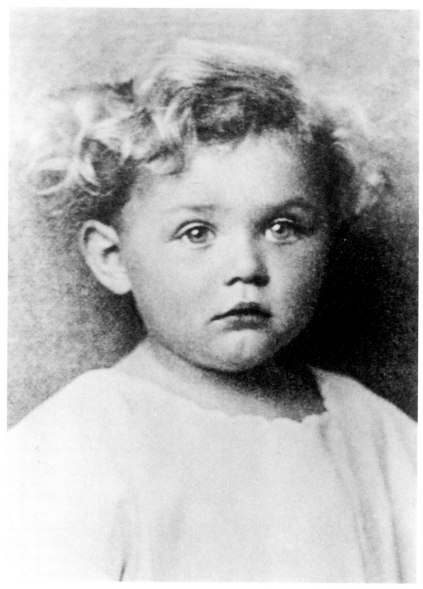

Miss Gloria Frances Stewart, age three.

Alice Deitrick Stewart as a bride, 1909.
(*Lorillard*)

Papa Frank Stewart, and me and Frank Junior
(otherwise known as Boy). (*Lorillard*)

GLORIA STUART

*As a Sculptor's Wife She Models a Plan
for a Screen Star's Successful Married Life.*

By Jack Jamison

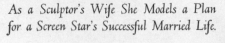

EDITOR'S NOTE—
"Gloria has just finished posing for one of the finest
pieces of sculpture her husband, Gordon Newell, has
ever turned out. We have
obtained a photograph of it
and reproduced it on this
page. It is a beautiful panel
for a door, carved of the
finest hardwoods. The carv-
ing, to some extent, is con-
ventionalized and 'modern-
istic.' The face, especially,
has been worked into an artistic unity, and so does not
particularly resemble Gloria's. But there, in Gordon's
new house, immortalized in
the glossy sheen of rare
woods, stands Gloria's slim,
lovely body.

GLORIA STUART has
taught Hollywood a new
way to look at marriage!
As perhaps you've heard, marriage in Hollywood is a pretty
shaky proposition. Few couples stay together long. To
date, Hollywood has had only
two viewpoints towards those
broken homes. Either you
broke frankly into the head-
lines with your divorce, and
let the public think what it
liked, or you kept on pretend-
ing you loved your wife or
husband (for the public's sake)
when really you wished he or
she were in the nearest ash-can.
Brazen it out, or hide it. It had
to be one thing or the other.

Few stars, indeed, have actually tried to *beat* the Hollywood jinx, which decrees that
marriage has little chance to
last, or to figure out a work-
able scheme which would help
them stay in love. Miriam
Hopkins' companionate marriage failed, and, though it is
true that Claudette Colbert
and Norman Foster live apart,
strong rumors have it that the
reason is not any attempt to
experiment, but rather, Claudette's Mama!

Gloria and her husband are
setting up two establishments,
in [Continued on page 59]

Gloria Stuart is the
provocation and de-
spair of her sculptor
husband.

Gordon Newell, hus-
band of our Gloria,
photographed beside
the bas-relief which
he sculptured from
his beautiful wife.

I may have been the "provocation and despair" of my sculptor husband,
Gordon Newell, but I was also his inspiration. The nude carved into the
wooden panel was me. (Silver Screen *magazine, February 1934. Courtesy of Marvin
Paige's Motion Picture & T.V. Research Service)*

And to think they called it "leg" art!

(*Magazine cover, Rio de Janeiro, November 1932*)

I was an international Movie Star—capital M, capital S!

CINÉ MONDE

PRIX : 1 franc - 2 MAI 1935
DIRECTEUR : JEAN-MICHEL PAGÈS

1fr

ÉCLAT !...
GLORIA STUART

The OLD DARK HOUSE

WEIRD!

Travelers on a mountain
road overtaken by a thun-
der-storm and torrential
rain, seek shelter in a
mysterious old mansion. It is full
of queer characters and uncanny
happenings. A remarkable picture
with a remarkable cast.

BORIS KARLOFF
MELVYN DOUGLAS
CHARLES LAUGHTON
GLORIA STUART
LILLIAN BOND and others

Directed by
JAMES WHALE

From the novel by J. B. Priestley

Universal Pictures

UNIVERSAL CITY, CALIFORNIA   Carl Laemmle   730 FIFTH AVENUE, NEW YORK
President

Shadoplay

DECEMBER

10¢

GLORIA
STUART

"SCANDALS"
of the
HOUR

CLICK
THE NATIONAL PICTURE MONTHLY

On my way! Being "mailed" to New York City via American Airways for
Air Mail publicity, 1932. *(Air Mail Publicity, Universal set photographer Ray Jones.*
Courtesy of Marvin Paige's Motion Picture & T.V. Research Service)

end, your agents, who are supposed to have your best interests at heart, are not answering the phone or are "away," or in conference.

It's humiliating. Makes a girl feel like she's been had.

It didn't help that, during a crying spell, my husband said to me, "You'll never be a famous actress, Gloria. You don't have it. Give it up."

Was that a salve to heal my rejections?

If one doesn't have it, one shouldn't keep on hoping?

Or was it a Swann-like maneuver to keep me to himself?

9

I shared double beds with my dear first husband and my last lover, but darling Arthur and I started out with separate rooms and beds.

By necessity. I was working and had to get up at 5 A.M. Arthur was working, too, but needed only four or five hours a night to sleep — the other hours he read. And he read. And he read.

So, as my breakfast tray was brought in, his reading light was just being put out.

Early in April 1939, reading the *Los Angeles Times* Sunday travel section — lo and behold! The towers of Angkor Wat!

What had Gordon Newell said to me once when we'd been talking about influences on his sculpture? "On my trip around the world, the most exciting thing I saw was Angkor Wat. Gloria, you have to see it before you die!"

I put my breakfast tray aside and walked into Arthur's room with the paper.

"Honey, how would you like to go around the world?"

He looked startled and answered with a twinkle, "When?"

"As soon as we can. I want to go to Indochina. I want to see Angkor Wat."

So, after a joke starting with "What is Wat?" we got serious. (So, what *is* Wat? It is the memorable temple of Angkor Thom, capital of the ancient Khmers, founded in the ninth century. Once as magnificent as India's Taj Majal, the temple is a mile outside the city walls. Both city and temple were in ruins when a French naturalist discovered them in 1860 in the middle of a jungle. The jungle was cut away so visitors could see these Wonders of the World.)

Arthur had finished at Metro and I had finished at Twentieth. Adolf Hitler was making a lot of trouble in Europe, the Japanese were already in China, it was very possible we were heading for another world war. We figured we'd better see the world before it exploded.

As we canceled social dates, called a real estate agent, called our families, Arthur cautioned me, "Don't tell me how much money we have — just make sure there's enough in the bank to see us through."

Early in our marriage, Arthur had said to me, "You keep track of the money. Don't bother me. Just take care of it all." And I did. With style. Arthur and I were never filthy rich — by today's standards at least — but when we had it, we had no qualms about spending it.

Mama worried about our finances — and that I was giving up what was, to her, "a brilliant career." But I was set on it. Reluctantly, but certainly with love, Mama accepted care of our Sylvia, age four, and promised to supervise the rental of our house and our two real estate properties.

We booked passage on the Pacific Steamship freighter line from San Francisco to New York City via the Orient and the Mediterranean, with the promise that we could jump ship and reboard at any time up to two years.

What I didn't happen to mention to Mama was that I wanted to stay in New York City after we landed — permanently. As Norman Krasna said later, "You're going to New York by way of China?"

We shipped ahead to the dock in San Francisco four extra-sized steamer trunks (the kind where the lid comes up and the two sides open up, one with drawers, the other with hangers), six pieces of more or less hand luggage, plus a four-piece tapestry luggage set for my shoes, hats, and lingerie. We kept our chess/backgammon set, two portable typewriters, a case for books and paper, makeup, jewelry, leftovers, and overnight cases with us.

Ever the practical person, prepared for any emergency, I packed a blue fox jacket and a three-quarter-length white ostrich feather cape (which was to prove a sensation at the French club in Shanghai!).

Eight days after sailing, May 23, 1939, I wrote in my diary (I couldn't write sooner because I was seasick), "The first sight of our boat at its dock was pretty disheartening. Small, 522 feet long, and low in the water." Thank heaven it was low. Our little USS *Polk* never pitched in rough seas, just rolled a bit — like a very pregnant woman out for a walk.

Our stateroom was the best. There were only six other passengers, and they left us in Honolulu. No press met us there. That was both an upper and a downer. I may have been giving up my movie star life — but I wasn't so sure I liked being ignored. A navy family joined us, going out to the Philippines. We all ate at Captain Hawkins's table and enjoyed lots of seafaring stories and little-known facts. Like, drowned women float faceup, drowned men facedown.

Quote from May 29 — "Intermittently I'm reading Stanislavsky's *An Actor Prepares* and find it exciting and oh so thorough." Still hoping, I guess.

In Yokohama, we were met by a goodly number of photographers and press — that felt good. Our first interviewer was a Nisei — and he and others asked why we had come to Japan and what about the proposed Hollywood boycott?

The rape of Nanking had taken place only two years before. Two hundred and fifty thousand defenseless Chinese had been raped, brutalized, and murdered by the Japanese army. Add to that the Japanese had long been pirating our copyrighted films, so it had been suggested that Hollywood no longer send its movies to Japan.

One classic remark, when I mentioned we were going on to China, was "We don't want to fight there! No one wants to fight. We just want to unite with China."

"Like Hitler has united with Czechoslovakia?" I asked.

"Yes!"

At the Imperial Hotel in Tokyo, the original Frank Lloyd Wright hotel, we met more reporters, and one American, Al Pindar of the *Japanese Advertiser.*

I was stunned by his question, put with scarcely veiled acidity: "Do you think you have hidden undiscovered dramatic talents, Miss Stuart?" Yes, I did, and I was on my way to their being discovered on the New York stage.

Evidences of the war in China were everywhere. No cameras allowed, marching recruits, truck convoys, flags flags flags. But we managed a Japanese film studio visit. The Ofuna Studios. And the great tourist venues — Kamakura, Kabuki theatre, Yoshimara's red-light district, a geisha finishing school. . . .

On to beautiful, green green green Nara, where we had been told to ask for Harajiho Yoshikawa, the "only English-speaking rickshaw boy there."

He was so tiny.

Arthur and I lasted about three minutes being pulled. We both felt it was degrading. My husband figured that the rickshaw cost less per hour than the ten-cent cigar he was smoking. So Yoshikawa became our walking guide for the magical day in Nara.

On the way back to the train station, Yoshi confided that he was no ordinary rickshaw boy. He owned a farm his wife and son worked on plus a Korean — "Cheap labor," he commented snootily, and winked.

On our last morning in Tokyo, we stopped in an antique ivory store. I had heard that Charles Chaplin, on his visit there the year before, had collected some fabulous antique netsukes. These rare and exquisite small carved pieces — in ivory, rare woods, jade, or other semiprecious stones — used to be hung from kimono sashes, daggers, or swords. I was not to be outdone! Fortune smiled on us that day. We bought seven for fifteen yen each. They had all been signed by classic artisans. Nearly thirty years later, when we needed money, we sold them — for thousands of dollars!

On to Kobe, where we visited an American, Henry Sanborn — a friend of Al Pindar's. He was as anti-American as you could get, anti–Japanese men, too, but delirious over Japanese women. He had been there for forty years, as contrary a character as we had ever met.

People have favorite jokes. Henry Sanborn's was "Mrs. Lindbergh was dealt an Ace, Mrs. Windsor a King, Mrs. Mussolini was dealt a Deuce, and Mrs. Roosevelt a Knave. She called for a New Deal."

Here, too, we unknowingly feathered our nest for the coming lean years. Being a Californian, Henry presented us with a minutely detailed painting on white silk, twenty-four by forty inches, of a side-wheeler that had sailed between New York and San Francisco in the 1850s.

I was so hesitant about accepting it — "You're a native daughter," he urged. "Take it!" I did, and in the sixties, short of money, I sold it to the book dealer and old friend Jake Zeitlin for three hundred dollars. He never would tell me who bought it — where it is. Today, it is almost priceless, of course.

The Yellow River flowing past Shanghai was jammed with sampans and junks, all flying Japanese flags. Foreign ships had their countries' flags painted on their sides. A few of the buildings on the Bund — the boulevard bordering the river — still had shell holes.

No press or cameras, but an assistant to Sir Victor Sassoon

met us, took Arthur through customs, and drove us to Sassoon's Cathay Mansions, one of his hotels on the waterfront.

Sir Victor was a tall, grayish, impeccably tailored man with a limp — offhandedly mentioned as an aviation wound from World War I — who talked constantly, quite authoritatively, fingering his monocle. White Russians and European Jews, tens of thousands of them, were flooding northern China on their way to anyplace that would take them. Sir Victor was their patron.

Emily Hahn, later a brilliant writer for *The New Yorker,* was Sir Victor's majordomo for the refugee camps that he had set up across the river in Hankow.

Early in our stay, Emily invited us to smoke opium in her house. Hahn announced she was "second wife" to Sinmai Zau, noted Chinese intellectual and publisher, and that she smoked two pipes a day. (An American doctor friend of hers confided to me that she was exaggerating. "Maybe the Chinese can smoke that many, but it is so foreign to the Occidentals' culture, we just can't handle it!")

My father had taken my mother on a tour of the opium dens of San Francisco in 1919 on their honeymoon. Several levels down into the earth, dozens of cribs occupied by addicts, dank, dark, scary for a country girl. She fainted. But I found reading about opium titillating.

Emily's gratuitous two pipes a day was obviously meant to shock. I don't shock easily, and when someone tries to shock me, I respond enthusiastically or as not impressed. So when she tossed that boast at me, I responded, "I've always wanted to try it — thank you, darling, we'll be there."

So we went one hot, humid evening to her beautiful house with an open lanai, full of screeching macaws and leaping, climbing, swinging gibbons. Emily was on the opium bed, in a pink satin robe. On the long low table in front of the bed was a tray full of implements, small boxes, four pipes, and a burning lamp.

We sat on the other side of the table, and Sinmai came in. Sinmai was a gentle, tall man with a large mole on the center of his left cheek. A long hair came from it and rested on his chest. (Later, a friend told me the mole-cum-hair was considered a thing of beauty. I didn't reply.) He half lay down next to Emily on the other side of the bed, put the tray between them, and she said, "Sinmai never lets me prepare my pipes, because I do it so badly."

He was very busy, catching up the molassesy stuff on a little metal wand, weaving it back and forth over the flame, turning and molding it into a little half-cooked, asymmetric capsule. This was put in Emily's pipe, and she held it over the flame, sucking on it noisily and rhythmically and hard, inhaling the resultant smoke.

Then Sinmai started and finished preparing his pipe.

The whole exhibition was not at all provocative, or glamorous, especially with the screeching macaws and trapeezing gibbons in the dripping heat!

They lost us.

We lost them.

These two brilliant people. No scintillating repartee, no togetherness, so we left. There went my — up until then — desire to try opium. Shall we say it was a downer?

But try caviar, yes! It was flown into Shanghai fresh every day from Russia. We'd never had it before. So we ate it at breakfast, lunch, and dinner. A big bowl cost less than a dollar.

We decided to take a French boat going from Shanghai to Saigon via Hong Kong, the *Messagerie Maritimes Athos II*. We boarded at midnight June 18, and Sir Victor and Emily came aboard with a beautiful Chinese porcelain bowl of flowering plants. Plus several of his rarest vintage cigars for Arthur, one of which Sir Victor gave to an envious Emily. When Arthur started to light one — we were on the afterdeck — Sir Victor recoiled in shock and admonished him in a strong voice never never *never* to smoke that or any other fine cigar out in the open.

Emily nodded, shaking her head.

Lesson learned.

* * *

Hong Kong.

Practically the only hotel there then was the Peninsula. Across the water were a few modestly high office buildings.

The streets were fairly inhabited, but the ambience was one of a provincial capital — and boring after Shanghai.

Journeyman reporters and photographers, the usual inane questions. Please! Gentlemen, that's enough! The first evening of a projected three-day stay, I said to Arthur, "Let's get the hell out of here!" Anchors aweigh for Saigon.

Saigon was not only French, it was fascinating in every respect. The Hotel Continental, with citizens of the world having drinks, tea, a "pipe" on its terrace, the French shops — deluxe — silver, lingerie, handkerchiefs made with such exquisite skill and delicacy, plus the most beautiful women in the world, the Annamese. They could walk on water and not sink, or fly with the wind, so narrow and fragile were their bodies.

Then, on our way to Angkor Wat. Finally!

We hired a driver and guide and drove all day through vast rice fields — past a small herd of elephants tearing up a distant field! — crossed the wide, fast-flowing Mekong River on a barge, its cables strung between the two shores, and arrived at our Hotel Royal in Phnom Penh.

After dining on touristy French food, we went to a little theater. It was a small wooden building filled with people on wooden benches — all in a happy, sociable mood. Most of them chewing betel nuts and spitting into cans.

The performers were clothed in gold- and silver-embroidered brocaded silks and velvets, had on necklaces, earrings, bracelets, anklets, white-painted faces, heavily blacked brows. Singsong delivery. The audience, being addressed quite often, responded to the players with spirit and gaiety, and the play went on and on and on, despite many private conversations in the audience! We finally left. With a heavy rain streaming down, we splashed home, led by the skipping lightning.

On to Siem Reap, crossing the Mekong River again, through a forest swinging with monkeys, flocks of pure white cranes in the bright blue sky — and two flat tires, cranking a cranky car to get it started again.

Finally, the Grand Hotel D'Angkor.

I breathed a small prayer to Gordon Newell. "Thank you, dear boy! You were so right!"

Because, opening the French doors onto our balcony, and peering into the obscure light above distant jungle trees, we saw the towers of Angkor Wat: blacker than the jungle, terraced against the sunset.

The next few days exploring the great complex of temples, I felt like a sponge. It was a never-to-be-forgotten immersion.

The complex was far more massive than we'd expected, far more beautiful, far more *everything!* The panorama from the northwest approach between two enormous lotus-filled lakes prepared one for the grandeur ahead. There were water buffalo on either side, just enjoying the lakes — we saw no farmer with them.

Pierre Loti wrote of this incomparable monument to the Khmer civilization when he first saw it, "The colossal temples barely showing above the verdant jungles, the twining strength of vines all embracing the vaulted arches, the battlements holding back the roaring of tigers, the raucous cry of elephants, and belling of deer."

Well, the jungle had been cleared, but we watched out for cobras, and tried not to mind the bats inside the temples. Seeing as how there were thousands of them screeching ceaselessly, it was useless.

Climbing up the steep stone stairs of the main temple, we entered the first gallery, its pavement lined with exquisite carvings of gods on one side, and through elaborately flower-and-leaf-carved pillars on the other, we saw the vast jungle spread itself.

Up to the second gallery!

The third!

High high high up from the lake, bats' dreadful screeching, but the view was awesome. Then down the steps (I went backward, on my knees, given to vertigo).

The very noticeable element that day was that we were alone. Not another soul, or, I should say, tourist. But a dear old man, his lips and chin betel-nut stained, brought us a lotus from the lake and asked for money. Our guide tried to shoo him away, but we gave him a franc or two.

On our way back, he and a friend met us at our car with an arm-load of lotus blossoms!

Then we drove to the ruins of Angkor Thom. Massive walls, incredible sculptures in stone — more glorious motifs of gods and nature — and an even larger temple — over fifty towers! — Le Bayon.

After the next day, and the next, of prowling the exquisite in all-enveloping silence, at dawn we left for Bangkok on a train with wooden benches in wooden cars with open unscreened windows.

At Bangkok's Imperial Hotel, our view was of an ever-changing scene of canals and people, temples, markets, all of it so colorful, so busy. Bangkok is where I first tasted the excitement of flying a kite — now one of my passions. We passed by a park where fliers were fighting each other with their saw-toothed knife kites. Others had humming kites, and many flew beautifully colorful kites just soaring peaceably. Arthur bought a hawk kite — not his style, certainly — but hand-carried it carefully all the way home.

Next, another train ride, this time one thousand miles down the Malay Peninsula. In my diary, I wrote: "At Haad Yai Junction, a couple who had been standing in the aisles for many hours got off with a bird cage full of birds, a large potted rubber tree plant, one cat basket with cat, several straw-covered wine bottles strung together, a large goldfish bowl full of water and fish! a large enamel tea kettle, a perch for a parrot complete with bird, a ten-by-twelve photograph of a young man, and two teapots strung on either side of a suitcase. All of this on a pair of shoulders and four arms!"

By this time we figured we'd lost the press. We had been basically left alone in Hong Kong, Saigon, and Bangkok. But the morning we pulled into the Singapore station, unwashed for several days, Arturo unshaven, and me only in lipstick and undone hair, lo and behold! A brass band; Singapore Joe Fisher — owner of dozens of Malayan theaters; Run Run Shaw — owner of many amusement parks (and our host for one hilarious evening); the Keith Goldsmiths — he represented Twentieth Century–Fox and she Helena Rubenstein Cosmetics in the Far East; the head of Metro Goldwyn Mayer for the Far East; plus photographers and newsmen and several huge bouquets of butterfly orchids and carnations!

We were told that several hours earlier a reporter at the Johore station had spotted me and alerted the Singapore group. I wanted to sink into a hole.

My misery intensified when I saw the grandness of our suite at the legendary Raffles Hotel. It was twenty-eight dollars Singapore, nothing for a grand Hollywood couple. But, we were running out of money — and I didn't want to tell Arthur.

Gin slings and gimlets on the Raffles' Veranda Bar helped a little.

We had been entertained in Johore — just across the straits from Singapore — by the crown prince. He and his father, the sultan, had a country club for two members — themselves. Racetrack, golf course, clubhouse with a "mile-long" bar, and a wild animal zoo. Also, in a separate building — under twenty-four-hour guard — there was service for thirty-six in eight-carat gold: candelabra, centerpieces, plates, flatware, given to Great-grandpa Sultan by Queen Victoria.

I wonder what the Japanese army did with it.

For *his* entertaining, Singapore Joe Fisher set up an air-raid alarm practice for us! The next night, in a blackout, ambulances, air-raid wardens, civilian "casualties" lying in the street, gas-decontaminating squads, volunteer firemen — we tootled about with him in an official inspection car. Everyone seemed to enjoy himself immensely, finding it great fun.

I understood from one of Joe's surviving nieces that when the Japanese struck Singapore, very few of the remaining citizenry survived, and the English who had been so dear to us were imprisoned and died there.

Our luggage came off the ship and I repacked — the only disappointment being my turquoise blue fox coat had turned a sickly ashes-of-roses color in the hot and humid hotel go-down (below-ground storage) — on to New York City.

Down to just a few hand pieces — chess/backgammon set, one typewriter, two suitcases, and the "throw everything in it" bag — we boarded Rotterdam Lloyd's *Slamat* for Java and Bali. It was full of Jewish refugees from Holland on their way to Australia and New Zealand.

Disembarking in Bandung, we did the usual Javanese touristy things — the zoo, the temples, the markets, slept well, boarded a train for Surabaya, ditto ditto, and took another train to Banjoewangi, where a small ferry would take us to Gilimanoek, Bali.

On that train, we enjoyed eight hours of breathtaking scenery and endured the scariest of storms and our one meal of cold canned corned beef, two thick slices of bread and butter, several bottles of beer, and a couple of bars of Dutch chocolate.

To quote again from my diary: "It started to rain as we started to come down the mountains. No *tiptoeing* over the canyon ravines by our Javanese engineer. He banged over those bridges like a bat out of hell, evidently figuring the sooner he got over them, the less time they had to collapse under us. Our train going through the tunnels screamed and clanged unbelievably. I knew the very vibrations could collapse those dripping tunnels."

Which apparently they did.

At the little Banjoewangi Hotel that night, the mistress told us there'd been a landslide behind us. By the next morning, three bridges had gone out, and the last tunnel caved in.

I'd sailed over the deepest ocean in the world, ascended the mountains around Fuji, crossed the Mekong River by cables, taken a train from Surabaya to Banjoewangi through a violent rainstorm, and now, according to the travel agent, we faced taking a tiny ferry across the Straits of Bali. There had never been an accident, but the channel was full of sharks and very strong crosscurrents, and he wouldn't take his family on it.

I remembered an old lady in Hawaii who had witnessed volcanic eruptions, tsunami waves, earthquakes, telling me, "I always keep repeating, I'm not afraid! I've never been afraid. I'm not afraid!"

I decided, looking at that frail little ferry (we were its only passengers), the great strait where the Pacific and Indian oceans met, and distant green Bali, I was not going to be afraid again. Ever! I was going to enjoy the perils of travel, even an airplane with a coughing engine. And I have — well, almost always.

Bali!

The gentlest people — full of grace, courtesy, composure. Children were invited to come and perform for us. Beautiful children, singing about what they wanted in their lives: a wife with long black hair, a husband who took no other wives, baby brothers.

We drove to Kota Beach, where friends of ours from the Beverly Hills Tennis Club had cottages. Their cook had been let out of jail in nearby Denpasar to prepare us dinner and next day's breakfast. There was no "rape" — that is, criminal rape — among the Balinese. A man took a girl home for several days and, if she was acceptable, married her, if not, returned her to her family. But the cook had violated a Polish woman, so he was jailed for several months. Except they had only a one-room jail in Denpasar, so to avoid crowding, he spent days in jail and came back to the hotel every night to cook.

Our hostess arranged performances of the Monkey Dance, the Flirtation Dance, and the Legong Dance at several temples and villages. All for us alone, sitting with the villagers.

My favorite story about the Balinese concerns the first Dutch governor. Shortly after his arrival on the island, he announced he and his wife would drive down Denpasar's main street the following Sunday, and he decreed the female citizenry cover their breasts. The day arrived, the couple started down the avenue in the open carriage, and the assembled women all lifted up their sarongs and covered their breasts, treating the new governor and his wife to a mile and a half of black pussy.

I didn't want to leave. Here was life seemingly serene and simple, joyous, familial. So unlike ours — we westerners'. I kept thinking, Gloria, how fabulous! You and Arthur are witnesses to these cultures, so special, and have had the pleasure of bonding with these pure souls!

But we had to move on, and soon enough — too soon — we were back in Surabaya, and down to our last three hundred dollars.

We met an MGM Far Eastern agent, an American, who asked us for lunch. I had remarked to Arthur that the treatment of natives in the Far East by the English and French was shocking. But, thank heaven, I hadn't witnessed any class-consciousness among the Americans.

As we sat down for lunch, our host apologized for the service. "A new boy," he said. He had caught his old "boy" wearing shoes in the house and had fired him.

It took about three seconds for me to digest this. "You *what?*"

"I had to fire him."

"Why?"

"I told you. He had shoes on in the house. It's not allowed. It's a sign of disrespect. You can't let them put on airs."

I was choking. "Maybe he wanted to wear shoes like you. Maybe he wanted to better himself, maybe . . ."

He interrupted me. "No! No! You have to make them understand they're servants, you . . ."

Arthur broke in. "Now, Gloria!"

I didn't thank him or say good-bye. An American in that mode? Unforgivable.

I recorded the evening on the Java Sea that night: "The black sunset clouds formed a long spewing dragon, half submerged, with his horned and curled tail lashing high into the heavens. Fire in the sky behind and in front of him spread evenly on the sea." Never to be forgotten!

We said fond farewells to our friends in Singapore and sailed off on the freighter *President Garfield* for Ceylon, India, Egypt, and Europe. One of the most memorable farewells was from a new-found "friend," Professor L. S. Rao, of Hatha Yoga persuasion. Joe Fisher introduced us, advising the professor was Very Special. He was. He ate a glass while we were having Singapore gin slings at the Raffles Hotel, and then, for nibbles, opened a package of phonograph needles and swallowed them. He promised our horoscopes would be there when we arrived in New York City, gave me a verry long python skin, and sadly announced his walking on water was not yet perfected.

"My feet are still eight to ten inches below the surface." It was difficult to give him advice, or comfort, about that.

The last we heard from him was a cable to us in New York, asking for $1,001, his price for our horoscopes. News to us — who asked him for horoscopes?

* * *

Ceylon . . . Bombay . . .

Curious. Knowing we were running out of money, I still kept buying things. Silver bangles, gold-embroidered slippers, a turquoise silk sarong, tie-dyed scarves, earrings, a pair of brass peacock curtain tiebacks. Maybe subconsciously I thought friends would rescue us. If I did, I was sadly mistaken!

Cairo. From the famous Shepheard's Hotel at 1 A.M., we drove on out to see the Pyramids and Sphinx in full moonlight.

Mrs. Larry Sherwood, a fellow traveling companion since Singapore, volunteered that her husband was cabling her money, and she would share with us. We had about nine dollars left!

I suggested that Arthur wire Groucho. He didn't want to.

Who else? Eugene Frenke, his Russian friend from UFA, that great German film company. Gene was married to the German actress Anna Sten. We had had a gemütlich friendship with Gene and Anna in Hollywood. Arthur had worked on a script or two with him and they were close friends. Frenke was debonair, always smiling, always up, up, up — or seemingly so — and full of projects. He was an elf, and brought out a mischievous quality in Arthur no one else did. Anna was charming and gifted, a lovely woman. She had been imported by Samuel Goldwyn as his answer to Marlene Dietrich and Greta Garbo. Goldwyn never really "got" her, never found her the right vehicle. Her films did not do her justice, but she always seemed to be sailing fair.

Arthur borrowed twenty dollars from our freighter's purser, and cabled Frenke. The next day, Mrs. Sherwood's money arrived, and we all rejoiced. And went shopping!

That night, in the bar, a Captain Bert Smith introduced himself, "I can't resist meeting a beautiful famous actress," he said, and offered the information that he was the adviser to King Farouk on air-raid precautions in Egypt.

We listened. He told us cisterns built by Roman invaders nearly two thousand years ago were being readied for shelters and supply depots, and also that enormous caves in the hills behind Cairo were being prepared for refugees.

Another world war was coming. No question, just a matter of when it would erupt. Although Arthur and I had contracts to work in England — this was my chance to become an international name — of course our professional lives were not to be considered. I truly deep-sixed any hopes, any dreams.

Our guide Moses had a brother who owned the Palace of Perfumes, and he invited us to visit it — and, we thought, to see how perfumes were made. So the next morning, we arrived and were asked into their parlor. It was lined with over-overstuffed sofas, big fat upholstered footstools for weary shoppers' feet, elaborately carved gold-leafed standing ashtrays, Oriental rugs. Sweet odors filled the air. We were offered lemon squashes (lemonades) — cigarettes, tea, coffee.

Moses hovered, and his brother called in two lovely young ladies in harem dress. With bottles of perfume. As they uncorked them and gently stroked our arms with the wet corks, names drifted down — pure essences called Mimosa, Amber, Kashmir, Attar of Roses, Taj Mahal Musk, Frankincense; fragrant blends named Scent of the Pharaohs, Royal Harem, Nefertiti's Promise, Song of Arabia.

By this time, several other male relatives had come in to see the action. The room was full of aromas, salesmen, and three Americans who had no intention of buying. Who smelled and sipped and complimented and inquired as to price, and then got up and said they'd be back tomorrow.

Total consternation!

Total outcries of bewilderment!

"What time will you return tomorrow?" We weren't sure. But we would. Cross our hearts. Honest and true. (Dishonest and false.)

Meeting us the next day, Moses was sad and fairly silent. We claimed allergies to perfume and expressed extreme gratitude to

his brother. Arturo observed it was the only country where we'd experienced the need to convince the merchant of our lack of need
to buy!

After another visit to the Cairo Museum, Moses suggested we
might like to see the red-light district. Well, we hadn't missed any
others wherever we'd been, so why not? Moses couldn't take us —
it was against the law for licensed guides — but he had a cousin
(were all the Egyptians related?) who could.

Into a very narrow street lined with curtained cubicles on either
side, each lady sitting in front of her own. The women were smiling, fat, with their cheap silk shifts taut over their breasts and tummies, young and not so young, all heavily made up. They called out
to us, "Yankees, over here!" and invited us in.

Their pimps were all over our carriage. I kept pushing them
away. "Girl fock dog, boy fock boy, girl fock donkey." Our driver
thought it was very funny.

I kept hollering, "Get away! Get away!"

But all of a sudden, Arthur asked one of the pimps, "How
much?"

Immediately, chaos! We were swamped, smothered in bargain-
ing men. Frightening.

"He's kidding," I yelled, pushing them off him and me. "He
doesn't mean it. He's kidding, get away!" I punched our driver's
back. "Tell them he's kidding! He doesn't mean it! Tell them
no money! Shame on you," I hollered at Arthur. "Shame, shame,
shame!"

Some of the pimps jumped off, a few stayed on. But finally, with
our coachman's help and me yelling and pushing, off they all
jumped.

Sad.

Mrs. Sherwood loaned us some money to settle our hotel bill,
then down we three went to the station to rejoin our ship in
Alexandria.

At Alexandria's train station, a Twentieth Century–Fox Some-

thing or Other greeted me/us with a huge bouquet of red roses —
why? (poor man, he had to know I was finished at Fox) — and
drove us all over the city in his open Packard deluxe! I thanked
him and hoped that was the end of greeters.

Onto the dock, into the water taxi, onto the ship, and off we
sailed for Italy.

Farewell the Orient, India, and Egypt. What we had seen soon
would be changed — agonizingly and irrevocably.

10

I had decided I would not disembark in Naples because I had signed several open letters to Benito's son, Vittorio Mussolini, in 1938 when he visited Hollywood as the honored guest of director Hal Roach.

"Vittorio, go home. You are not welcome here" were the opening words on full pages in *Variety* and the *Hollywood Reporter.*

Vittorio, an aviator, had written a book describing his air victories in Ethiopia — the bombing of a village that "opened up like a rose" from a direct hit! About fifty of us signed the letters, creating a bit of a brouhaha among the local fascist sympathizers and political idiots.

So Arthur went ashore, hoping for money from Eugene Frenke. And it was there, in an office dockside — one thousand dollars. He came quickly back, also announcing in a slightly sarcastic but amused tone, "You're right! The Italians hate you! Mussolini and Ciano hate you! Your puss is all over the magazine stands. You must have made twenty covers! Now will you go to Rome?"

Yes, indeedy, I would go to Rome to see the *Pietà* at St. Peter's, the marble column where Caesar fell. And to Pompeii, with great emotional quiverings, looking at ash-smothered, running figures — imagining the terror and pain of that kind of death.

But there were so many posters of Il Duce everywhere, it was suffocating. Duce Duce Duce. It was on everything. The Italians we talked with assured us Italy would never join Germany. Weren't we allies in 1914?

Back on the ship, we prepared to disembark in Marseilles, spend a little time on the Blue Riviera — not Cannes or Monte Carlo, called the Gold Coast — before going to England, where Mrs. Movie Star was supposed to make a film for Gaumont-British playing an American fiancée of an English naval officer, and Mr. Screenwriter was supposed to doctor a musical featuring a top English comedienne.

Landing in Marseilles, we checked our luggage at the dock and headed for the most recommended restaurant there for bouillabaisse! Another first, and still in my culinary repertoire. And pondering maps as to where we should settle for the couple of weeks we had to kill before our work began in England.

La Ciotât Plage was it. Very close to Marseilles, right on the Mediterranean, not fashionable or expensive. Its only hotel, Le Rose Thé, had a cottage for us in the rear. Perfect!

We cabled Christopher Mann, our agent in London, that we had arrived and stood "at the ready!"

At Le Rose Thé there were few guests. There was a Dutch woman with her nine-year-old son, Pierre; an English couple, he a Suez Canal official heading home; an English priest; and a charming Czech couple with their ten-year-old daughter.

For the first time, everyone — the hotel proprietor, staff (the cook and waiter were Moroccans), guests, café keeper in the village, all — seemed on tippy toes about war.

And well they might have! From our arrival in France on the fifteenth of August to the twenty-fourth, only nine days, Hitler had annexed Danzig, signed a pact with Stalin, not answered a letter from President Roosevelt urging arbitration, and been warned in a speech from Churchill — now First Lord of the Admiralty — that if he invaded Poland, England would declare war on him. That speech came through our radio loud and clear. Here is an excerpt printed in the London *Daily Mirror,* August 24: "For four long years, Nazidom has been breaking treaties, spending a thousand million sterling a year on armaments, terrorizing its neighbors, or actually annexing their territory. Nazi leaders seem to indulge the hope that if they gained initial sudden successes against Poland they could then offer peace to the Western democracies. Let them clear their minds of such illusions."

Indeed, all hell *was* breaking loose!

Arthur and I were the only ones who had a portable radio, and between the small company, eight languages were spoken. We also listened to Chamberlain, Hitler, Daladier, Mussolini — bedlam!

I think the Führer had forgotten his line in *Mein Kampf:* "The fact of forming an alliance with Russia would be the signal for a new war, and the result of that would be the end of Germany!"

On August 25, Nazi-sympathizing Irish terrorists exploded bombs in several taverns in Coventry and Broadgate. The Fascist-favoring Japanese cabinet resigned, but its army blockaded Hong Kong. Italy, according to Count Ciano, Mussolini's son-in-law, seemed undecided — our cook and waiter were called up. Most of the stained glass windows were being removed from La Sainte Chapelle in Paris. The mayor of La Ciotât Plage asked for *"calme avec sangfroid, discipline, bonne volonté"* (calm with composure, discipline, freely given) of the *Ciotadens* (Ciotât citizens)! Thousands of children were being evacuated from Paris and London to the country. German-made gas masks were being distributed in London.

August 26, the entire coast — probably all of France — went into a blackout. All of us at Le Rose Thé helped paint the windows dark blue.

We still hadn't heard from Christopher Mann, and wondered how to get to England. The French were mobilizing. Sitting on the front porch of our beach hotel, we were so saddened, disturbed, to witness the straggly line of farmers shouldering what looked like

Napoleonic muskets, leading their big old dray horses and asses into town. It was so unlike the French, being silent and grim.

Watching one of these small slow columns of men late one afternoon, the English priest commented, "The French uniforms are so sloppy. Really, so ill fitting! How much do you have to pay for a suit in the States, Mr. Sheekman?" Answer. "Really? Why, in England one can get a magnificent suit for fifteen pounds, and quite a decent one for ten. Really, the French should do something about their uniforms!" He left very soon, said he had connections in high places that would get him out — and home. He was not missed.

The twenty-ninth, the Polish government ordered mobilization. Ribbentrop assured Denmark and Lithuania of their neutrality and safety from military action — Germany just needed to "right the wrongs" of the Polish government. In France and England, all international telephone calls and telegrams were now subject to censorship.

The thirtieth, the Duke of Windsor (generally recognized by now, I think, as a fascist sympathizer) appealed to the little king of Italy to intervene. The value of gold, bedrock of most economies, soared to an all-time high. The labor unions of England and France appealed to the workers in Germany. And then a Nazi broadcast to the German public announced that ration cards were being issued. They were completely unaware of their situation, and in shock! All foreign ships in European waters were leaving for home.

And still no message from Christopher Mann.

September 1, Hitler's warplanes bombed ninety-three towns in Poland, and Mahatma Gandhi sent condolences to the Polish people. The Pope appealed for a general conference to revise the Treaty of Versailles, Shirley Temple's film *La Vie en Rose* opened in Marseilles to charming notices(!), Hitler wired Mussolini that the great German army didn't need help, and, according to the Personals column in the *Times* of London, several marriages between

young ladies and gentlemen of the armed forces were either quietly taking place or being postponed.

September 2, we all hung on the radio. The Englishman's wife
had disclosed that she was Italian, born in Germany, and why
didn't everybody just let Hitler alone and let him "annex" Poland?
We jumped all over her, her husband shushed her, so she retired to
her room in a pet.

The Dutch woman — we nicknamed her "Holland" — was distraught because her lover was French, had been called up, and
now, again, she was alone with her little Pierre.

The cook and waiter had left, so the owner and his wife took
over the cooking. They were very sad. Their son had decamped a
few months before with twenty thousand francs and a chorine
from Marseilles and had returned that afternoon without either.
He had received his summons to report to army headquarters.
"And we had forgiven him, madame," his mother said to me. "We
had so generously forgiven him."

The Czech couple and their daughter, Nora, kept quietly,
tensely, to themselves. We asked what their plans were.

Leopold Kraus had been a lawyer in Prague. He had written
anti-Nazi articles for the leading newspaper there before the Nazis
moved in. Being threatened constantly by the Gestapo, and being
Jewish, they had fled to Switzerland many months before. There
they received permission to go to South America, so they went to
Italy for a boat. But by the time they reached Genoa, their South
American country had called a halt to immigration. Fearful of remaining in fascist Italy, they went up to San Remo, paid to get on
one of the small boats ferrying refugees illegally into France,
landed in Nice, and their consul got them a temporary permit to
stay. They had made their way to La Ciotât Plage and this modest
pension.

They had relatives in Chicago, but Leopold's wife, Gertrude,
said, "Now, if war comes, we stay, and my husband will fight. It is
our destiny, it must be. Then we should have peace once more."

Leopold repeated with a wry smile, "If war comes . . . will war come, war will come, will war come, war will come; we are like opera chorus bassos, sopranos, tenors, singing together."

We did not envy them their future.

Headline in *Paris Soir* September 3: "ERICH VON STROHEIM WISHES TO JOIN THE FRENCH ARMY."

The celebrated German cinema film actor Erich von Stroheim has telegraphed the Minister of War to offer his services to the French army. "I wish," he wrote, "to show my gratitude to the French people who have so warmly opened their arms to my return from Hollywood. If France doesn't accept my offer, I will join the American Legion being formed now by Colonel Sweeny and General Reilly."

September 3, France and England declared themselves at war with Germany.

We received a cable — finally! — from Chris Mann:

Dear Gloria,

Film contract canceled, British navy busy elsewhere!

Love

Christopher

And there was a companion wire from the American consul in Marseilles. We were to take the SS *President Adams* home in three days.

We had decided we would stay in Europe if we could, Arthur as a war correspondent, I as a hospital or armed services volunteer. Our consul refused us any help at all. "Go home" was his order. "You have to go home."

Deeply frustrated, we said good-bye to our little band in Le Rose Thé and on September 7 boarded the ship. Jammed with Americans who had boarded at Cairo and Naples, it was the last

American ship to sail for home. The very small swimming pool was drained and single men bedded down in it. The recreation room was also full of beds — just a little room left around the bar.

In Marseilles I had bought scads of knitting wool and needles for volunteers to knit sweaters or scarves or caps for the Czech Foreign Brigade while we crossed. I put a note in the ship's paper and was immediately swamped with knitters. The next morning, the purser found me on deck knitting and said the captain wanted to see me.

Captain Cullen greeted me sternly, and said I had violated the neutrality of "his" ship with that notice, and I was to gather up all the wool and forbid the volunteers to go on knitting.

I was shocked! Responding to my question, "How will the Germans know we're knitting for the Czechs if and when they board our ship?" he replied that, with the notice in the ship's paper, it was on record and discoverable.

I looked at a large framed photograph on his desk. A greeting from Count Ciano. There were also two little crossed flags, American and Italian, on his desk. The name over the bar came to me — Club Marco Polo. And the passageways were named Via Napoli, Via Capri, Via Sorrento, and so on.

"Do you have relatives in Italy?" I asked. "Is Ciano a friend of yours?" He was.

It wasn't much, but it was enough.

I made the rounds of the ship, quickly informing every lady not to let the captain see her knitting. But to keep going.

At Gibraltar, they opened the submarine nets to let us through.

We arrived in New York City with sweaters, mufflers, caps, all the wool gone.

As we passed the Statue of Liberty, Arthur said to me, "How much money do we have?"

"Two hundred dollars," I replied.

"No, no, I mean altogether — in the bank at home."

"Two hundred dollars — and it's here, not there."

"What about the money in the bank?"

"There isn't any. This is it. Two hundred dollars."

We both fell into contemplative silence.

"Ah!" I thought. "Greenwich Village. *La vie bohème* again — what I've yearned for." At last!

I never asked Arthur what he thought at that moment. I guess I was just so targeted, I didn't care, and I was not about to give up my old dream.

I was on my way! On my way to becoming a New York City stage actress.

And my brilliant husband would, of course, now write plays — for me to star in! We would become a dazzling success story. We would be the envy of the theatrical world. I could finally say to my family and friends, "See? I told you so!"

11

There were lots of reporters when we landed in New York in September 1939. Again I was Gloria Stuart of Hollywood. But more than that, I was a movie star returning from the war zone.

We found a one-room walk-up apartment in — guess where? — Greenwich Village, just opposite the lovely old Hotel Marguery. The Frenchwoman who owned the apartment was very cordial and anxious that we were "accommodated."

Our kitchen/bathroom occupied one end of the room. Arthur, not being used to such an arrangement — not being used to housework of any kind — somehow managed several times to turn on the shower while rinsing dishes.

I loved walking around the Village, I loved feeling "bohemian" — a state my mother never had any sympathy with — "given a choice," as she had often put it. It reminded me of my years in Carmel with Gordon — artists, sculptors, poets, actors, crazies, all celebratory and broke.

And so here I was, embarking upon a second bohemian chapter in my life with my second, less-bohemian husband.

Arthur called our savior, Gene Frenke, told him that we had landed, and thanked him for the thousand dollars. Gene said he was coming in to New York City with his friend, Adrian Conan

Doyle, the son of Sherlock Holmes's creator, Sir Arthur Conan Doyle. They were partners in a film venture.

Several days later, Gene called. He was at the Waldorf Towers with Mr. Doyle and the crown prince and princess of Austria-Hungary. The crown prince was giving a dinner party for the maharaja and maharani of Jaipur. Would we come?

Would we?

Arthur, of course, wore his tuxedo. I wore my gold satin bias-cut dress with diamanté straps (the Joan Crawford one) and no underwear. And my rosy (formerly blue) fox jacket, my twenty-carat two-inch-wide gold bracelet, star ruby earrings, ring to match — and away we went!

How?

By subway! We couldn't afford a taxi from Tenth Street and Fifth Avenue to the Waldorf Towers — Fifty-first and Park. Frenke was so effusive and dear greeting us in their suite, and, I guess, the others appraised us as Hollywood Somebodies, because they were gracious, too. I can only report that we were Somebodies in the subway too, but seemed to be Weirdo Somebodies! Those glances! Frowns! Shrugs!

After a lengthy, luxurious dinner served in the suite, we all left for the nightclub El Morocco.

The crown prince asked me to dance, and, in the middle of the dance floor, pressed his charms too familiarly against me. I pulled myself free and walked off the floor, leaving him stranded. Not wishing to embarrass his wife, I simply smiled at the startled questions.

On we went to the supper club "21," and eventually, back to the Waldorf. We thanked our hosts, excused ourselves, walked out into the deserted streets and down the nearest subway station steps.

Approaching our apartment, I realized we had no keys. Arthur was never one to carry keys or money — just attached things like a wristwatch or ring. Absentminded to the nth degree, you see!

So, four o'clock in the morning, I felt we couldn't wake our landlady, or sit on the stoop, so we went into the Hotel Marguery without luggage, and convinced the desk clerk to give us a room.

Waking at noon, I gave the desk clerk my last traveler's check, and we walked across the busy street, still in our finery. More looks!

Entering the dark, shabby room did it. I started to cry. Arthur tried to comfort me. All the mistakes, disappointments, fears of the future, really did me in.

La vie bohème had lost its luster.

Frenke came down that afternoon and counseled us in a fatherly fashion. He was shocked at our apartment, we must move, we must get an agent "tomorrow." He would loan us more money.

"Now, we go out and have a good dinner, no?"

Yes!

I started packing that night. The next morning, Arthur found us an apartment in the Beaux Arts hostelry. I called Mama and asked about Sylvia. "She's fine, bless her heart, but she misses you and I think the time has come for you to send for her."

That rocked me. I hadn't included baby care in my immediate plans.

Spurred to action by our physical and financial status, Arthur called an old friend from newspaper days, Margaret Shane. She lived in Ridgefield, Connecticut, with her writer-husband, Ted, and their two daughters. Arthur had a unique idea for a play.

I was euphoric. My boy was on track! And there was a leading-lady role in it for me!

By December I was struggling to keep alive professionally, and agreed to do a guest shot on one of the day's most popular radio quiz shows, *Information, Please,* for the princely sum of $150. The regulars were writers Clifton Fadiman and Carl Van Doren, the columnist F.P.A. (Franklin P. Adams), and the brilliant and witty concert pianist Oscar Levant. These men were encyclopedists, and experienced in the format. I was out of my element, getting only one question right. Not a promising beginning for the New Year, 1940.

Then Dorothy Thompson and Fritz Kortner wanted to see me about a play they'd written, *Another Sun;* I was "right" for it! Somehow, Celeste Holm ended up with the part, but the play didn't last long.

Next the Theatre Guild called, asking if I would read for *The Fifth Column,* their next play; Ernest Hemingway was the playwright! Frances Farmer, the actress set for the role, was sick. My diary entry is, "Kay Schwartz, whom I called to accept a cocktail party date next Sunday, told me Frances was *very* sick. I hope so." Today I shudder at the inexcusable reaction. The role went to Katherine Locke.

There was so much theatrical activity noted in *Variety* and the New York newspapers, I couldn't believe I was still standing outside the window, my nose pressed against the glass.

I began to realize I was tainted. I was a "movie star." All those unhappy years I had worked, striving to make a reputation as an actress, had gone for naught. The elitism of the New York theater people proscribed them from hiring movie people. I should have come to New York cold, as a twenty-two-year-old, pounded the pavements, and remained pure, unsullied by Hollywood.

Once in a while I was allowed to read for playwright, director, and producer, sitting in a darkened, empty theater, their expressionless faces dimly outlined.

The stage is lit, the stage manager hands you your "sides," walks out on the empty stage with you, introduces you, and reads with you. You finish, and look up, smile if the lines are amusing, look solemn if they aren't ("thoughtful" is effective, too), and you hear a "Thank you, Miss Stuart," or a "Very nice, thank you, Miss Stuart." You respond, and walk off the stage with an empty, sinking feeling or sometimes a tremor of hope that you will be called back.

Another radio show, the *Hobby Lobby,* called. The producer asked, What about my hats? Were there adventures collecting them? Was I chased by coolies in a rice paddy? Or wild elephants attacking our Javanese chauffeur whilst I bargained with him for his? Or did an honorable fly fly into my eye in Cairo whilst buying fezzes?

The *Lobby* would have paid me two hundred dollars if the material had "jelled." It didn't.

Mama wrote from California: "My darling Gloria" on a "Friday evening":

> I am deeply grateful for your financial help and it has taken quite a lot of strain off my taut nerves and moody outlook. Am worried about you however, and I guess I am always to be worried. Can not remember since a little girl being free of fear and trembling of tomorrow. I have loved deeply and been loved lightly by all, and the very fact that I placed love and duty before self esteem and a demand for equality as it were, has defeated me. . . .

We had room for Sylvia now. We even went to the city pound and got a dog for her — black and white spots — we named it Beau. I wrote Mama to make arrangements. A week later, she wired us, "Sylvia leaves Wednesday, Streamliner City Los Angeles, lower berth right P24 arrives Chicago, Friday, January 26, 12:15 P.M. noon, Northwestern Depot Canal and Madison Sts, wire reply by Western Union. Mother."

In these villainous days, would you have your mother put your four-and-a-half-year-old daughter on a train in the charge of a stewardess all the way to Chicago from Los Angeles? We did. It was done in those days.

It was too expensive for both of us to pick her up in Chicago. But Arthur's family was there and they had never met our child. They were overjoyed at the prospect of seeing Sylvia, and of seeing Arthur, famous columnist, screenwriter, husband of movie star, now great playwright-to-be.

On the train to Chicago, Arthur wrote this note:

Dear Beau,

Please take care of the carpets while I'm gone. I like them better just plain green.

And if you must eliminate in the hotel halls, do it when no one
is looking. I do not like to see Mother embarrassed. How would
you feel if she suddenly decided to relieve herself in the elevator?

Tell Mother I would write but nothing has happened. I haven't
found any cardsharps on the train, although I've gone around shuf-
fling a nicely marked deck.

Tell Mother I love her and to leave the dishes in the sink. Sylvia
and I will do them Sunday.

Father

He wired me the next day. "Oh Darling, she's wonderful and so
eager to see you. We loved your telegram and both adore you.
Arthur."

So! They arrived. Sylvia was full of hugs and kisses, and sitting
on our laps, playing with Beau, and then she took a nap.

Arthur and I looked at each other and panicked.

This was going to be it? Trapped in a little apartment with no
help, a child to take care of twenty-four hours a day — cooking,
marketing, doing laundry?

He was sympathetic. He'd never done any fathering either.

We started with Campari sodas, having bought six bottles of it
in Naples, feeling it would not be available if there were a war.

We followed them that afternoon and evening with more than
enough martinis, made with gin, naturally, and stuffed olives.

The next day, January 28, I note in my diary:

"I cried all day long. Arthur went back to bed early with a mi-
graine headache. Sylvia kept asking, 'Why do we have to stay in
this old place?' and 'When can we leave?' Beau piddled often, and
our sad little girl knocked over a rickety table holding a chicken
and its broth, then cried hysterically from exhaustion and shock
and strange circumstances."

Another letter from Mama:

Dear Gloria and Arthur:

I am sorry to bother you but Daddy and I have decided to call it quits. Out of a clear sky this noon over the sum of $1.50 that I was short to pay for your box and trunks and which he had to advance, he vented such wrath upon me, that while I have heard them many times before, and agreed to forget them I can not take them any more.

It comes at the worst time of my life. I had hoped to weather it out since the all-kind and just God allotted us three score years and ten, and as I will be fifty six on August 12th, figure it out for yourself.

I have known for many years the fate of a woman no longer able to work. But I've thought a lot about it, perhaps a housekeeper's job or the care of children, but even that will be preferable.

No he can't be made to support me since the one and only check is for $350 each month and comes to him in the Company's name. He has suggested I get a job in the laundry, and the big joke is I couldn't even do that. . . .

I need about two hundred dollars, and if you can or have to borrow it, I hope you will. I am going to try to pawn my ring but may not get enough.

Fred borrowed $500 on my car last month to meet insurance and such, so no go there.

Following is an accounting of the $80.

Fare	59.85
Food	4.00
Suitcases	7.25
Sweaters	2.00
Leggings	1.98
Drugs, etc., Ribbons	1.00
Tip to porter	.25
Freight on box and transfer charges	8.11
Bicycle crated	1.00

Now I may be a spendthrift, but it was the cheapest I could do it for, and Fred felt the care of Sylvia was too much for me and nagged me constantly until there was no joy in it, just a battle from beginning to end.

Of course I am no bargain, having change of life and a million things the matter with me. I guess he is pretty smart at that.

I am so shabby as to clothes, I dread going down to the post office to mail letters, and the pitying remarks from friends has me backing away from any social contacts.

Now, nothing matters to me but to hide away and figure it out. You have helped others out, Gloria, please help me.

Your loving
Mother

What could I write?

How could I comfort her? Aside from sending the money? Everything she wrote was true. She had been abused by Finch for years, his failings in the business world being progressively oftener (Arthur and I had helped him out of bankruptcy once), he laid it on my mother heavier and heavier.

His suggesting "a job in the laundry" reminded me of his suggestion to me, "I'll get you a job washing elephants."

Cruel, cruel man.

We tried to think where we could get two hundred dollars. We were committed to helping Arthur's mother, too, and had just about exhausted loans from our friends. I wrote Mama we'd send it soon.

At that point in my life, I didn't know how to make any money, but I still knew how to look like a million bucks.

My dear friend from Carmel, Catherine Turney, came into town with her collaborator, Jerry Horwin, and their play, *My Dear Children*, starring John Barrymore — JOHN BARRYMORE?!! It opened to, and I quote from *Vanity Fair,* "the most distinguished audience of 1940," come to see "the most distinguished actor of his generation."

Cathy and her husband, George Reynolds, took us. And for the first time since l'affaire Waldorf Towers, I wore my Jean Harlow bias-cut, gold satin dress without underwear and with my rubies and fox jacket.

Walter Winchell was there and nodded hello. To quote his column several days later, "Gloria Stuart is the blonde's answer to Hedy Lamarr." Thank you, Walter, but where the hell is a play for me?

We now had many friends — a lively, brilliant and warm, gracious and successful group.

Kyle and Mae Crichton — Kyle, argumentative, vigorous, was a contributing editor of *Collier's,* a *Saturday Evening Post*–like magazine, and author of the ultraliberal books *Reading from Right to Left* and *Redder Than the Rose* — were wonderful hosts in their rambling old house in Bronxville. Kyle was a Communist Party member, Mae a devout Catholic. One gave to the Party, one gave to the Church, but they had profound respect for one another.

And there was Joe Alex and Maxine Morris, Frank and Kay Gervasi, George and Beatrice Kaufman (or whoever else he was with at the time), Marc Connelly, Paul and Millicent Osborn, Samson and Dorschka Raphaelson — all in journalism or of the theater.

Of course, the war in Europe was always the main subject of conversation, and the leading argument was should we or shouldn't we go in? The several members of the Communist Party in our group naturally followed the Soviet-Nazi party line. So infuriating, so contentious, so stupid!

But I think their friends never felt these radical members were making bombs in their basements or plotting the overthrow of our government by assassination. At most, by the ballot! And fortunately, there weren't enough of them to make a difference.

We felt sorry for them — so misguided, so illogical, so misled by the Comintern. That was about the extent of our condemnation.

Besides, several of them were very witty people — very amusing to have around, devoted, generous friends.

Meanwhile, Paul Osborn's *Morning's at Seven* had just opened to critical acclaim. He and Millicent decided to move to the country and let us take over their "railroad flat" on Fifty-sixth Street near the East River. To the uninitiated, that was several rooms running straight through a building, with no "sidecars." We were so grateful, especially because a beautiful lady from Harlem, Ella Vesha, joined us.

She and Sylvia were inseparable. Dear Beau had been left behind at the Beaux Arts with the elevator boy, who had promised him "a good home." "You're giving me a good home," Arthur replied.

Ella was elegant. Lovely manners, soft voice, sweet smile and disposition (with an equally dear husband, Leedy, and a son, Clarence, who later became a judge in Cleveland). Sylvia called her Ellee, and she took care of Sylvia and the house. (Sylvia told me years later that, after parties, she and Ellee polished off all the unfinished bottles of beer!) There were many, many weeks when I couldn't pay her, but she managed to stick, and we always managed finally to pay her. Ella was a godsend for me. I could devote most of the time to *me!*

So! Summer Theater! Summer theater was a lovely, gemütlich happening, then principally on the East Coast. Actors met and worked with accomplished playwrights and directors, the audiences were warm and responsive, and runs were very short so one could perform in a variety of plays.

Henry Lewis, of the very important William Morris Agency, signed me, and, all of a sudden, as of June 7, I had a contract to open the season at the Town Hall Playhouse in *The Animal Kingdom,* in Westborough, Massachusetts! My salary was $250 to rehearse six days and perform six days. According to the "Admissions Tax and Box Office Statement," the theater's total gross that week was $1,007.10.

I couldn't wait to go on to Ridgefield, for a July 8th opening in *The Night of January 16th* at the New England Playhouse.

In summer theater that season, I also appeared in *Accent on Youth, Route 101, Mr. and Mrs. North, The Pursuit of Happiness, Sailor Beware,* and — the high point of my career as a stage actress — played Emily, with Thornton Wilder as the Stage Manager, in his play *Our Town,* which had opened on Broadway to enormous success a couple of years before.

We opened the Amherst (Massachusetts) Drama Festival August 19. Mr. Wilder directed. I learned my lines *before* we started rehearsals, not during. I could tell he was happy with my work.

Thornton said to me at the end of the week, "I have a play coming in with Tallulah Bankhead — *The Skin of Our Teeth.* There's an ingenue in it. I'd like you to play her."

I suddenly remembered that Arthur had said in Hollywood, when the studio and agents had let me go, "You don't have it, Gloria. Give it up."

So! Arthur Sheekman, I *did* "have it"! *I did!*

12

That heady signal from Thornton sustained me for many months. I didn't know then that his wishing didn't make it so. It seems so immature, so unrealistic a commitment to me today, looking back, but it wasn't then. It was a bright and shining marquee in the sky: "GLORIA STUART — STAR!" I kept wanting, hoping, believing that it would happen, with Thornton my godfather!

I thank my natural exuberance, my happiness at being a person — or personage — mezzo-mezzo talented, in love with an amorous man who was in love with me, mother to an adorable daughter, popular with friends, fairly young, quite beautiful — kept me going.

And working alongside my peers those summers, Gertrude Lawrence, Laurette Taylor, Pauline Lord, Sinclair Lewis, Luther Adler, Sylvia Sidney, gave me heart, said to me, "Gloria, you can do it."

And Arthur's progress with Peggy Shane on their play, *Mr. Big*, said, "He's doing it."

The Hungarian matinee idol Francis Lederer called. He wanted me to tour with him in *Pursuit of Happiness*, but Arthur nixed that. Arthur went into his silent mode when I went on "locations" in Hollywood. He was always convinced I was engaged in some on-set hanky-panky. Looking back, he must have *never* trusted me, from the first evening we spent together.

Guy Palmerton, the owner of a theater in Fitchburg, Massachusetts, asked if I would consider stock the next year.

Arthur said no. (Summer stock meant being in residence at the theater for the duration of the season.)

We moved to an inn at Ridgefield, Connecticut, La Bretagne, and Arthur and Peggy began working on *Mr. Big* every day.

September 16th, a wire from Lawrence Langner and a phone call from Theresa Helburn — both "high-mucky-mucks" of the Theatre Guild. Would I come in for a reading tomorrow of Leonard Kirsten's new play, *First Stop to Heaven*?

That same day, my agent called. Harold Clurman of the Group Theatre wanted to see me about Irwin Shaw's new play!

The two companies I'd rather work for than any others.

The next day, a large leading story in the "News of the Theatre" column in the *New York Herald Tribune* — Charley Ruggles and Gloria Stuart sought by the Shuberts for the production of *Mr. Big*.

The gifted director Joshua Logan called Arthur on October 10th and asked him to help rewrite *Charley's Aunt* for José Ferrer, so Arthur went into the city and stayed in the Hotel Astor in Times Square, working eighteen hours a day. Money had not been mentioned, and it wasn't until many weeks after the gala opening, October 17th, that my lad received one hundred dollars. One hundred dollars!?

The producer Richard Aldrich announced his fall production plans. I sicced my agent on Aldrich, whom I had worked for in summer theater on Cape Cod. He was married to Gertrude Lawrence, the fabulous English comedienne and leading lady opposite Noel Coward — we had met them socially several times.

October 24th I went to read for the playwrights Sam and Bella Spewack, *Out West It's Different*, Sam Levene directing. Nothing. *Niente*.

October 29th the playwright Edward Chodorov called from Aldrich's office that he had a "good part" in his new play for me, and could I meet him at Sardi's tomorrow? And then my agent called and wanted me to see John Shubert about another part also tomorrow.

My note in my diary read, "Hey! Hey! Comes the deluge!"

Arthur and I went in to New York. I was interviewed by the Aldrich group, coddled — by experts, I might add — and left for the Crichtons' house in Bronxville for the night.

Dear Mae loaned me her silver fox coat and new hat with red feathers for the next day's interviews. I shouldn't be caught dead in the same outfit I'd worn the day before!

Meeting with Edward Chodorov, his cowriter, Hy Kraft, and their director, Otto Preminger, at lunch resulted in their hiring me! We settled on a two-hundred-dollar-a-week salary, and they were so enthusiastic, I agreed to tell John Shubert I couldn't do his play.

So, parting with many embraces and hand shakings, I walked over to Mr. Shubert's office and regretfully told him I was going to do the Chodorov play. He was very "flattered I had taken the trouble."

Arthur and I celebrated at the Algonquin Bar. I couldn't stop thinking about the brilliant "Algonquin Round Table." (From the early twenties, members including Alexander Woollcott, Harpo Marx, Dorothy Parker, Robert Benchley, Marc Connelly, George Kaufman, Heywood Broun, Edna Ferber, Robert Sherwood, Neysa McMein, Harold Ross, and Alice Duer Miller got together for lunch on weekdays at a big round table at the Algonquin Hotel dining room.) Many were friends of ours. Possibly Arthur could join them.

The next day, back I went to Aldrich's office. Chodorov, Kraft, and Preminger were discussing casting the leading man and fairly ignored me. I finally asked, "What am I doing here?"

Chodorov replied, "Why, to sign a contract, I guess."

I went out to make a phone call in the outer office. Coming back I heard, "I know a brunette who is a *grand* actress." Mumble mumble mumble. Then Hy Kraft, "But is Gloria confident enough?" "Oh, sure!" Mumble mumble mumble. I went cold and stiff all over.

Aldrich showed up at that moment. "What are *you* doing here?"

I answered that the other men had asked me to come in. He shrugged and went into the office, closing the door.

After ten or fifteen minutes, he came out and said, "We'll get in touch." I fled. And burst into tears in the elevator.

Back at La Bretagne, Arthur said I was crazy. It had to be a "done deal." They hadn't even bothered to ask me to read. We had talked salary. They had asked me to reject Shubert.

I was too demoralized to call John Shubert and ask for another crack at his part.

Arthur had just wired Groucho for money. *Mr. Big* was still in the works, although optioned by the producer Dwight Wiman, with Josh Logan to direct. We were down to thirty-six dollars.

He went back into the city the next day to see *his* agent. He called at noon. The producer of Willie Howard's new revue, *Crazy with the Heat,* had offered him a *contract* for five hundred dollars a week, a five-week guarantee, and 10 percent of the gross!

Whoops! Whoops! Whoops!

That was November 2.

He had a couple of meetings with Kurt Kasznar, the character actor who was producing the show, about what Arthur would contribute to the revue. Arthur was eager to get started — rewriting sketches, bringing in new sketches.

November 11th was Black Monday. *Mr. Big* was dropped by Dwight Wiman, because of Josh Logan's collapse. Logan had almost had a nervous breakdown — was truly unable to function as the director — and had begged off. Kasznar dropped Arthur from *Crazy with the Heat* — why? Just because (!) — and the Aldrich office wired me I was "not suitable" for their play.

I sat up knitting on a sweater for my husband until 4:45 A.M., writing and rewriting devastating letters to all these callous villains.

In my head.

To quote from my diary, Tuesday, November 12, 1940: "His lousy luck I can take because I know he'll survive handsomely — mine is but a natural result of mediocrity."

I received two letters from Mama. The first one echoed again her inability to understand and/or sympathize with my forever and a day ambition to be a New York theater actress. The second was so sad. I could see Mama — standing proudly and independently, socially at the top with her old friends, suddenly having to admit bankruptcy — "on the way to the poor house" as the saying was — to her closest friends one devastating afternoon in Santa Monica.

> My dear old friends, Pansy, Rheba, and Maribelle and I were playing bridge the other afternoon, and, hearing a hammering in the front door, I opened it to someone nailing a foreclosure/bankruptcy notice on it. In other words we are closed out, done, broke, and with trimmings. But, of course, you will probably be experiencing the same thing soon, only with not such a wrench at your vitals since it is of your own choosing.

What a gentle rebuke — "of your own choosing." We had a little money in 1941, from this and that and the rentals of our two houses. However, we finally lost our half block of commercial property on Vine Street in Hollywood, because our two closest friends refused to help us with its mortgage. And we still owed dear Gene Frenke quite a bit.

Stacy Keach, director of the Savannah (Georgia) Playhouse, invited me there to play opposite him in *Accent on Youth* in May. It was a heartwarming success — not only good notices and very receptive audiences but a happy, skillful cast.

And Southern hospitality always.

(Which sometimes I could do without. The first morning on the way to rehearsal, several of the cast picked me up at my hotel, and stopped by a drugstore. We sat down at the soda fountain, and they ordered "an ammonia dope"!

What that is, is Coca-Cola with a shot of ammonia.

Ammonia? Yes, ammonia.

Not me, not then, not ever!)

Arthur and Peggy had kept working on *Mr. Big*. Finally, it was going into rehearsal — Lee Shubert was producing and George Kaufman directing for a September opening! So much publicity — for Arthur, Kaufman, Hume Cronyn, the lead, and me, understood to be the leading lady in the part of Paula.

In late summer, I was playing a week's run near the Harvard University campus in *Here Today,* a George Kaufman and George Oppenheimer play. I called Arthur every evening, and one evening, before I asked about *Mr. Big* and what was happening, he said casually, "Oh, by the way, we cast Fay Wray as Paula."

I couldn't believe my ears. "Fay Wray?" Arthur had written the play, had 100 percent say and approval as to casting. "Fay Wray?"

I truly don't remember the rest of the conversation, but I do remember I quietly hung up on him.

No doubt now, or ever again. Arthur did not want me to be anything but a nonprofessional wife. A hausfrau.

I'd show him! He could *never* "do me in" as a stage actress. I would just keep going. Trying for those classic roles. And the brand new ones.

My resolve met his.

And he lost.

Mr. Big's rehearsals went so well, and the opening in Boston was so well received — the notices were raves — George Kaufman told me, "Send for the furniture!"

I immediately rented a town house in Turtle Bay Gardens — our neighbors were Katharine Hepburn, the couturier Elizabeth Hawes, and Dorothy Thompson, the great war correspondent then married to Sinclair Lewis — and sent to California for our furniture.

Opening night in New York City, the Crichtons and I left Arthur in our house (he said he couldn't witness the opening), had dinner, and went to the theater. Because Lee Shubert was producing the play and George Kaufman had directed it, the opening was gala and important.

Mr. Big had a wonderful plot.

The curtain went up. Actors were taking curtain calls. As the star took his final bow, he was shot dead. Pandemonium. Hume Cronyn, as a clone of Thomas E. Dewey (then New York City's district attorney), arose from the audience, took charge on stage, and the investigation began. The audience became part of the performance.

In Boston, the tension had held.

Here it collapsed. In the two weeks since, influenced by the great hit of that period, a frantic *Hellzapoppin,* Kaufman had added lots of physical business. Popcorn salesmen up and down the aisles, photographers realistically "shooting" individuals in the audience, a body falling out of a balcony, a "customer" fainting and being carried out. The whole mystery and suspense of the murder investigation was lost.

Very little applause at the end of Act One. Questioning frowns, shrugged shoulders.

Act Two. "Let's see it through, friends, all the way."

To witness the death of a play is, to the uninitiated, not much. To the participants, unbelievable torment.

So! The Crichtons and I did not go to Sardi's — the Mecca of First Nighters. We went back to our Turtle Bay Gardens house, sick at heart.

We found Arthur had just wrestled an unknown intruder to the floor and was sitting on him. The victim, or victimized, was quite drunk. We called the police. They came and took the man away.

The notices that morning were brutal.

My feeling of failure was indescribable. One's ego, one's hope is obliterated — bombed — thrown into a ditch and shoveled over. "Benumbed," as in *Webster's* — "to make numb physically or emotionally, deaden the mind or feelings, to stupefy the senses" — doesn't even begin to describe it. You're throwing up, you can't swallow, you have headaches, you wish you were dead.

We sold one of our two houses in Hollywood.

We sold our antiques and moved out of beautiful Turtle Bay Gardens to a walk-up flat around the corner. The building had been a brothel and it faced the Third Avenue El. Everyone assured us we wouldn't hear the elevated trains after a while, and I must admit, even though at first they seemed to go through our living room every few minutes, in time, we didn't hear them.

Arthur and our friend Ruth Goetz went to work on a comedy drama called *Franklin Street*. Groucho was to star in it, George Kaufman to direct it. A teenage newcomer named Lauren Bacall had the ingenue role. Three weeks before the opening, Groucho canceled. His replacement was completely inept. Opening in Baltimore, this comedy drama managed a deathly silence from the audience during the entire three acts. It could have closed there, but the authors, director, and producer hoped for a miracle, so, after the last performance — past midnight — we all boarded the train for a week in Washington, DC.

Relaxing in the club car, and knowing the play would close in the capital, we watched the very young boy in the cast as he approached Arthur.

"May I ask you a question, Mr. Sheekman?" Arthur nodded yes. "Was it a hard climb, the ladder to success?"

Yes, it was. And it was a hard climb down, too.

Looking back, I realize the incompatibility of my ambition and Arthur's talent. I had a dream: My husband was a writer — he could be a playwright. He had the wit, the skill, the discipline. From the thirties to the fifties, the giants of comedy and drama were playwrights — William Saroyan, Noel Coward,

Eugene O'Neill, Maxwell Anderson, Thornton Wilder, Tennessee Williams, so many others. Film, in my opinion, was still second class. Kudos were for the Theater.

Arthur opted for the more popular genre of not-too-introspective comedy. George Kaufman's and Moss Hart's brilliant comedies were his models. Besides, wasn't he "the fastest wit in the West" according to Groucho?

I should have urged him to write about his mother, his father — a dedicated lady's man — his own childhood and coming of age, his heritage. Those stories were American classics.

But I didn't.

It was time to head back to Hollywood.

Well, it was likely that in Hollywood, Arthur again would be very successful. And I could be successful again in Southern California theater.

Still hoping!

13

From the day it opened in 1927, the Garden of Allah was the place to stay for show people from all over the world. In the heart of old Hollywood, convenient to everything, you could stop for a night or forever, rent was reasonable, daily maid service was included, and almost everybody was there.

The Garden was the brainchild of Alla Nazimova, brilliant Russian stage and silent screen actress. Today it would be called a resort — three acres luxuriant with banana and orange trees, bougainvillea, hibiscus, ferns, and bamboo, with a swimming pool in the center shaped like the Black Sea (Nazimova was born in Yalta). The hotel that accommodated short-term guests may have faced Sunset Boulevard but it resembled a large Mediterranean villa. Both its sunny restaurant and dim bar gave onto an elegant patio by the pool. (In four years, I never saw the inside of either restaurant or bar — never had reason to!) Across the pool and filling in the rest of the property were a couple of dozen bungalows — whitewashed, tile roofs, small courtyards and arcades — Southern California–cum–Morocco. The bungalows were divided into apartments called villas, some one story, some two, none alike. The compound was connected by flagstones set in grassy earth, with small stone fountains here and there. All was serene and peaceful.

In the middle of a city in the middle of a war, the Garden of Allah was Paradise.

Vacancies seemed to be handed on from actor to actor, writer to writer, musician to musician, director to director. Conductors and classical performers like José Iturbi, Paul Whiteman, Xavier Cugat, and Tito Guizar were at the top of the path next to the hotel, in Villa 1, while popular musicians like Benny Goodman, Artie Shaw, Woody Herman, and Frank Sinatra stayed catty-corner to us in Villa 17. Our two-bedroom Villa 12 was at the bottom of the Garden, in the writers' and actors' end.

Robert Benchley — the incomparable humorist, actor, critic, journalist, screenwriter, father of Nathaniel and grandfather of Peter, and member of the Algonquin Round Table — stayed in Villa 16, a few doors over. I found Bob to be one of the most engaging, attractive persons I'd ever known. In retrospect, he still is, with a charming twinkle in his smile and speech, and constant delicious wit ("In America there are two classes of travel — first class and with children. Traveling with children corresponds roughly to traveling third class in Bulgaria. They tell me there is nothing lower in the world than third-class Bulgarian travel—"). His manners were polished, he was warm and outgoing, gentle in criticism or comment, and the author of the best martini mix ever:

> Three fingers of gin, a frosted glass, slowly open a bottle of dry vermouth, and quickly pass it over the filled glass. Recap it, plop an olive or an onion into the glass, and drink. Salud!

Bob's best friend, the comedian Charles Butterworth, was next door to him at Villa 17. Charlie was droll. He was also modest. I never knew he had a law degree from Notre Dame — I found this out in a book, one that describes the roles he played in those days as "a reticent, indecisive, balding bachelor of the leisure class."

Charlie's ex-wife, Ethel, is one of the wittiest women anybody ever knew. At the time divorced from Charlie and married to the publisher Ernest Heyn, Ethel was out from New York on a visit. She was hugely pregnant. For some reason, everybody still referred to her as Ethel Butterworth, and eight-year-old Sylvia asked, "Why does Mr. Butterworth live downstairs and Mrs. Butterworth live upstairs in a different villa?"

The Garden's sophisticated and cozy atmosphere was conducive to living casually near one's ex. Our darling Natalie Schafer was in the second-story Villa 5 and downstairs in Villa 4 was her former husband, Louis Calhern, living with silent screen and stage actress Dorothy Gish. Gish was the great Lillian's sister and had been in our friend Paul Osborn's play *Morning's at Seven*. Calhern was a superb character actor and was making movies like *Heaven Can Wait, Up in Arms,* and *The Bridge of San Luis Rey.*

Calhern was Sylvia's good friend. Sylvia had mostly grown-up friends at the Garden because there were never enough children to play with. So she was delighted when John Carradine moved next door with his boys. David Carradine (who grew up to be the *Kung Fu* star) was a little younger than Sylvia but he was a playmate. She remembers one late night when there was a fire in the Hollywood hills — we could hear the fire engines tearing by — and she ran outside to watch. All the Carradines came running out the door in their pajamas. David grabbed her arm and said, "Come on!" and off they raced. After that, I had to stop Sylvia from dashing outside in her pj's!

On the other side of us lived the playwright and screenwriter Edwin Justus Mayer. Eddie was a bachelor (as I remember, once he hinted he'd had an affair with our opium-smoking China friend, Emily Hahn). Eddie was a big man with white skin and droopy eyes. His shades were usually down in the daytime, so I guess he worked all night. Around the time we arrived, he was writing the screenplay of *To Be or Not to Be* for Carole Lombard and Jack Benny — to be directed by Ernst Lubitsch. Brilliant satire.

Nunnally Johnson kept a pad at the Garden for a while. When he and the actress Dorris Bowdon were first keeping company (she appeared in *The Grapes of Wrath* and *The Moon Is Down* — Nunnally wrote both scripts), they went over to Benchley's for drinks one night. Charlie was there, and Bogey (he was staying in Villa 8), and the men got talking. There was a pitcher of Bob's martinis on the table next to where Dorris was sitting.

Dorris was a young girl and she'd never had a martini. She helped herself, and eventually emptied the pitcher. When the men finally stopped talking, they had to carry her back to Nunnally's. Dorris says that was the first and last time she ever got drunk.

Nunnally once told Bogey that if anybody ever wanted to hit him — remember, Bogey got obstreperous and abusive when he drank — that he should sit down, because nobody would hit anyone sitting down. So at a party, Bogey got obstreperous and abusive and this man said, "I'm going to kill you," and Bogey sat down. The man picked him up by the scruff of the neck and hit him.

I heard these stories from Dorris, but they could have come from Ben the bellboy. Ben always had interesting gossip to murmur into interested ears. Probably in his thirties, he was a treasure beyond measure, every man's and every woman's Friday. He went across Crescent Heights Boulevard to Schwab's if you needed something from the drugstore, and bought your groceries at the market next to Schwab's, or brought deli and spirits from Greenblatt's across Sunset Boulevard. He got anything for you, if he could, at any hour.

Because of the war, we had ration tickets for meat, butter, oils, and fuel. Hard liquors were in Very Short Supply.

Ben got Scotch or bourbon when you couldn't find any without having also to buy four bottles of Kahlúa — a tidy swindle. Gin was pretty easy to come by — you didn't have to buy Kahlúa, just two bottles of Dry Sack sherry!

Ben was a darling man. I wonder now when did he sleep? And where?

Other come-and-go guests in his keeping were Kay Thompson, later *Eloise*'s creator, but then working at MGM as a voice coach — for Judy Garland, among others (she was Liza Minnelli's godmother) — and as arranger and songwriter for the *Ziegfeld Follies*. Kay was married to William Spier, who was working on his marvelous radio show, *Suspense*. Elliott Nugent, Broadway leading man and director, was there with his family, acting in movies. Clifford Odets, whose *Waiting for Lefty* had caused a sensation on Broadway a few years before, wrote the screenplay and directed *None but the Lonely Heart* for Cary Grant and Ethel Barrymore (she received an Oscar for her performance). Odets lived around the corner from Charlie, but I hardly ever saw him.

Coming back to Hollywood after a nothing life in the New York theater, I knew I had to keep my chin up. I tried for work in movies again. My former agents were so uninterested in me, the humiliation of accepting their half-assed offer to take me on was *molto difficile!* They managed to get me *Here Comes Elmer* with Stuart Erwin in 1943, and, in 1944, *The Whistler* with Richard Dix, and *Enemy of Women*. I was back where I had started, and finished, once again — B pictures. But Mama was delighted. And so were our debtors.

I wanted terribly to volunteer for service overseas with the USO, but Arthur wouldn't hear of it. He didn't want me near the Hollywood USO either — all those strange men, female hungry! But I did finally get an assignment to travel with Hillary Brooke, visiting hospitals in the Southwest and the southeastern United States. Hillary was a tall, willowy blonde, a bit younger than I. During that period she was working hard in every genre of film — as I had done in the thirties — from *Jane Eyre* to *The Road to Utopia* to *The Enchanted Cottage* to the *Big Town* series, in which she was the leading lady. We enjoyed one another's company, which helps when you're on the road, believe me!

In between times working for the war effort and praying for a good part, my own morale boosters were the cast of characters we lived with at the Garden, and stories Arthur brought home from the studio.

For example, when he was working at Paramount on the musical *Blue Skies* for Fred Astaire and Bing Crosby, he told me that he'd had lunch that day with our friend Harry Tugend — by then head of production at the studio — and several other writers. Y. Frank Freeman, head of the studio, stopped by, and was invited to sit down and join them at the table. They were discussing the new plan for giving blood at the Red Cross. Harry said to Y. Frank, who was from the Deep South, "What would you think, Mr. Freeman, about having a transfusion of Negro blood?"

"Why, Harry," he said, "I feel that if I had a transfusion of Negro blood, I would be considered part Negro."

Harry said, "Mr. Freeman, have you ever been vaccinated for smallpox?"

He answered, "Why, yes, I think I have. I think I have, Harry. Why?"

Harry said, "Because if you have, Mr. Freeman, you are not only part horse, you are part *sick* horse!"

I became the Den Mother of the Garden of Allah — most of the "permanents" gave me their ration tickets, because not one of them, to my knowledge, could cook. But I could make chicken in the pot with matzo balls, delicate buckwheat blini without caviar, once in a while a lamb or beef stew, all kinds of pasta and rice — especially after accumulating a lot of ration tickets!

In Java, Arthur and I had loved the great Dutch invention rijsttafel — rice table. The idea is to have a big bowl of rice in front of you, and as many servants as one could have pass by you offering different dishes from both right and left hands. It can be a "six boy" rijsttafel — twelve varied dishes — or a twenty-boy tafel.

I decided to do a two-boy tafel, but with twenty-six dishes! The "boys" hired just had to come back into our kitchen — elbow room only with a two-burner stove and tiny oven, plus fifty-pound icebox — and refurbish the plates.

We invited eighteen guests, who gave us their ration tickets. I cooked for three days on Benchley's stove, Eddie Mayer's stove,

Natalie Schafer's stove, and ours. Used all their iceboxes and dishes, hired two professional waiters, ran up fair imitations of Javanese turbans and sashes for them, and thoroughly enjoyed myself!

Here's the entry from my hostess book, more than fifty years ago.

May 29, 1944

Albert Hacketts	Eddie Mayer
Ned Russells	Robert Benchley
John Reinharts	Mary Baker
Natalie Schafer	Phyllis List
Arthur Schwartzes	Thornton Delehanty
Marion Herwood & *Mari*	Cathy Turney & *Mari*

~ ~ ~

Chicken curry & rice	*Pimento strips*
Filet of sole & oyster mold	*Chopped eggs*
Fried shrimps	*Chopped onions*
Chinese vegetables	*Chopped green peppers*
Bean sprouts & sesame seeds	*Crushed peanuts*
Shish kebabs	*Crushed chilies*
Butterfly fritters	*Chopped raisins*
Lentils Omar Khayyam	*Major Grey's chutney*
Bieten met Appelen	*Red pepper relish*
Broiled tomatoes cinnamon	*Pickled mushrooms*
Broiled bananas ginger	*Mustard pickles*
Creamed radishes	*Preserved kumquats*

Eggs with anchovies

~ ~ ~

Beer ~ Gamay Rosé

~ ~ ~

Fresh pineapple sticks
Almond paste crust
Coffee   Grog

~ ~ ~

It's hard, in these days of plenty, to imagine how tightly rationed everything was, and even if one had the tickets, one had to find the precious goods — oils, butter, beef, et cetera.

Because gas was restricted, everyone carpooled. Arthur carpooled with William Faulkner when they were both at Warner Brothers. I was thrilled — *William Faulkner!*

Arthur was somewhat less thrilled. Faulkner in the mornings was usually either very hungover and silent or else very verbose and slightly belligerent. Arthur and the other two members of the car pool were upset because he usually asked the driver to take a side trip — the laundry, the cleaners, the shoemaker, post office, liquor store. Faulkner didn't have a car, and his requests weren't exactly sporting.

I had met Faulkner when I was at Universal. Now he was working on a film about California gold. I was collecting Californiana, and I lent him several rare and expensive books for research. When he'd kept my books for some time, I wrote him a kindly, affectionate note about them and gave the letter to Arthur to deliver. Arthur reported that Bill had put my letter, unopened, in his pocket.

One day Faulkner asked the studio if he could work at home. "Of course" was the answer. They soon discovered he meant way, way home — Mississippi! By the time I got around to reminding Arthur to ask about my books, Faulkner was gone.

One Sunday brunch I made an elaborate cold vegetable salad — with bottled dressing — for Benchley and Butterworth.

The next day, on Garden of Allah stationery — paper was in short supply, too — typed in the old black and red ribbon, dear Robert brought over these recipes:

NEW ENGLAND BOILED DRESSING FOR
BOILED NEW ENGLANDERS

1/4 tbs. salt
3 teaspoons mustard (this is for jaded palates.
The rule calls for 1 teaspoon)
1 1/2 tbs. sugar
Few grains cayenne
2 tbsp. flour
1 egg or yolk of 2 eggs
1 1/2 tbsp. melted butter   ha! ha!
3/4 cup of milk
1/4 cup of vinegar

Mix dry ingredients, add yolks of eggs slightly beaten, butter, milk and vinegar *very slowly*. Cook over boiling water till mixture thickens — strain — add pepper from peppermill, and cool.

MOULDED SALMON

Use same rule as for boiled dressing. When cooked, add 3/4 tbsp. granulated gelatin soaked in 2 tbsp. cold water. Pour over contents of one can of salmon (rinsed in hot water and separated in flakes). Fill mould and chill.

Serve with

CUCUMBER SAUCE

Beat 1/2 cup heavy cream (ha-ha) until stiff (ha-ha-ha). Add 1/4 teasp. salt, few grains pepper, and gradually 2 tbls. vinegar. Then add 1 cucumber, pared, chopped and drained through cheese cloth.

Then take off all your clothes and call
VILLA 16

Benchley and I were very naughty. When we could, with our double martinis carefully balanced, we would sit on the back stairs of one particular villa listening to late afternoon, or early evening, lovemaking.

Our darling daughter was in the second grade when we arrived back in California. Across the street was a private school, the Eunice Knight Saunders School, so convenient, and seemingly taking good care of the children.

Sylvia was very busy alongside me whenever I was home, and I'm sure her culinary art and appreciation and creativeness started with her sojourn at Mama's, and then progressed as my apprentice, or as she once described it, scullery maid!

Early in 1943, M. F. K. Fisher wrote in *The Gastronomical Me*:

> I know a beautiful honey-colored actress who is a gourmande, in a pleasant way. She loves to cook rich hot lavish meals. She does it well, too.
>
> She is slender, fragile, with a mute other-worldly pathos in her large azure eyes, and she likes to invite a lot of oddly assorted and usually famous people to a long table crowded with flowers, glasses, dishes of nuts, bowls of Armenian jelly and Russian relishes and Indian chutney, and beer and wine and even water, and then bring in a huge bowl of oxtail stew with dumplings. She has spent days making it, with special spices she found in Bombay or Soho or Honolulu, and she sits watching happily while it disappears. Then she disappears herself, and in a few minutes staggers to the table with a baked Alaska as big as a washtub, a thing of beauty, and a joy for about fifteen minutes.
>
> But this star-eyed slender gourmande has a daughter about eight or nine, and the daughter hates her mother's sensuous dishes. In fact, she grows spindly on them. The only way to put meat on her bones is to send her to stay for a week or two with her grandmother, where she eats store ice cream for lunch, mashed potatoes for supper, hot white pap for breakfast.

"My daughter!" the actress cries in despair and horror. I tell her there is still hope, with the passage of time. But she, perhaps, because of her beauty, pretends Time is not.

Yes, as W. H. Auden put it about our dear friend M. F. K. Fisher, "I do not know of anyone in the United States today who writes better prose." Her books — *The Art of Eating, Sister Age,* a translation of Brillat-Savarin — are delightful classics.

But, as an intimate of hers once observed, MF wrote about life as she *remembered* it — or as it suited her fancy. And fanciful she could be. Sylvia did not "hate" my cooking at all. And MF never had a meal at Mama's table, so how would she know what Sylvia ate there!

MF had been friends with Gordon Newell, Ward Ritchie, and Larry Powell since college days. MF and I met in 1932 when she was married to Alfred Fisher, her first husband. She and Al were living in a cottage in Laguna Beach. MF and I instantly bonded and remained intimate friends for years. I was the *only* member of that extraordinary group that was earning good money — $125 a week. So, always on visits, Gloria and Gordon arrived at the Fishers' house or Ward's studio with a basket of goodies!

We weren't in touch much after that until MF and her second husband, Dillwyn — Timmy — Parrish, returned from Switzerland and were living at Bareacres, the house they bought on a hill overlooking the fields and orchards of Hemet Valley. During the period of Timmy's catastrophic illness, MF and I began corresponding.

Once, when we were living in New York, she had written me complaining that a novel she had written had been "Jew-disapproved — a year's work gone with a libel suit threatened." She said she'd like to loan us the $5,000, which she hadn't, to accept the Marharajah of Jaipur's invitation for a shoot in India that spring (we had been invited through Gene Frenke). She had started another novel. . . .

I was so busy being *me*, I didn't ask her who might be involved in the libel suit. And, anyway, MF loved little hints that her personal life flowed with mysterious currents. So I didn't rise to her "Jew-disapproved" bait. It would not have been seemly. Arthur shrugged.

When Arthur and I returned to Hollywood, MF was living by herself at Bareacres. In between studio work, I drove the three or four hours alone (about a hundred miles due east) many times to visit with her. We talked and talked, walked and walked, were convivial at meals with wine, and prepared special dishes for each other.

Not long after our return, MF came into town to work as a junior writer at Paramount. It was wonderful to have her so close — on the phone, with us at the Garden of Allah.

One morning she called with an amazing message. This was during the war and she said it was very hush hush. The army was sending her on a secret mission and she couldn't tell me where, or what, so not to expect to hear from her for a while.

I was *that* impressed!

Many months later, in the fall of 1943, she called, back at Bareacres. She had a surprise for me. It was a baby girl she said she had adopted in the East, after she'd finished her assignment. The baby had dark hair and dark eyes and was a beauty.

I was so thrilled for MF! I drove down to Bareacres with baby gifts and champagne, and we celebrated by reading together most of a novella I had written about a fantasized love affair — its threats, its follies, its pursuit. Rather a diary of desire and frustration.

I had written my little novel ardently, and, I thought, rather well — skillfully, with panache. In fact, MF was very complimentary, and I went to bed full of happy thoughts about my future as a writer.

The next evening, after dinner, she said to me — very quietly, in her soft, confidential voice, slowly enunciating, "Gloria, I think you should burn the book."

At my startled, "What?" she said, "Arthur's going to think it's a diary faked up into a novella — that you really are having an affair. You have to burn it." The possibility of having to convince my wildly jealous husband that his suspicions were false — for weeks and weeks and weeks and maybe forever — was monstrous, unacceptable!

"We'll put it in the incinerator." And she did — that night.

It was a dastardly act. Motivated by jealousy? Why didn't she suggest I hide the manuscript in a safety deposit box? But in my immediate reaction to what she had said, I thought about it no further. For a very long while.

A month or two later, Arthur and I were at a dinner party. The conversation came to a remark I could hardly believe I was hearing:

"Did you know that M. F. K. Fisher had a child by Val Burton?"

Val Burton was a writer. A married man.

I angrily reprimanded our host with, "How dare you? How can you say such a thing? MF is my best friend, and it's not true, not true at all!"

The moment we got home, even though it was almost midnight, I called MF. She listened without exclamation, or questions. I said, "MF, you have to do something about this. You can't have people saying this about you. Val Burton! It's dreadful!"

Her reply was even-toned, unruffled. I was not to pay any attention to all this, she said. Gossip is gossip, or some such calming comment.

I couldn't believe her lack of concern. Her indifference to a scandalmonger. And as long as I knew her, over sixty years, she never mentioned it again.

*　*　*

A year and a half later, MF complained a great deal about her uninteresting situation. She was lonesome, she was looking for more excitement in her life, certainly another lover — whatever. The fearsome forties were upon us! Arthur and I advised her to go either to New York City or Washington, DC. Opportunities were there, and certainly a change of pace!

We called Kyle and Mae Crichton — our dear, generous friends in Bronxville. They invited MF to stay with them when she arrived. They gave her a party, to introduce her to their friends. Donald Friede, a dashing bookman (Covici-Friede Publishers), was there.

He proposed marriage that night, and MF *accepted*.

MF called us, the Crichtons called us, and we were shocked.

I told MF I knew about Donald from his first wife, our old friend Evie — now Mrs. Peter Dunne. Donald and Evie had divorced for several reasons, and I begged MF to take more time to get to know him.

She laughed and said, "Kyle says he proposes to everyone he meets."

I answered, "MF, he's known for that!"

It didn't faze her, and they married three weeks later.

We had them for dinner when they returned, and were actually pleasantly surprised at their seeming happiness.

MF always seemed concerned about social status. She was proud to have gone to the elite Bishop's School in La Jolla — where I had longed to go when I was a girl. And I seem to remember her mentioning a relationship with Swedish aristocracy. Friede was a bon vivant and gentleman. Quite a catch. However, as stupid as it was, in those days, agents, literary or theatrical, were, like other riffraff — actors, for example — not invited to join most clubs. I have no idea whether or not MF knew this when she married Donald, but I think she must have been very surprised when she found out. Because Donald had come out to Hollywood as an agent.

They had a daughter, Kennedy (MF's family surname), in 1946, and their life seemed serene.

But in time, MF did write me from Bareacres that Donald was not well and would undergo major surgery to find out why.

She indicated unhappiness, and a lot of quarreling.

Eventually, he went back to New York City and they divorced.

One afternoon in our garden a few years later, as MF and I were finishing our tea, Sylvia came home from junior high school. MF got up to leave, and Sylvia offered to get her coat.

"And purse," I added.

Sylvia hurried into the house and came out with a happy smile. Accepting the coat and bag, MF purred to me — in front of Sylvia — "My! Isn't she the busy little bee, trying so hard to please. Isn't she a bit much?"

I led Sylvia into the house and left MF standing there, and didn't speak to her or answer her letters for about thirty years.

She never acknowledged the break.

14

Well, lucky for me, save for one, the many *many* friends I've had in my life have not played games with our friendship. Actually, it isn't luck. Friendship takes constant paying attention.

The first Christmas we were in residence at the Garden of Allah, I decided to have only Mama and my brother and his wife, Marjorie, for dinner. As I walked past Benchley's villa with groceries, I saw a knitted bright red penis before two large green balls hanging in his door window.

I rang the bell, and when he appeared, asked where did he get it, where could I get one. Some girl had given it to him. Disappointed, I brightly asked, "Where are you having Christmas dinner?"

"No place," he answered.

"What do you mean, no place?"

Here was one of the most sought-after bachelors in Hollywood, famous as a writer, actor, bon vivant, not asked to Christmas dinner? Unbelievable.

"Well, we're only having my mother and brother, Bob, but we'd love to have you, if you'd like."

"I'd love to, Gloria. I really would. It would be just great."

I put my grocery bags down and gave him a big hug. Oh, jolly! Jolly! Happy, happy holidays!

I'd been in our villa about fifteen minutes when the phone rang. It was Benchley, and he asked, "Gloria, can Dottie come, too? "Dottie" was his dear friend Dorothy Parker.

"Of course, Bob. I didn't know she was in town. We'd love to have her."

About ten minutes after that, Bob called again. "Gloria, Charlie would like to come, too."

Charlie Butterworth hadn't a Christmas dinner invitation either. "But of course! Welcome! Welcome!"

I dashed back to the butcher, the baker, the grocer, and called Mama.

"Guess who's coming to dinner? Robert Benchley, Charlie Butterworth, and —" I paused for dramatic emphasis — "Dorothy Parker!" My mother was indeed impressed, as my newspaperman brother would be, too.

So! Mama arrived the next afternoon, all done up in her best, and sat down on the sofa, with rosy anticipation of Parkerisms about to fall from those notable lips. Except that Dottie's humor could stun. Her most famous poem would have snapped Mama to Kingdom Come:

> *Résumé*
>
> Razors pain you;
> Rivers are damp;
> Acids stain you;
> And drugs cause cramp.
> Guns aren't lawful;
> Nooses give;
> Gas smells awful;
> You might as well live.

When she was working at *The New Yorker*, Dottie hung a sign on her office door: MEN.

And the day someone came to lunch at the Round Table and said President Coolidge was dead, Dottie said, "How can they tell?"

The threesome arrived. Cocktails all around, even though Miss Parker seemed slightly high to start with and in a bad mood. She had on a black sweater, rumpled black cotton skirt, black stockings and shoes, and never stopped talking about her dogs on her farm in Bucks County, Pennsylvania, having ticks ticks ticks and no one taking care of them and what could she do? Sullen sullen sullen.

Bob tried to shush her a couple of times, unsuccessfully.

Mama looked unbelieving. My brother was past caring — he was loaded. Arthur and Charlie and Bob tried holiday cheeriness, and Sylvia and Marge and I cleaned up.

When we weren't eating chez Stuart, we usually went across Sunset Boulevard to Preston Sturges's restaurant, the Players. Benchley wouldn't walk — or dash — across Sunset Boulevard with us. He would order a cab to cross the street.

One of our delights in people-watching was in observing a man named S. P. Eagle at a table by the window, host to a flock? covey? bevy? of beautiful young ladies clustered over a lazy Susan of fresh caviar and all the trimmings — chopped yolk of egg, chopped white of egg, minced green onions, melba toast. Caviar during wartime? But at some point, he stopped appearing; Sturges banned him because of his unpaid restaurant chits.

He later took back his real name, Sam Spiegel, and produced such illustrious films as *The African Queen, On the Waterfront, The Bridge on the River Kwai,* and *Lawrence of Arabia.* And I'm sure that if the restaurant had still been in business, he would have paid his bills.

We surreptitiously watched Charlie Chaplin one night at Chasen's. He was seated with several friends in the Number One

Table in the front room. We were with the Bogarts, sitting across from him. When Chaplin's tab was presented, he read it very carefully, and then put down some bills on the tray (no credit cards in those days). The change was brought back, and first he put all the money into his jacket pocket. Then he took out some change and a bill and put it on the tray. Then he took the bill away and pushed the change around on the tray. Then he took a piece of change up, hesitated, and put it back.

Leaving maybe some fifty-odd cents finally!

We ate at Dave Chasen's because most of our friends who lived in Beverly Hills ate there. Chasen's wonderful chili and ribs were a hearty welcome to new and old friends. Other main restaurants were Musso & Franks — still with us — Perino's, the most elegant, and the Brown Derby.

And Mike Romanoff's — Prince Romanoff to us peasants. His elegant restaurant was financed by several New Yorkers, including Benchley and Jock Whitney. When Mike opened his restaurant on Rodeo Drive, my friends and I lunched there often. Kay Schwartz, married to Arthur Schwartz, the fine lyricist-composer; Kay Cromwell, John Cromwell's wife — I had worked for him in the Lionel Barrymore film *Sweepings*; Gertrude Hatch, wife to Eric — humorist-writer; Irene of Bullock's Wilshire, designer for the elite; and Decla Dunning, elegant scenarist and writer.

We all started with martinis, gin of course (who knew from vodka?). We had a lot of yatata! yatata! to say to each other, all sorts of gossip (except sexual, which was not discussed) from our varied lives. We considered ourselves sophisticates, and sardonically referred to our lunching as "contributing to the war effort!" (Not quite true. We all *were* in volunteer work of one kind or another.) We dressed for luncheon. Hats, gloves, jewelry, boutonnieres, but then, everyone dressed for dinner, too, and the theater and the movies. We all smoked cigarettes. I favored a black enamel holder with a gold band set with tiny diamonds. It had been given to Susan Marx, Harpo's wife, by Joseph Schenck, an early film mogul, when she was a *Ziegfeld Follies* star, and she gave it to me when she quit smoking.

Decla and I became best friends. I remember one time at Mike's, we were still talking at four-thirty, and the headwaiter came over and asked us please to leave so they could get ready for dinner.

These were seemingly happy times, but I was also desperately, and at times despondently, looking for things to do. That lingering desire for fame and fortune was still with me, but not all-consuming. The war was raging. I started a mammoth scrapbook, and clipped articles from the newspapers practically every day. My favorite headline was: "DE GAULLE CALLS FOR AN ERECT FRANCE."

The time came when I decided I needed to add to my charms on hospital tours.

First, I took singing lessons. Cloris Leachman, the nimble and charming comedienne, offered to have a twosome act with her playing piano, me singing, for Southern California convalescent hospitals.

I tried.

Sylvia says she remembers her fascination at my sitting on top of our small upright piano, legs crossed, singing "Jenny made her mind up" — "The Saga of Jenny" from Weill and Gershwin's *Lady in the Dark*. Only at parties with our poor guests' indulgence — when I was a little high (otherwise, I would never have put them through such a dipsy doodle). For our tours I also learned to sing "St. Louis Blues" and "St. James Infirmary."

But after a few stints, Cloris quietly removed herself and me from performances. No more volunteer bookings. Was I really that off pitch? Skirly?

Next I went thrice a week to the most famous dance school in the country, Arthur Murray's, which agitated my Arthur greatly. He was afraid that I might fall in love with one of the dance teachers, I guess. But it was wonderful dancing again. The Charleston had come and gone. Now it was swing dancing. A lot of turns, a lot of dancing apart. And to all the great bands on records — Glenn Miller, Tommy Dorsey, Harry James. . . . I loved it.

One great thing about those lessons was that we were wearing very full skirts with beautiful petticoats. So they swished and billowed and flirted as we danced.

Dancing with strangers at Arthur Murray's was a release for me. It gave me a sense of freedom from responsibilities and commitments — what I've always sought and valued.

In the hospitals, Hillary and I cozied up to the wounded men and women, sat on their beds, and held their hands. Our conversations were about where they were from, were they married, any children, had they been to California — always with such sweet, soft, sad responses. We danced with them — the paraplegics, too — played softball, watched movies, all with the loving help of their orderlies.

All those dancing lessons had an unforeseen benefit — but it took nearly forty years.

It was 1981 and I had been out of work for quite some time when one day my agent, Pat Amaral, called. Richard Benjamin, the charming actor-director, wondered if I would play a small role with Peter O'Toole in *My Favorite Year*. "You have no dialogue, Gloria, so I told him I was sure you're not interested, but I have to tell you about it."

I hollered, "Peter O'Toole? Are you crazy? Of course, I'll do it. For nothing!"

"That won't be necessary! Please! Don't say that! I'll call him."

I was to meet them in two or three days.

So I called Benjy, my handsome twenty-two-year-old grandson. "Benjy, you've got to come over. I'm going to be dancing with Peter

O'Toole. I haven't danced in years. I need to practice." Benjy came over for two days and whirled me around my living room in his inimitable fashion.

At Metro Goldwyn Mayer, the production assistant took me into a small anteroom on the soundstage. Two women were seated there. I did not recognize either of them, but, of course, I wouldn't have. I mean, what recognizable character actress wants a non-speaking part for one day?

I asked them, "Have you met him?" They hadn't. One said she was a dance teacher, the other was a dress extra.

I thought to myself, "You really are hard up, Gloria." And then, "But you're doing what you want to do — be grateful!"

The production assistant came and called me first. I was so excited, I was trembling! Richard Benjamin met me, we had a short exchange — I admire him so as an actor.

"You'd consider doing this part? No lines?"

I answered, "Well, maybe during the scene I can say 'Hello' or 'Good-bye' or 'Thank you!'"

He kind of smiled and said, "Hmm, I don't think so. But we'll see. Anyway, I'd like you to meet Peter."

We walked over to where he was sitting with several men, and Big Blue Eyes stood up, with that quizzical smile, and took my hand.

I burbled something like "This is a great honor!" He indicated with a shrug it wasn't, turned me around, and said, "Shall we dance?"

He led me to a big patch of smooth flooring, sounds of the "Anniversary Waltz" suddenly filled the stage, he put his arms around me, I rested my hand on his shoulder — it was a stretch, he's so tall! — and we started to dance.

Tremble tremble!

Stumble stumble!

An agonizing performance — and irretrievable.

As the record ended, he dropped his arm, my arm, and looked down at me.

I looked up sadly and said, "I bet you'll never ask me to dance with you again, Mr. O'Toole!"

He kind of smiled, and replied, "No, no, it was fine."

I thanked him and the director, sick at heart, thinking, "I've lost this part. No way I'll get it," and left for the anteroom. It was a long walk back, alone. *But,* I had time to plot!

I opened the anteroom door, half closed it, leaned against it, raised my eyes to heaven, let out a heartrending half sigh, half sob, dropped my head, closed the door, and whispered, sotto voce, "Oh, my God!"

The two waiting women said, "What? What? What's the matter? What happened?"

"Well! O'Toole is so tall! And he really doesn't help you! And the dance floor is like sandpaper, it sticks to your feet, and it's hard to move! And there's only a bunch of men in there — and they're no help! They don't give a damn! Nobody does! It was one of the worst experiences of my life!" The hand goes to my brow, I drop my head, shudder, groan, and really give quite a performance. Wobbly exit. Barely making it.

What happened, I don't know. But my home is about a twenty-five-minute drive from Metro. By the time I got there, my agent had called and said, "Gloria, they want you." So either I spooked those women so completely that they were paralyzed, or Mr. O'Toole just said, "That's it. Let's not bother with anyone else."

It was one of my better ploys.

Peter O'Toole was one of the very few actors I have ever worked with who really cared about the other performer. He said to me the Monday of the week that I worked, "Miss Stuart, we have a few days before we dance together on Friday. Would you like to rehearse every day? So that when we shoot, we will be used to each other?"

I said, "I would love that. That's very kind of you, Mr. O'Toole."

So, every day, sometimes twice, there was a little floor set up on the stage, and the prop man would play "The Anniversary Waltz," and Mr. O'Toole and I would dance. On the Wednesday or Thursday before the Friday we were to dance on film, he asked me to have lunch with him in his magnificent trailer outside the soundstage.

I was thrilled! We talked about his childhood, the prestigious performers he had worked with, certainly the roles. Then I ventured to enquire, "Mr. O'Toole, how could you ever let go of your wife [Siân Phillips, unforgettable in *I, Claudius* and today, *in Marlene,* as Dietrich]. She's so beautiful and talented."

His reply was, "My dear, booze and broads . . ."

Me, "Dear, dear!"

"But we're still friends. And we have two beautiful daughters, both interested in the theater."

He was so charming. Such a beautiful actor. It was a great privilege to work with him. Even though I never got to say a word onscreen!

Back to the Garden of Allah. Because it was clear I couldn't get arrested as an actor, I threw myself into so many activities, so many directions — cooking and entertaining, singing and dancing and French lessons, touring hospitals, sewing a tutu for Sylvia's ballet recital — I often met myself coming and going.

For example, there was the time I took up handwriting analysis and studied it thoroughly. We were at a party one night for our host's brother who had just arrived from the East, and I mentioned that I was studying it. Someone suggested that I read somebody's handwriting. One of the samples given to me was very tiny, very legible, very precise. I said about it, "Oh, this person is very secretive, very much within themselves, very manipulative, very organized." It turned out to be the guest of honor.

Going home, Arthur was so upset with me. He said, "How dare you do a character analysis that is so uncomplimentary?"

I answered, "The man had very small handwriting, very organized sentences, he's a closed person, and he was entitled to what I said." Well, several years later we discovered that he was a member of the Communist Party, and had come out from the East to elicit membership in the Party among the movie colony. The year he produced the classic movie about anti-Semitism, *Crossfire,* he was indicted by the House Un-American Activities Committee for contempt of Congress. One of the Hollywood Ten, Adrian Scott was his name.

By the fall of 1945, Arthur was working steadily, the three of us were crowding each other in three rooms (to say the least!), a lot of our friends at the Garden had left, so we decided to sell our last house in Hollywood that we'd hung on to for so long, and rent something larger somewhere else.

We rented a Spanish-style furnished house up a near-perpendicular road in hilly Laurel Canyon. (Groucho refused to drive up it.) It was only a quarter of a mile from the Garden of Allah, still close to Greenblatt's deli, Schwab's pharmacy, and Preston Sturges's Players restaurant! We were told Ethel Barrymore lived next door, but next door was a steep climb. So we never attempted a neighborly visit. But neither did she.

I had a garden again — at last. Sylvia had a small swimming pool for herself and friends, Arthur had a study, and we had a housekeeper-cook.

We went to a lot of parties. If I had to pick one — just one — I think the most exciting evening was at the Ira Gershwins' when both Judy Garland and Frank Sinatra were there.

Lee and Ira were gracious hosts. After dinner we sat around with brandies and liqueurs and chatted. With only one thing on our minds. Would *they* sing? They would and did. Solos and duets, "and then I sang . . ." Or, "Do you remember . . . ?" Until about 2 A.M. It was an evening to treasure forever.

And we continued giving lots of parties. December 22, 1944, the entry in my hostess book lists a Chinese dinner for Kay and Groucho Marx (Kay had to drive him up our hill), Betty Bacall and Bogey (*To Have and Have Not* had just been released), Dorothy Parker, Frances and Albert Hackett (writing *It's a Wonderful Life* for Jimmy Stewart), Nunnally Johnson (he was writing *The Dark Mirror* for Olivia de Havilland and Lew Ayres), the Adrian Scotts (we were becoming friends — his production of *Murder, My Sweet,* with Dick Powell and Claire Trevor, had a script based on a Raymond Chandler novel), the Nat Perrins, Celeste Holm, Ruth and Sol Siegel (fairly new to our circle — Sol had just produced *Kiss and Tell* for Shirley Temple and adorable Robert Benchley), and Chick and Don Hartman (also new friends).

I hired a Chinese chef to come in, and I was his sous-chef with the spareribs, egg rolls, sweet-and-sour pork, almond chicken, pineapple chicken, lobster chow mein, chow yuk, and fried rice. Followed by litchi nuts, kumquats, coconut candy, and almond cakes.

It may sound like a rather mundane menu today, but in the mid-forties it was *très exotique!*

In fact, it was such a triumph, it became clear to me I needed to concoct an equally gourmet presentation for our Christmas party. I decided on Roast Piglet.

Ordered one from the Farmer's Market in Hollywood, brought it home — too long for my oven! So I sliced him in half — or was it a her? — and started the roasting.

I'd had our florist make a rosy wreath, bought the reddest ever Delicious apple, cut a bed of greenery from the garden — bought a beautiful silver-plated platter. All set for a splendiferous presentation!

The guests assembled, dinner was announced, and in comes Gloria bearing this beautiful offering (once again full-bodied).

No ecstatic cries greeted me as I glided around, lifting Itself up to be happily admired. It really didn't dawn on me until after Piglet — the buffet's centerpiece — was sliced that there were very few takers.

I mean, Very Few.

The next morning, asking my closest friends "Why?" to a woman they said it was "not very appetizing."

I was "making busy" but unhappily so. Very restless and crochety. Poor Sylvia, poor Arturo, poor Mama.

The garden and gardening have always nurtured me. Calmed and filled unspoken needs.

I remember sitting in the grass near the swimming pool one afternoon pulling weeds, and Mama, who was visiting, coming over to me, saying I should stop wasting my time and try to get back into the movies.

But that was no longer available to me. No theatrical agent was interested, no casting directors ever called, my husband kept disabusing me of any hope to "do" theater. So in my darkened room, I climbed into my bed and stayed for a while. And cried a lot — at least that's what my daughter tells me; this, I don't remember. Mama hovered, Sylvia was full of generous "What can I do, Mother? Can I get you anything?" (She is a born nurse, be it for friend or foe.)

It was healing.

I think I was in the midst of having a mild — what in those days was genteelly called — nervous breakdown.

And for once in my life, it wasn't my cherished friends who pulled me through. It was silence.

I think that dreaming is the kindest, the gentlest, the most rewarding part of conscious contemplation. Certainly lying comfortably in the comfort of a warm bed and dreaming about what one needs, what one wants, what one feels, about any given situation, any friend, any ambitions, any disappointments, any happiness, looking forward to the future, blocking out unhappy situations, quietly in the dark, is most rewarding. I would encourage anyone with problems to indulge themselves, to take the time and the energy and the imagination to indulge in contemplation, to write a poem in one's head, or write a letter that needs to be written, or ought to be written. One can make one's way through any labyrinth. One can enjoy an experience, relive it, rejoice in it.

"The quiet darkness, it can nourish you," my mother said to me once a very long time ago. She loved the quiet of the night, the emptiness, except for one's own self, being alone.

I love it, too. I love to just stretch under warm blankets in winter, and in the summer under a sheet — my body well lubricated with my favorite cream. Bird songs are so much more poignant in the dark, and you don't miss out on the rustlings coming in through an open window, the intrigue and excitement from small creatures in the trees or bushes — even a cat in heat. A barking dog is not included, because a barking dog is alarmed about something or commenting on something that one can't know, doesn't see, usually doesn't hear. And it's more an alarm than a song.

But once as I lay there, surveying the canyons of an ocean deep, I said out loud, "Fuck you! Fuck you! I don't give a shit about being a good wife *or* a good daughter *or* a good mother *or* a dear friend! I want to be a great actress. And I won't be. . . ." And the tears would flow.

15

There are some people who are possessed by the need to express themselves creatively — in the arts, in business, the social sciences. Make a mark as an individual.

"I want to be *me!*"

"I did it *my* way. . . ."

I'm one of them.

I was truly creepy-crawly with ambition, dreams, what-ifs. Whatever I'd done I'd tackled with an intensity that surprised even me.

But I was so demoralized.

I was neglecting the garden. I was losing interest in haute cuisine. I stopped studying Culbertson and Goren for my bridge game. No more knitting, embroidering, writing poetry, brushing up on my French, reading aloud all the fascinating Shakespearean heroines, playing solo Scrabble and reading the dictionary. Having a Mozart festival while lying down was about it.

Dead in the water.

What to do?

It was then that the art of découpage came into my life.

Webster's defines découpage as the "art of cutting out designs or illustrations and mounting them on a surface in a decorative arrangement."

With this art, one can be witty, striking, laid back, scenic, poetic.

Right up my alley!

Arthur's studio had sent us to New York City to see a new show, *Dream Girl,* starring Betty Field. The studio gave us a suite at the Plaza Hotel, we met friends in the Oak Bar, a limo was sent to take us to the opening! Very gala, all on the cuff (show business term for FREE!).

While there, I called Sylvia Keefe, wife of Willard, Arthur's best friend from his early newspaper days in St. Paul, Minnesota. She was a gifted decorator. I told her I was beside myself to find something artistic to do.

She said the magic word: "découpage."

When I looked blank, she said, "There's a ninety-year-old woman I'll introduce you to. She will show you, and, if you like it, she'll give you lessons."

In my soon-to-be teacher's studio, she showed me drawers of prints, some hand tinted, some not. Variety? Animals, fruits, flowers, trees, objets d'art, statues, French fashion models, English crests, sea creatures — I wanted them all! Light, fantastic compositions floated in my head. Birds and flowers and bonnets and cats and clouds and and and . . .

My teacher cut out a seated gorilla, a wreath of flowers for his head, a delicate lady seated in his lap, tree branches behind them — flowers, birds, blossoms everywhere. She glued them onto a glass plate, and then painted on the back of the glass — a turquoise sky.

I have it today in my bathroom. The twelve-by-twelve plate in a nineteenth-century gold-leafed pier glass mirror.

Eureka! I was given the source of the special glue, for applying cutout prints behind clear glass. The glue has to be so clear it's invisible — because behind the glued-on prints, is either gold- or silver-leafed or painted glass in the desired color. I haunted the New York City shops featuring antique and modern prints. She gave me the name of the glass factory that would furnish blank lamp bases. I bought a bevy of nineteenth-century embossed gold paper medallions and strips, French boxes in all sizes of unfinished white wood, lots of English tin trays, and, finally, when I got back to Hollywood, some really charming chests, chairs, bureaus, mirrors.

It occurred to me recently that almost every creative act, besides writing, I have ever done has evolved from my childhood cutting out of paper dolls and fitting their wardrobes on them with minute detailing — hats, coats, dresses (no slacks then), little shoes and purses, changes of hairstyles — and furnishing them with pet companions, trunks for travel. I did it from the beginning in cutting out patterns, dressmaking for Sylvia and me. Then again later in ikebana — the formal Japanese art of arranging flowers according to strict principles of shape, size, color, and spiritual meaning.

And now I was experiencing the flowering of my childhood art, from the intricate scissor work to combining subjects in my style.

My first crystal lamp base featured an ape wearing a bonnet and a contemplative gaze and holding another bonnet. He is at the bottom of the sea among delicate fronds and sea ferns, gently floating fish, and marine invertebrates.

I saw an advertisement in the *Hollywood Reporter*. "Shop for sale. Location La Cienega Blvd. Chinese antiques. Call . . ."

I went down to the shop. The woman had lived in China many years, left before the Japanese arrived, and had a very small but very fine collection of Chinese porcelains, bronzes, furniture, scrolls.

I bought her out and took over her lease.

Now I was a shopkeeper! I called my shop Décor, Ltd.

I couldn't wait each morning to leave our house, put the key in the door, open it, and welcome the rest of the world to my art!

I bought the finest scissors, the finest cutting knives, and sat alone in my shop designing, and applying, and admiring the lamp bases, the boxes, the trays I'd decorated.

I hired an assistant to do the cutting whenever needed. I would design and assemble the prints inside clear lamp bases. She would paint the background or do the gold or silver leafing. After I designed decorations on tables or chests, trays or screens, she would cut and glue with me.

Busy busy busy.

Came the opening cocktail party for my shop. My great and generous friend Chick Hartman led the parade of friends who said (and I really got tired of it), "It's all so beautiful, Gloria, but what will you do next?"

After a few months, I hired a helper in my shop, and several more ladies who did cutting at home.

I finally hired a representative, Cy Miller, who peddled my lamps, trays, boxes, and screens to my clients — Lord & Taylor in New York City, Neiman Marcus in Dallas, Bullock's in Pasadena, Cannell and Chaffin in Los Angeles, and Gump's in San Francisco. If I may say, the crème de la crème.

But the labor costs, the fine fine cutting, applying, finishing — sixteen coats of lacquer on the boxes, tables, screens — did me in. I had one competitor in New York City, who paid by the piece. I paid by the hour, and lost forty thousand dollars in three years.

I went into wholesale the last two years, because I got sick of customers coming in looking for antique china or glass or objets d'art, and exclaiming, "My mother had some of this," or "Why is it so expensive?"

My business lasted four and a half years.

But happily customers of many years ago still seek me out, and tell me how much they love what they have of what I did!

And my helper from those years is still in my life — Ruth Golden Gottlieb. She was my left and right arms, second head — you name it! We are still very close, loving friends.

And . . . good things were happening!

Arthur was back in his creative element. In the previous two years, he had written the screenplay for *The Trouble with Women* for Ray Milland and Teresa Wright, collaborated on *Hazard* for Paulette Goddard and Macdonald Carey, *Saigon* for Alan Ladd and Veronica Lake, and *Dear Wife* for William Holden and Joan Caulfield.

Now he was adapting a Samson Raphaelson play, *Mr. Music,* for Bing Crosby. In the back of his mind he was working on an original comedy, *Young Man with Ideas,* which he would write for Glenn Ford, and the screen version of Howard Lindsay's *Call Me Madam* for Ethel Merman and Donald O'Connor.

Meantime, he was house hunting. It was Arthur who always sniffed out the great houses in our lives. Interesting. You'd have thought it would be me.

This time, he had found a Craftsman* house from the twenties in Brentwood for us. Brentwood! I remembered little brooks, mellowed hills and dales, and rabbits and squirrels where Mama and Boy and I had picked wildflowers. Now it was completely inhabited by people, landscaped with hundreds of green lawns, flower beds, and paved streets with lights, power lines, and, occasionally, a sneaky coyote who rejoiced with us at the upgrading from a rental in Laurel Canyon.

The cedar-shingled house was on a quiet tree-thickened, sweet-smelling acre north of San Vicente Boulevard, on Burlingame Avenue. Two stories with a magnificent flying redwood overhang. Its owner was an English horticulturist for Evans and Reeves, one of the finest nurseries in Southern California. He had gardened this property for twenty years but was no longer able to care for it.

There were huge, tall pines and Cedars of Lebanon in the front; magnolia, bougainvillea, avocado, sapote, and apricot trees in the back, and Land, Land, Land!

I became a whirling dervish of creative renovation.

For Sylvia's upstairs bedroom suite, Mama and I hand quilted a green-flowered bedspread. I had the walls painted peach pink, painted her furniture black, découpaged each piece with beautiful scarlet and peach pink roses with green leaves.

---

*In the spirit of the Arts and Crafts movement of the late ninteenth and early twentieth centuries — there are many in Southern California.

For Arthur and me downstairs, we added two new bedrooms, dressing rooms, and baths. My suite was all in mauve. Loving words, *mauve* had always been one of my favorites. Serendipitously, it was also my favorite color! I sent for a pair of hundred-year-old merry-go-round horses made by a master carver in the South. I had a wood frame made for my double bed and set a horse at the head and foot, galloping into the room. The horses and frame were painted mauve, then I gold-leafed and bejeweled the horses' saddles. For their tails, which were missing, I tucked thick, heavy gold yarn up their sweet little asses. Smashing!

To bring the whole long living/dining room together, I decided to paint it in a very soft, subdued, pale creamy avocado. I created a sample for the painters. The first company of painters quit because they came back three days in a row and still couldn't match my color. After two more tries — and two more weeks — I did find painters that got it right. The dining room table and upright piano in the living room were lacquered to match the walls.

Open to the kitchen we added a huge breakfast/storage/laundry room. Its west wall was glass, affording a full view of the back garden. For pizazz, I had the south wall covered in a Saul Steinberg railroad station paper — brilliant black and red line drawings on a white background.

What to do after the remodeling was finished? The garden, of course! I had two greenhouses built, lath and hothouse. "Why not try and raise orchids, Gloria?" Why not! Dozens of orchid plants went into the hothouse. In the lath house, I experimented with grafting various stone fruits on one trunk. Hopefully, a garniture of peaches, apricots, and plums!

I had an aviary built. Filled it full of tiny lovebirds, cockatoos, cockateels, little nest retreats, food, water, and greens. It was under a wonderfully gnarled old tea tree beside a brick patio I'd had laid. That gnarled old tea tree by the aviary was perhaps my favorite thing in that garden. Most mornings, I ate my breakfast beneath it. The old tree reminded me that age can be beautiful. The *act* of aging can be beautiful — its final result identification with the earth — contemplative, harmonious.

But what had been happening to what I consider to be my numero uno creative act, daughter Sylvia?

By the time she was a senior in high school, Sylvia and I had become very close friends. She had always been a most affectionate child, and I, a most casual mother.

I had really been "playing" those years, playing at mothering, playing at being a wife, partying, gardening, shopping, shopkeeping, any attempt to keep my mind off the fact I was not acting.

So it almost took me by surprise to discover I had become a caring Mommy. I worried about my darling's appearance, her popularity, her grades, her choices for the future — actress, writer, doctor, lawyer, "merchant chief."

All of these involvements made it particularly difficult, very upsetting, when we realized Sylvia was very very involved with us emotionally, familially. And so, we decided to push her out of the nest into a place where she could develop as an independent, resourceful, stimulated — and happy — person. She chose the University of California at Berkeley! My alma mater!

We two drove up in August to find her lodging. We drove along the coast route, those lovely stretches of ocean beaches and longer stretches of oak strewn hills and seemingly uninhabited ranches — their thousands of acres then in autumnal fallowness. Both of us feeling an enveloping sense of mutual affection, surrounded by a native landscape dear to our hearts and inheritance.

For a long time Sylvia's departure was much sadder, more traumatic than I ever would have imagined. And how could I have imagined, through my tears when Sylvia left the nest, that the occasion of a visit to her a couple of years later would felicitously turn my life around!

16

In the spring of 1954, Arthur and I traveled to Paris to visit Sylvia, who was doing the second half of her junior year at the Sorbonne. After several days of sight-seeing — Notre Dame, La Sainte Chapelle, the Louvre, Chartres, a boat trip on the Seine, the Flea Market, Folies-Bergère, and a brace of crummy night-clubs — Sylvia took us to the Jeu de Paume and l'Orangerie. These were the museums with the collections of the Impression-ist and Postimpressionist painters such as Monet, Manet, Seurat, Fantin-Latour, Degas.

Seeing those paintings for the first time sent me into near hys-terics. Having paused forever in front of each canvas on the way, looking at Rousseau's *Sleeping Gypsy* at the end of the first gallery, I burst into tears. Sylvia gave up trying to calm me, and led me up-stairs to the restroom. I don't remember much more, but I know this was one of the defining moments of my life. I returned the next day, and the next, alone. Was I trying to sober up from this ob-sessive intoxication? I was beside myself. Such beauty, such emo-tion, such style, and for real! Poor Arthur and Sylvia! I couldn't think or talk about anything else.

The end result of this happening was my resolve to become a painter.

I knew I could do it!

The U.S. government had recently introduced a new tax policy of no federal income tax if one lived and worked abroad for a minimum of eighteen months. We seized the chance. Bogey had raved about Italy, and Rapallo in particular, so we decided to settle around Rapallo, a small town on the rocky Ligurian coast just south of Genoa. It had a lively collection of Americans and Brits, including artists of all stripes.

We had been handed on to the Doctors Bacigalupo. They were physicians to the expatriate community around Rapallo — lots of interesting patients! Perhaps the most interesting had been Dorothy Gish (our old Garden of Allah neighbor), Ezra Pound, and Sir Max Beerbohm.

We looked for a house, and Frieda Bacigalupo found Villa Glicini — *glicini* are wisteria — halfway between Rapallo and the village of Santa Margherita. It was on the estate where the Treaty of Rapallo had been signed and within walking distance of the heavenly little port of Portofino. Four stories high, with practically no furniture. On the second — main — floor were a sofa, round table, and two chairs in the living room, four chairs in the dining room. Empty bedrooms were on the third and fourth floors. The kitchen was below garden level and had a dirt floor, so standing at the sink (with one cold water faucet), you looked straight out the window onto a tiny flower bed. It had no appliances or furniture, only an underground cave for storing sundries.

We needed a housekeeper, and Frieda sent over Angela, a young, beautiful woman. In parentheses, I have to record that we were told to "keep the icebox locked," that servants did not eat the same food as employers, that they were on a wine ration, too, just so much, nothing more. The sleeping accommodation for the help was an attic room. The bed had a straw mattress. There was a small chest of drawers, a chair, and a thunder mug.

Viewing it, I protested to Frieda — It's hot and close, no rugs, and what is that mattress? She said it was fine — no more, no less than usual. Angela seemed content. She was to live in but have afternoons off. Two mornings later, she tearfully announced her husband didn't want her sleeping in. She would have to leave.

We called Frieda and she arrived with Tina, a hearty, single woman.

Please recall the kitchen and fourth-floor "bedroom."

Angela handed Tina the household keys, saying, *"Benvenuti á paradiso!"* Welcome to paradise! Was it the open icebox and wine?

I had to buy a lot of things for the villa — beds, mattresses, tables, mosquito netting (it was the Mediterranean seaside in summer!), linens, dishes, silverware, and so forth. I had already rented a two-burner gas ring with a removable tin oven and a wooden icebox — literally an insulated box that held twenty-five pounds of ice! I was so anxious to drive into Genoa for art supplies that I got the household things together in two days!

In Genoa, I bought an English-Italian dictionary, an easel, various-sized canvas boards, oil paints, turpentine, varnishes, brushes, and, I almost forgot, a book in Italian on "How to Paint"!

My first painting was a large autumn-colored leaf of a plane tree, with the hint of a male nude figure sketched into it. The next was a portrait of a wild celery blossom sustaining a dangling spider.

I loved what I was doing.

We had met the author and playwright S. N. Behrman years before in New York. He dropped by soon after we arrived. Sam was going to see Sir Max Beerbohm, who lived close by, with the intention of writing Beerbohm's biography. The brilliant writer/caricaturist was now in his eighties, very fragile, and very poor.

Sam was upset. He had just come from visiting Somerset Maugham at his villa in Cap-Ferrat. He repeated his conversation with "Willie" about Beerbohm. "'One can't imagine it!' I said to Willie, who is a multimillionaire, 'Why don't we all get together and give Sir Max a monthly allowance so he won't worry about eating or the rent?' And Willie replied, 'Well, of course he's broke. He hasn't written anything in twenty years!' So no help from there!"

We knew that Sir Max was on thin times. When our friends Lee and Ira Gershwin heard we were going to Rapallo by way of Paris, Lee ordered goodies from Fauchon, the great Parisian grocery, and asked that we pick them up and take them to Sir Max. After Behrman left, we made a date.

Sir Max was adorable. Dressed in English country gentleman whites and navy blazer (they had seen better times), his jaunty straw hat tipped against the sun, he instantly greeted us with a twinkly smile and extended hand. He had lived in Rapallo with his wife, Florence, since 1910 and had been widowed just a few years.

Now his companion/secretary was Elizabeth Jungmann. She had been secretary to Gerhardt Hauptmann, the German playwright, poet, and novelist who won the 1912 Nobel Prize for literature. Miss Jungmann graciously seated us in the garden gazebo, and they opened the Gershwins' basket with modest joy.

After that, we visited with them several times. When Elizabeth heard how much Arthur loved figs, twice she came to our door with a basket of ripe figs for him. Very dear.

Once after tea in their small garden, Sir Max said, "Come into the study. I want to show you something."

In that little book-lined room, he reached toward a series of books. "I want to show you the collected works of Arnold Bennett." He deftly pulled out a four-inch long, six-inch-high piece of leather denoting these works, and there was nothing behind it.

I've often wondered — was there a feud, or was this just Sir Max's pixieness?

Sir Max married Elizabeth on his deathbed. Frieda told me Iris Tree, his niece, had hurried from London to claim his estate, and had been more than surprised to meet the new Lady Beerbohm at the gate. Iris evidently hadn't been "close" or attentive to her dear uncle. Lady Beerbohm inherited the tiny estate.

When Groucho and his new wife, Eden, came to visit us, Arthur, who was working on a play — huzzah huzzah — was delighted to see them. But I confess that, as much as I loved entertaining, for the first time in my life, dinner parties interested me less than my new calling. Painting! Painting! Painting!

My second figure in oils began with a dark-haired girl framed in the cerise-colored window of a *villino* down the road. Then I painted our housekeeper, Tina, with her cat, Piccolo, in our living room. I painted ships in Rapallo Bay gaily festooned with bright lights and brilliant fireworks splashed overhead. Then seascapes nearby — the secluded port of Camogli, enchanting Portofino, and the cliff-hanging villages of Cinque Terre . . .

After three months, Frieda brought the head of Rome's Instituto delle Arte over to see my work. He was so full of praises, and bows, and arms around my shoulders! I was a true naïf, I was so *spiritosa, belissima, è buona!*

Ah! Those *gentile* Italianos!

I felt I was on my way — that I was going to be a success!

Paint! Paint! Paint!

I dismissed any thought of trying for the mainstream. In that period, anyone who was anyone was an abstract artist. But I agree with France's leading art critic — a friend of Gertrude Stein's — who, on viewing Picasso's shift to abstract, burst into tears, crying, "France has lost a great artist!"

Caricature line drawings of girls with three tits, crossed eyes, and a blue bum on the end of her leg really don't grab me. Or black smears on black with a misplaced dot, dash, or hole cut in the canvas.

Surrealism I love.

Les Naïfs I love.

The voluptuousness and sexuality of Hindu sculpture.

Alexander Calder.

Oh, quite a few more! You get the idea.

In June, Sylvia took the train down from Paris and joined us. The next day, Frieda introduced her to Orsina Cavriani, an elegant young woman with a broad circle of friends. I don't think we saw Sylvia again for more than twenty minutes! In September, she returned to her junior year at Berkeley via Venice, Rome, and London.

In September, we headed for London, where Arthur was to rewrite a treatment of an old English musical, *Evergreen*, with Jessie Matthews. The days there seemed about four hours long. By the time we finished breakfast and reading the London *Times* and the *Manchester Guardian* — Arthur and I were, and I still am, devourers of morning newspapers — and I had marketed, prepared lunch for my husband and the secretary, answered a phone call or two, and written a note or two, it would be two-thirty in the afternoon and the light was gone! What light had been there in the first place. Pale, thin, misty.

I simply couldn't paint. I longed for sunshine and Southern California.

The highlight of our London stay, after going to Parliament to hear Sir Winston Churchill speak, was the night we were watching TV and the BBC announcer dramatically informed us that for the First Time in History, the queen and prince were going to call on the prime minister at his residence, 10 Downing Street. It was Tuesday evening, April 5, 1955. Churchill was resigning.

I said to Arthur, "Let's call a cab and go. I think it should be very interesting — fun!"

So we did, and as we got into the cab, Arthur said to the cabbie, "Ten Downing Street."

"Right, Gov'" came the response. It wasn't very far from our flat, and as we approached the short street, we noticed a phalanx of people lining both sides of Whitehall. The cabbie drove straight into Downing Street, past bobbies on both sides keeping people back, to the Front Door!

I, by that time, was yelling, "He didn't mean it! We're not invited! Turn back! Stop! Please, stop!"

Well, he did stop, right at the end of the walk up to the prime minister's house.

A very puzzled — shall I call him an equerry? — opened the

door, Arthur was paying the cabbie, I was saying, "We didn't mean it, really, I'm sorry," as a bobby took us both carefully and quietly across the street, under the ropes, into stunned witnesses of our transgression.

It was all in slow motion, smooth, no hitches, silent, polite.

Imagine what would happen to the likes of us today?

Meanwhile, back in Berkeley, in February of 1955, our darling daughter met Eugene Allen Thompson, a writer in graduate school who was renting an apartment in the Berkeley hills from Norah Barr. Norah was M. F. K. Fisher's sister. Norah had introduced them, and they fell instantly, madly in love. Gene proposed on their second date, and Sylvia accepted. She was nineteen and he was thirty. She wrote that they wanted to marry as soon as her finals were over in June. Their urgency was that, in those days, living together outside of wedlock was not done, and they were hungry to be together. (Sylvia says that when she and Gene walked down the street, people would turn around and stare at them, they were so wildly in love.) But because of our eighteen-month tax deal, we couldn't come back until August.

Arthur wrote, asking Sylvia to come spend the summer with us, saying that when we returned we'd give them a big wedding at the Bel-Air Hotel. He braced her by saying that if she was as much in love as she said, a couple of months should make no difference.

Her answer was a polite but heartfelt, "No, Daddy, thank you, but I just couldn't be without Gene that long."

Lots of telephone calls to MF, who loftily assured us that if her sister Noni approved, we needn't worry. To Groucho, who had known this young man since he was sixteen (when Gene had been a writer on Groucho's radio show). To the Hartmans, Siegels, Tugends, and Perrins, who had met Gene when he and Sylvia came down for a friend's spring wedding.

Their assurances were 100 percent.

They called after the ceremony. I cried, Sylvia cried, Arthur and Gene were, shall I say, stalwart?

In the fall, the Thompsons moved to New York City. I think, I hope — because we were coming back, Arthur with a play, me with canvases — to be with us!

Looking for an apartment, I was driven all over midtown Manhattan by a real estate agent. I found one and said, "Yes, we'll take it, it's lovely." We went back to the agent's office, and I phoned Arthur and said, "You'll be crazy about it."

The woman brought out the lease and said, "You know one very good thing about this, it is classified HCH."

I said, "What is that?"

And she said, "Well, the owner only takes high-class Hebrews."

I said, "What does that mean?"

She said, "Well, you know, they only take the very best kind."

And I said, "Well, I'm Hebrew and I'm not high class at all. I'm very much lower middle class." She went absolutely white. I said, "My husband, he's even lower, near the bottom, and there's no way that we could possibly sign a lease with you. They wouldn't accept us." I picked up my purse and walked out.

Sylvia and Gene immediately got copywriting jobs in advertising. It was wonderful being in the same town with them. They were so young, giving — so appreciative of our admiration of them.

Back in the groove of painting again, this time in a dark apartment, I went with Arthur to an auction at Parke-Bernet. The paintings were mostly French Postimpressionists. We bought a small Moise Kisling, *Girl with Kerchief.* It was *so* exciting, such a charming painting! Friends we went with had brought Moses Soyer along — brother to Raphael Soyer. They were two of our best American painters of that period, much influenced by the Ashcan school, portrayer of middle- and lower-class urban American life.

After the auction, we invited our friends and Mr. Soyer back to our apartment for midnight supper.

My paintings were all over the place. Drying, stacked, on my easel, and against a wall in our living room. In the kitchen, I was leaning down over the broiler full of cheese toasts when I heard, "Are these paintings yours?" I looked up. It was Moses Soyer.

"Yes."

"Where have you studied?"

"I haven't."

"What do you mean?"

"I'm self-taught." Long pause. I pulled the toasts out of the broiler. I looked at him, wondering what was coming next.

He replied, "I'm a teacher. I teach art. You're a true primitive. You musn't take lessons. You musn't go to shows. You musn't read art articles. You must stay pure." I didn't have any answer, and I couldn't think of any questions. He reiterated, "I teach. I beg of you: Never take lessons." Taking the toast off the broiling pan, I agreed I wouldn't. "How often do you work?"

"I work every day. Or every day that I can."

"Good!"

In 1961 I had the first of many shows, my one-woman show at the Hammer Galleries in New York City. For the show, my dearest friend Chick Hartman drove across the country to join me. My sister, Pat, came down from Rome, New York. Marjorie Cummings, a New York City/Hollywood friend, made a most generous gesture. First she booked me for most of the day at Elizabeth Arden — a unique treat! — then she persuaded the gallery to let her put her red dots on several canvases before the show opened. "It always helps to get people going at a vernissage* when there are already red dots." My show sold out!

Since then, there have been many more, both one-woman shows and those in which I've shared the gallery with one or two other artists.

---

*Pretty French word that literally means "varnishing," and has come to refer to the reception for the artist on the opening of his/her show.

My favorite subject in figure drawing is Adam and Eve in the Garden of Eden. In my first painting — I've managed three very large versions — a black Adam is taking the apple from a white Eve, stretched out on a bottom limb of the tree, her arm around a gorgeous green snake coiled between her legs and all the way up the tree. Eden's landscape contains a field of fluttering butterflies and exotic erotic blossoms, with an elephant, giraffe, deer, llama, rabbit, owl, and monkey as witnesses. Sylvia and Gene have my second, *The Naming of the Animals,* from the Bible. Here, I reversed the colors, a beautiful black Eve and handsome white Adam — with a diaphanous winged angel on high recording the names — in Hebrew! — of bears, leopards, zebras, monkeys, and extra added attractions like flamingos, frogs, and leaping salmon!

Inspired by the English decorative fashion of flowers on striped fields, I composed a series of three very large canvases I called *Artist's Toys,* still lifes with striped backgrounds, the foregrounds filled with relevant objects. One, with lively toys, fans, whirligigs, paper garlands, and flowers; the second, to do with the sea — boat-shaped bowl, anchor, compass, feather duster, figurehead, seaman's watch horn, wreath for "man overboard." The third is more toys, more amusing masks, hands, fans, fortune sticks, a Siamese umbrella.

The subject of my two most important accomplishments is the Watts Towers — also large canvases, which took about three years of very detailed painting.

The Watts Towers? Simon Rodia, an uneducated Italian immigrant with extraordinary engineering and architectural skills and talent, spent thirty-three years erecting and decorating three tall towers in a poor section of Los Angeles called Watts. The towers rise ninety-nine, ninety-seven, and fifty-five feet, respectively, into the smoggy Los Angeles sky, three colorful, graceful towers of steel lacework, with tile and shell and glass mosaic walls.

"I wanted to do something big and I did," he said.

The naughty stupid children in his neighborhood chose to be-
devil him as an "enemy alien" early in the Second World War
years. In my paintings, the towers are shown nearly as they were
when Simon Rodia turned the key in the gate and his back on
them in 1939 and moved to Northern California.

The last time I was there sketching the Towers, I saw the great
director Jean Renoir (son of the painter, Auguste), with an assistant holding a video camera. Renoir was talking, gesturing with
great vivacity, while the man was filming. With my frail French, after he stopped, I asked how he knew about the Towers.

"They are known everywhere, madame. They are true primitive
American art. They are masterpieces!"

Years later, I sicced my grandson Benjamin, who was studying
film in Paris, onto the French Film Institute. There is no record
there of Renoir's documentary, and Madame Renoir has no knowledge of it. But I have photographs of Monsieur Renoir filming the
towers. Find that film!

Though always greeted by viewers with genuine astonishment
and enthusiastic praise, my chef d'oeuvres still hang in my studio.
They are priced at fifty-five thousand dollars, only to be sold as a
pair to a museum or public building.

Portraits of masterpieces of American primitive art, anyone?

I was composing a lot of verse these years, and surprise! surprise!
so was Arturo. For his 52nd birthday party's banner he wrote:

> Lord, what a whimsical
> Thing to do
> You made my spirit twenty
> And my body
> Fifty-two
> — A.G.S.

17

When we arrived back in Los Angeles, we had to sell our dream house in Brentwood. *Evergreen* hadn't materialized in London. Arthur's play had flopped in New York. It was 1956 and my husband's most recent movie credit was four years old.

We found a small Spanish-style apartment near the UCLA campus, two bedrooms up, one down, plus a dining room — no garden, just a long, sunny cement terrace. My studio, my own private workspace, was the small bedroom downstairs. Arthur worked upstairs, in his bedroom.

And Arthur did work — as he always had. Two movies in two years, and then perhaps the film he was proudest of, turning James Jones's novel into a sensational *Some Came Running* for Dean Martin, Frank Sinatra, and soon-to-be star Shirley MacLaine.

Flush again, naturally we returned to our Hollywood habits, and several nights a week went out with friends for dinner at Romanoff's or Chasen's or Perino's or the Brown Derby, or I cooked for friends at home. We went to screenings of new movies on studio lots or in a friend's projection room, I shopped in San Francisco for Christmas presents, and we both loved going to gala happenings like the engagement party for Grace Kelly and Prince Rainier (note in *Variety* after their wedding: "Bride is film star, groom non-pro").

But what really sustained me through lovely times and dismal ones has been our Poker Group, which has met every Saturday night for nearly forty years!

The game has had an extraordinary cast of characters, changing with deaths and removes from Hollywood.

Originally, the game included Robert and Edie Soderberg — Bob was first a screenwriter, then worked with enormous success on soaps for many years; Edie's play, *A Roomful of Roses,* was a Broadway success. And Di and Henry Jaffe — she was the novelist Diana Gaines, and he was head of radiology at Cedars of Lebanon Hospital. And Ruth and Ira Steiner — Ruthie is a highly regarded therapist, and Ira was a top theatrical agent.

Then Paul and Decla Radin joined. Paul was a producer — his *Born Free* is a classic film — and, as Decla Dunning, Decla wrote for *The New Yorker* and with Herman Mankiewicz on screenplays at MGM.

Then Doris and Frank Hursley. They had been schoolteachers in Minnesota, decided to write in Hollywood, came out, and created the enduring soap, *General Hospital.*

When everyone was playing, there were two tables of six. Only with wild cards. For example, one could lose the pot with a hand holding 5 aces and a perfect low of 1 2 3 4 6!

All the women were intimate friends, and all except Ruthie and I were writers. Again, with Ruth and I as exceptions, there always seemed to be petty female tensions — pairing off one time, not speaking another, but always showing up, or hostessing. The Group!

I remember when the Perrins came into the game, Helen saying to me, "I'm not sure I can handle those women and all that *hazerei!*" Nat had been my Arthur's collaborator during the Marx Brothers days, and went on to become a producer-writer at MGM, and Helen had been George Burns and Gracie Allen's private secretary for years. She was one of my dearest and oldest friends, a woman of great charm and wit.

The Soderbergs and Jaffes moved away, so Fay and Michael

My all-time favorite portrait,
1936. *(Set photographer Ray Jones.
Courtesy of Marvin Paige's Motion
Picture & T.V. Research Service)*

With my beau,
George Oppenheimer,
at my first Hollywood
party, given by the
Donald Ogden Stewarts
at the Trocadero Café
in 1933.

Some of my favorite leading men...

Charles Laughton in *The Old Dark House*, 1932. *(Courtesy of Marvin Paige's Motion Picture & T.V. Research Service)*

Claude Rains (as *The Invisible Man*), 1933. *(Courtesy of Marvin Paige's Motion Picture & T.V. Research Service)*

Michael Whelan in
The Lady Escapes, 1937.

Jimmy Cagney in *Hey, Sailor*, 1934. (*Courtesy of Marvin
Paige's Motion Picture & T.V. Research Service*)

Dick Powell in *Broadway
Melody*, 1937.

Boris Karloff in *The Old Dark House*, 1932. (*Courtesy of
Marvin Paige's Motion Picture & T.V. Research Service*)

From the sublime...

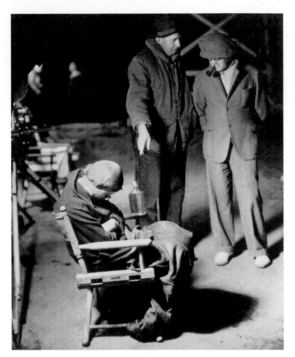

With legendary director John Ford (with pipe)
while filming *Air Mail* (Universal Pictures, 1932).

With the one-of-a-kind director James Whale (*Kiss Before the Mirror*,
Universal Pictures, 1933).

...to the ridiculous

Okay, Shirley Temple was adorable, but I wanted to be a *serious* actress! (Rebecca of Sunnybrook Farm, Twentieth Century Fox, 1938)

What's a working girl to do?
(Courtesy of Marvin Paige's Motion Picture & T.V. Research Service)

In between takes during the filming of *Roman Scandals* "Princess Sylvia" was lying on a velvet chaise, reading a Chinese newspaper, when a deep voice behind her said, "You're holding that thing upside down." The rest, as they say, is history. . . . *(Samuel Goldwyn Studios, 1933)*

Arthur Sheekman and I, quite the glamorous married couple, at *The Life of Emile Zola* Hollywood premiere in 1937. (*Dell Publishing Company, Inc., October 1937*)

La Belle Sylvia's first photo, July 1935. Less than one month old and already adorable! *(Courtesy of Marvin Paige's Motion Picture & T.V. Research Service)*

Trying (none too well) to hide my pregnancy in *Laddie*, with John Beal. George Stevens proved a very considerate director. *(RKO Studios, 1935)*

The world was about to
explode in war. By day,
we toured the Shanghai
International Settlement as a
Japanese sentry stood guard.
By night, we danced at
Shanghai's French Club.
(Above: *Lacks News Photos*)

What's Wat? In 1939, I took Arthur around the world and showed him
Angkor Wat, Cambodia.

How beautiful Bali was! And how beautiful its people!

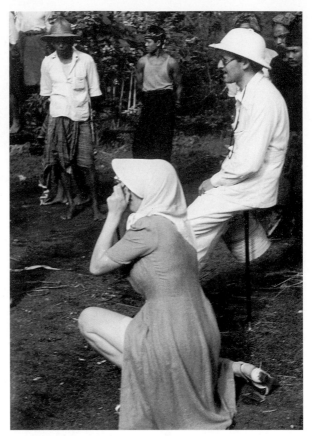

Photographing a magnificent funeral procession in Bali, July 1939.

Look at Hong Kong back then—no skyscrapers…hell, no buildings!

Wherever we went journeymen, reporters, and photographers hounded us. Please! Gentlemen, that's enough!

The Evening News
of India

16   BOMBAY: FRIDAY, JULY 28, 1939.

FAMOUS FILM STAR IN BOMBAY

"SCREEN CAREER NOT A BED OF ROSES"

GLORIA STUART AND HER HUSBAND ON HOLIDAY TRIP

GLORIA Stuart, beautiful hollywood film star, and her husband Arthur Sheekman, film writer, celebrating the fifth anniversary of their wedding in Bombay.

They arrived in the city in the case of a round-the-world holiday in the s. s. "President Garfield" y. Bombay Pressmen were among the first to congratulate the couple on board the steamer on the happy event.

Mrs. Sheekman who has been connected with films since six years has played the leading role in many pictures including the 20th century films "Three Musketeers" "It Could Happen to You" does not regard a film career as a bed of roses, though she admitted that she did not think of any other profession or her own limitations. If one was exceptionally good at comedy it was no good to try and change for any other kind of role.

Mrs. Sheekman was amused and interested on hearing that an Indian film star recently resorted to hunger-strike for obtaining redress of what she regarded as her grievances, and remarked that film artistes in Hollywood were strongly organised.

At one time, the Union of Film Actors and Actresses, including feature players, stunt men, chorus girls and men, and other extras had a membership of over 24,000.

Earning Of Artistes

With the exception of the feature players, a large number of artistes earned only about 100 dollars a year.

Caption: Gloria Stuart, the famous film star, and her husband, Mr. Arthur Sheekman.

Liner Adams Docks with 160 From War Zone

'Round-World Vessel Also Brings Million in Gold from Bombay

With 160 passengers overflowing her normal capacity, DS. the President Adams of the American President Liner docked in Jersey City at 1 p.m., having steamed into the war situation in Naples, Genoa and Marseilles while on the last leg of a round-the-world cruise. Of her passengers 160 were Americans fleeing the European war zones.

The President Adams brought $1,000,000 in gold bullion from Bombay and many experiences and speculation regarding the war.

"The Mediterranean is not going to be a war zone this time," Capt. Gregory Cullen, master of the President Adams, believes. "Mussolini in Italy and France in Spain are he figured in bankrupt over and both of them are disgusted with Hitler because of his recent agreement with Russia."

Compares with World Trip.

This was the captain's 66th round-the-world trip. He is a veteran of the last war when he commanded a transport and was decorated with the Navy Cross for distinguished service.

The terminus rain was turned into a lord's dormitory, with 40 cabs. There were cots also in the social hall. Capt. Cullen prohibited the use of fresh water for bathing in case the vessel should pick up castaways at sea and these castaways additional.

Caption: Safe in Port from the War-Churned Seas

Julius Augustus Guggenaster, Austrian, saved by Capt. Gregory Cullen of the President Adams from internment in France, pictured with his American bride.

Gloria Stuart, Hollywood star, aboard the President Adams, who was forbidden to manufacture non-neutral sweaters—but did.

THE CHINA MAIL, JUNE 23, 1939

Hollywood Intellectual Passes Through Hong Kong

MISS GLORIA STUART (OR MRS. ARTHUR SHEEKMAN, AS SHE PREFERS TO BE CALLED WHEN OFF THE SET), ONE OF HOLLYWOOD'S FEW STARS WHO COMBINE BEAUTY WITH INTELLIGENCE AND A UNIVERSITY DEGREE, ARRIVED IN HONG KONG LATE LAST EVENING IN THE ATHOS II.

Most of yesterday, she told the "China Mail," she spent in arguing with her husband, one of Hollywood's better scenario writers, try-

---

South China Morning Post

JUNE 23, 1939.

LOVELY VISITOR

Hollywood Star Passes Through on Athos

MISS GLORIA STUART

Expected in Hongkong for several weeks, Miss Gloria Stuart, charming

We figured we'd lost the press, but no such luck. After three unwashed days
coming from Bangkok, they discovered us at the Singapore train station.
Photographers, bouquets, and V.I.P. greeters. A bit discombobulating!
(*Photo copyright Starits Times Press, Ltd. Singapore*)

La Ciotât—Hôtel Brasserie Rose Thé. Our last stop before heading home.

Darling Harpo Marx with Helen Vinson, Fred Perry, Barbara Stanwyck, brother Groucho, and me at the Beverly Hills Tennis Club, 1945. *(M.G.M. Photo by Grimes)*

Arturo's fiftieth birthday party—guests included Harry Tugend, Groucho, Harry and Eileen Ruby. Brentwood, California, February 5, 1951.

Doing our bit for the War Effort, signing autographs at the Hollywood USO, 1944.

Activist Days! Hollywood's "Declaration of Independence." Members of the Committee of 56, composed of film stars, sign a document to be circulated throughout the nation in an effort to secure the names of 20,000,000 people who would observe an economic boycott against Germany. Left to right they are Claude Rains, Paul Muni, Edward G. Robinson, Arthur Hornblow Jr., Helen Gahagan, John Garfield, me in furs, James Cagney, Groucho Marx, Aline MacMahon, Henry Fonda, and Gale Sondegaard. Seated are Myrna Loy, Melvin Douglas, and Carl Laemmle.

"Gloria Stuart, former movie actress arriving in Chicago for the Democratic National Convention, which opened yesterday. The former star is a delegate from the Hollywood district." Published July 20, 1944, *The Inquirer.* Photo by ACME NEWSPICTURES, Inc. *(Courtesy of Marvin Paige's Motion Picture & T.V. Research Service)*

"Gloria, are you a Communist?" my very Republican mother asked. No, just a Democrat. *(Chicago Sun Times)*

With my all-time
favorite actor—
Peter O'Toole in
My Favorite Year, 1982.

In my (more or less)
happy sixties.

Kanin came in. Mike had won an Oscar for his screenplay *Woman of the Year* in collaboration with Ring Lardner Jr. Michael was also a brilliant artist. Fay often wrote with Mike, but her long suit was serving as president, first of the Writers Guild of America, then of the Academy of Motion Picture Arts and Sciences.

Then the Hursleys left us for Santa Barbara and Ann and Julius J. Epstein came in. Ann is an artist, and Julie a most gifted scenarist — famous for his collaboration with his twin brother, Philip, on *Casablanca* (another Oscar winner among us!), as well as more than two dozen other distinguished movies.

Norman Panama, of the team Panama and Frank — the Crosby-Hope "Road" comedies — joined us for a few years, but recently withdrew. Lily Carter, the ne plus ultra Beverly Hills travel agent for most of us, had left her Big Game with Lee and Ira Gershwin, Angie Dickinson, et al., so she was invited in — but last year decided to join her daughter in Florida. In Lily's place came Nancy Lee Freed — widow of the fine character actor and Screen Actors Guild activist Bert Freed — by profession a publicist, and now a tireless volunteer for good causes.

Most recently, Ray Evans, our lyricist ("Mona Lisa," "Buttons and Bows"), joins us occasionally. We've discouraged his suggestions of dealing out conventional poker games. "You mean, nothing's *wild*?"

Arthur was never a good poker player. But he was good enough so that he could stay in the game and not lose always. I think that he was mostly with us, but with Arthur, there were levels of concentration. The concentration at the top was on what he was writing. Story lines. Characters. Conversations. Background. That kind of thing. And next what he was reading. And next probably his personal relationship with me. And I think way at the bottom layer of his consciousness was the rote of playing cards. Dealing them out, arranging them, and so forth and so on. However he was a very good loser. And a very good winner — when and if, which was very very very very very very seldom.

*   *   *

I'm a Scot. No gambler. Except for our penny-ante poker game — our game starts with a big-sounding hundred-dollar stack of chips, but in fact the chips only represent ten dollars, so that three to four dollars is usually the largest loss — I don't gamble.

Well, our first Labor Day weekend in Vegas with Groucho and Eden and the Krasnas, I did play roulette. It was a dime a game in those days, the earlier, happier fifties.

Zeppo Marx was our host. He had made a fortune on a small patented invention used by the army or the navy or the air corps to manufacture something they needed. Zep was up in Vegas a great deal (we always wondered if he was in a gambling syndicate). It was a very crowded weekend, and our hotel, one of the most popular in town, was jammed with people. Reservations, of course, were very tight, but because we were with The Boys, we had a lovely room.

While I unpacked, Arthur went downstairs to the little credit kiosk, and they asked him what his limit was. He didn't want to seem excessive — but he also didn't want to be extravagant. Instead of saying, "The sky!" which was his style, he said, "Two hundred dollars." Well, by the time he got back up to the room, the hotel had made a terrible mistake! The manager had made a terrible mistake! The desk clerk had made a terrible mistake and our room had been rented! The message was we had to vacate by 3 P.M.! Of course, they wanted it for the high rollers. We had to get hold of Zeppo. It was early in the afternoon, Zeppo was nowhere in sight, and Groucho couldn't help us. It was only Zep that could. We had him paged, we left messages on his phone, we knocked on his door and slipped notes under it, and I started repacking. Finally, Zep surfaced and we were allowed to keep our room.

The rules of hospitality, shall we say, in Vegas — at least in those days — were something. The next morning, Arthur was standing at a slot machine. Not the dollar slot machines, but the nickel slot machines. One of the bosses walked by and said something to him like, "I thought you learned your lesson. . . ." It was a warning. He should have been at the dollar slots. One of our friends, Grace Kahn, the widow of the wonderful songwriter Gus Kahn, was downtown playing at one of the cheap casinos that day, and evidently a spotter from her hotel saw her. By the time she got back to the hotel, she was out of a room, too.

Going to Vegas with the Marx Brothers was fun. We putt-putted on Lake Mead and went fishing, and, of course, dressed for dinner every evening, which was lovely for the ladies. Everything was very luxe, very gemütlich, always the best table at the shows, and acknowledgment of our presence from the stage's performers. One could play blackjack or craps or baccarat, and in those days you could play dime roulette, so I did. Arthur played blackjack and was wiped out every time. Groucho never gambled (years later, he said he'd never play Vegas, it was run by the mob). Eden never gambled. The Krasnas didn't either. But we had a wonderful time. The food was great. The entertainment was great. And we were treated royally, all on account of Zep.

Vegas was a gala galaxy.

I hate to confess it, but I am known in our poker game as the worst loser of all. I never threw the cards, but I certainly shoved them into the center after a game. Although I never liked to think that it was the money, losing a dollar and a half could throw me into a tizzy fit!

When we first played, I had a glass of wine to accompany me. But many years ago Decla said to me, "When you drink during the game, Gloria, it changes your whole character, and you have a bad temper. You shouldn't do that." I listened to her. So now I very seldom have a glass while I'm playing. And — it's taken me years and years — I have conquered my bad manners, my ill temper, my ridiculous resentment of bad cards. I'm not quite sure how or why, but I now almost always amicably accept losing. Almost. It's very rewarding. Of course, bad calls in poker, or bad strategy in bridge, or bad memory in gin can be cause for self-pity and self-anger. But it should only be, must only be, for that particular deal.

The love of card playing must run in the family. More than cooking, more than the garden, Mama was crazy about cards. And she and Sylvia played gin rummy from the time Sylvia was ten. My dear niece, Deborah Finch, and her daughter, Kimberly, are professional dealers, and, I understand, my several-times-removed cousin, Jesse James, dealt out a doozer of a game!

In terms of what I'd expected, the hand Arthur and I were dealt was as lousy as they come. Such a brilliant and witty man . . .

In the late fifties and through the sixties, things were tricky, but we had managed. Until now — this was early in the seventies — despite increasing moodiness and confusion, he had managed to finish his assignments. But now deadlines were looming for a movie script for Elvis Presley and two television scripts for Debbie Reynolds that a fuzzy but stubborn Arthur would not/could not finish. And if he didn't meet these deadlines, he wouldn't get paid.

I was frantic.

Arthur and I had been delighted when our daughter, Sylvia, became a writer — and when she, too, married a writer. By coincidence, like Arthur, Gene had also written for Groucho and other comedians when he was young. Now he was writing television comedy for the likes of Bob Newhart and Lucille Ball, and dramas for shows such as *Columbo* and *Mission Impossible*. Many of his scripts are considered classics.

Gene and Sylvia and Arthur and I had been close friends from the start of their marriage. At this point, the Thompsons lived twenty minutes away, in Malibu, with their four children. Gene greatly admired Arthur and in the past often sought his opinions, whether on the long novel he was writing at night or a current television script. Now, their positions were reversed. Gene had to step in and secretly finish Arthur's work.

And Arthur's jealousy was becoming more and more irrational. It focused on lovers he was sure I had. In my film days, he had watched like a hawk for signs of on-set entanglements. By this time, I couldn't go marketing, lunching with friends, or have an afternoon of bridge without nasty accusations when I got home: "I know where you were and what you were doing! You can't fool me!"

There were attractions over the years. I'm human. But I never did anything about it.

One of my great refuges and comforts was my collection of bonsai. Bonsai is a Japanese art form in which a tree or plant is dwarfed by growing it in a pot in mere inches of soil, and, over many years, carefully, artistically, training it with wire and pruning it judiciously to shape it pleasingly so that it mimics its full-sized kin in nature.

I first paid attention to bonsais one evening at dinner at Joe Cohn's, an old friend from Arthur's Metro days. I was fascinated by Joe's centerpiece — a classic bonsai in an antique Chinese pot. I asked, "Where did you get it?" He said it was one of his own trees. He'd been studying bonsai for many years with Frank Nagata, the dean of bonsai masters in Southern California. He said I could, too. The class was taught every Sunday afternoon at Nagata-san's home downtown.

I went down the next Sunday. About eight students, ages twenty to eighty, were seated before Nagata-san in his small lath house, with their little trees in front of them, watching Nagata trim and wire his tree. He had a small radio in his shirt pocket, broadcasting a Dodger game, and, during the demonstration, a saucy blue jay flew in, sat on his shoulder, and squawked for a peanut — instantly retrieved from the same pocket.

I was hooked!

I took up bonsai with a passion partly because I had no place, no earth in which to garden. Mama's people were dirt farmers, and I hungered for a garden. With bonsais, at least I could have growing things around me on the apartment's patio. Soon I had over one hundred miniature trees set along the patio wall.

Once one of my grandchildren asked that I bring my bonsais and potting tools for a show-and-tell at his elementary school in Malibu. I took some tiny trees up there. I demonstrated how these little giants were trained and shaped — that the point was one (that is, you/a tree) can survive with grace and beauty and strength no matter what Nature throws at you.

The children were completely simpatico — it was so rewarding!

As a matter of fact, a dozen years later, that same grandchild, Benjamin, and I found ourselves strolling through the royal forest surrounding the palace at Fontainebleau, near Paris. On our walk, we filled our pockets with French black oak acorns. When I got home, I planted them as three bonsai forests. Seventeen years old now, the tallest trees are eighteen inches high, their leaves, instead of being a man's palm size, are two to three inches wide. And, true to my bonsai master's dictum, in their arrangement, there is space for the birds to fly through.

My bonsai — and the friends that come with it — among them John and Alice Naka, Frank and Margaret Goya, Kay Komai, Joseph Locke — are still an abiding comfort and joy!

Arthur's obsessive and unfounded suspicions were kindled early on in our marriage by a bizarre source.

When I was in film, after finishing a movie, once or twice a year I would go up to San Francisco and stay with a dear college friend,

Georgena Keller. We were very close, poetry and plays were the food on our table.

In San Francisco in 1939, the night before Arthur and I set out on our trip around the world, we had dinner with my old friend. Georgena confided in Arthur that my visits to her had been adulterous. Of course they hadn't been. But the damage was done. Her "revelation" colored Arthur's and my relationship forever. He didn't speak to me for our first week on the ship. He didn't tell me about what she'd said until we were back in Hollywood four years later.

What could have been her reason?

One day I asked her. She was very candid about it. She said she'd done the same to other friends. As a writer, she was interested in the effects such a story would have on the marital relationship.

And I had thought Georgena loved me.

Arthur wasn't the only one in our crowd possessed by jealousy. But his was at least private — it didn't show. My friends were never aware of it. I bore it in secret. Not so another friend.

In the thirties and forties, one of our favorite getaway spots was the Springs — Palm Springs, a three-hour drive due east through small farms and orange and grapefruit groves. No housing developments or shopping malls or take-out joints. Not one!

We were with Helen and Nat Perrin, Jean and Harry Tugend, and Miriam and Dore Schary — Dore was production head at MGM. We all were sitting around the pool under the palms one afternoon when Ginger Rogers strolled over to say hello. Ginger sat down next to Dore in the only available chair. He was attentive — a very sweet man. I watched his wife. She never took her eyes off the two of them. We all were talking pleasantly, Ginger was laughing, Dore was laughing, we were all very merry. All of a sudden, Miriam got up, threw her glass of lemonade all over Ginger, and left.

Dore scrambled to wipe Ginger off, we all offered our towels. She got up as Dore apologized, "Oh, Ginger, I'm so sorry." She smiled politely and walked silently away.

Now I would say that as powerful as Dore was in Hollywood, he was also Mr. Straight Arrow. A devoted family man. His wife was a talented artist who worked long hours in her studio at home. She was very quiet, very reclusive. These were not the sort of people to get involved in a poolside *petite scandale*.

Cut to a resort called the B-Bar-H Ranch another time in the Springs. At lunch dear Helen Perrin was being very charming to Dore — we were all very charming to one another, it was no big deal. All of a sudden, Miriam came over and slapped Helen in the face. Helen looked up, she was so surprised — we all were — and Dore said to his wife, "Oh, please, don't do that, stop that, Miriam! How could you do that?"

She left.

The next night we were all sitting around the fireplace after dinner. Mrs. Schary got up and leaned over to put another log on the fire and Helen got up and kicked her right in the fanny. She stumbled toward the fireplace, put out her hand to stop herself, then started for Helen, and of course the two husbands kept them apart. Helen had done it very pleasantly — let's say, with a smile on her face.

For a long time I thought Arthur's jealousy was just a provincial attitude. As I've said, I never ever discussed this with any of my friends. It was none of their business, actually, what he felt about my lunching or even having a conversation with another man. I never wanted to put him in a position of being made fun of, or for people to think he was strange. The truth is, he was just sick jealous, that was his problem.

One morning I met Joe Cohn by chance at a downtown bonsai show. We both belonged to the Beverly Hills Tennis Club — I'd played bridge with him there, with Charlie Lederer and Gilbert Roland many Sundays. He was an official of some kind at MGM, much older than I. He invited me to have lunch with him at Mike Romanoff's. He drove his car there, and I drove mine. We had a pleasant lunch, said hello to Mike and a few other friends, and finished about three-thirty. I went on shopping at Sak's and Magnin's, and was home by five-thirty or so.

I do not know why men feel that the price of a meal, time spent in conversation, a compliment here and there, necessarily adds up to a romp in bed. But when I got home and told Arthur Joe and I had had lunch, he had seven kitten fits. You would have thought that I had been in a motel with this man rather than in plain view at Romanoff's.

When Arthur quieted down the next day, I said to him, "I don't understand the reaction. Why can't I have a male friend without sex being involved?"

He said, "It doesn't work that way, Gloria. You have lunch with a man several times, he expects it."

I said, "But whether he expects it or not, he's not going to get it from me. So, what's the problem?"

He said, "Well, I don't want you to do it because I don't want you to be in that position with a strange man."

I said, "He's not, and they're not, strange men. Arthur, these are men that I see at parties, men that I meet at bonsai clubs or SAG committee meetings, or book clubs, these are not pickups."

He said, "Well, I don't want you to do it. You have to promise me you won't do it anymore."

I promised. It wasn't worth the emotional stress.

I remembered the unconscionable quarrels and fury we'd had over my desire to volunteer to the USO (United Service Organization) for overseas theatrics, or for hospital work; to walk with Martin Luther King to Selma, Alabama, for human rights; to go with the Bogarts — and a Hollywood citizens' group — to Washington, DC, protesting Senator McCarthy's red-baiting.

Yelling, physically hitting him, unrestrained resentment and anger.

Hatred.

Constantly accused and humiliated, I was desperate. What was I going to do with this man for the rest of my life!

Just when I thought I couldn't bear it any longer, my yoga teacher, Anne Graham, saved me. I had been taking a class from her at the local Y for only a few months. At the end of the next session, she gave me the tool, the power, to resolve my problem.

As we lay on our mats, our eyes shut, breathing deeply, contemplating in our imagination the blue sky, the clouds going by, the soft grass, the birds singing, butterflies flying, she said, "Some of you are of an age where anxiety and hurts take on a prominence and importance that they shouldn't. Problems can seem insurmountable. Your friends, or someone in your family, hurts your feelings, or picks on you so that you feel put upon, even resentful.

"Well! What you must understand is that their slights or meanness or unjust accusation is *their* problem, not yours. And so you must let go of it. Put it out of your mind. It's *their* problem!"

Eureka! She changed my life with that remarkable — and completely new to me — idea. I had been worrying about Arthur's worrying about me!

I couldn't wait to get home.

I was met with the usual, "You didn't have to put on that gym suit to try and fool me. . . ."

"Sit down, Arthur," I said. "I want you to listen to me, and listen good." I took a deep breath.

"You know, darling, you have a problem. You suspect me of infidelities, but they are delusions. I evidently can't help you get rid of them. They seem to nourish you. You seem to enjoy them, in a sad, bad way.

"So I want you to have them. Keep them close to your heart. Don't let go of them. Be my guest!

"Because, honey, I don't have any of these problems and I don't want to share yours. I just want you to have them all by yourself. Forevermore!"

He did not answer me. He looked as though I had slapped him in the face — or hit him on his head with a mallet — and, figuratively speaking, I had.

From that moment on, I never defended myself or denied anything. I just isolated myself from that kind of abusive behavior. I have used this infallible recipe for composure and understanding, and gone ahead with my life, lo these many years.

Nevertheless, Arthur's jealousy had grown out of control. He accused me of banging the box boy, the postman, the Chevron man, his friends. . . .

I was in my sixties!

(Although, now that I'm almost ninety, I feel free to say that I looked pretty damn good in my sixties. A part of me, the actress in me, still made sure I was Ready for the Big One — should it ever come. Keeping in shape meant ten to twelve hours' sleep a night, half an hour of calisthenics, such as they are, morning or evening walks, dieting, extra special hair and skin care, time for meditation. My most favorite position was flat on my back, my arms by my side, palms up. As a matter of fact, it's a great position, even with one's palms someplace else.)

At his best, Arthur was a bad driver — mindless and inattentive. Once his license was suspended for a year, and another time he was put on probation for six months — "You mean, Mr. Sheekman, you made a U-turn in the middle of Wilshire Boulevard at five o'clock in the afternoon?"

Arthur was changing, at first subtly. I began to get puzzling phone calls. He would call, laughing, and tell me he was in Santa Monica at the ocean when he had set out for the UCLA library two blocks away. Then the absentmindedness grew alarming. He was supposed to meet Groucho at Nate 'n Al's ten minutes away in Beverly Hills, but instead, he'd driven in the opposite direction for half an hour to the San Fernando Valley.

Again and again, I asked him not to drive, but Arthur was nothing if not stubborn. I'd hide the keys, but when I was out he'd call a locksmith and have them come make a set. Once, I lay down in the driveway in front of his car, because I knew that if he took it out, he could get dangerously lost, or kill himself — or someone else.

Finally, I asked my son-in-law simply to drive the car away and sell it. He did, and Arthur wouldn't speak to either of us for a week.

The day came when I realized that something was truly terribly wrong, that my husband was more than his usual preoccupied self.

It was the spring of 1971. I was getting our papers organized for our tax man. It had taken me three days to arrange all the bits and pieces of a year's receipts in dozens of little piles on the dining room table. Arthur watched me sorting as he shuffled back and forth in his slippers through the dining room to the kitchen several times a day.

The morning I finished, I went off to the market. When I got home an hour later, I found him standing at the dining room table, bent over in concentration. He was carefully moving the scraps of papers around. Every pile had been demolished. It was an unholy mess.

He looked pleased with himself, smiled at me, and continued the spoilage.

My heart sank. I was furious. I couldn't believe he could do such a thing. It seemed like deliberate sabotage. Why?

But that night — or the next day, or the next, I can't remember — it dawned on me that such an irrational act might be part and parcel of something else that was going on with Arthur. Something more subtle, but also more insidious and disturbing.

Finally, I had to face up to it. Arthur had seemed non compos mentis in many areas for quite a while. I had to get help.

My defining moment came in Dr. Rex Kennamer's office. His diagnosis of Arthur's illness: "Gloria, it's pre-senile dementia."

I stopped breathing. I recognized "senile" and "dementia" and tried to let go of what they meant. I had a crazy man as my partner?

Dr. Kennamer counseled me. I would probably have to have help to take care of Arthur. "Probably!" Yes, probably. It was a progressive disease. In those days none of us used the term "Alzheimer's." No doctors mentioned it. But I gradually understood Dr. Kennamer's warning. It was going to get much worse.

So many negatives crowded my mind, I sat speechless. Rex patted my hand, said to let him know how things were going, and left me stunned and trembly.

Driving home, images of my life came and went like a film — a "movie movie," as we always called a major film.

How I dreaded having to face our friends with our predicament.

Think of the Hollywood years, Gloria. The years traveling and living abroad. The Garden of Allah. The Burlingame years. Your painting, your hostessing. Yes, Arturo and I had had a fabulous run together. A life given to very few.

Those years won't disappear. You can't let them disappear. They will be with you always.

And they will surely light your way from now on. . . .

They will?

To where?

18

As Arthur's Alzheimer's advanced, he grew increasingly petulant, demanding, suspicious, unpleasant. I felt surrounded, hemmed in, roped and tied. What was even more discouraging was that when Arthur wasn't making me feel claustrophobic, pushing my back to the wall with his imagined, hateful accusations, he was withdrawing from life.

Talking with Sylvia on the phone one morning, she mentioned Mama. Afterward, thinking about it, I realized with a shudder that in her later years, Mama's miserable relationship with her husband, threadbare social life, and perpetual lack of money was exactly what was happening to me.

Unlike Sylvia and me, my mother and I had never been close or intimate, sharing each other's thoughts, being physically demonstrative — there were few hugs and kisses — and certainly we were geographically separated much of our lives. However, when she did call on me for help, naturally I responded with affection.

The call always had to do with my stepfather, Fred J. Finch. He had been a big problem in my life since I was eleven. He was a vulgar man, a braggart. I know that he physically abused my mother.

One day back in the fifties when Arthur and I were living in

New York City, Mama called and said my stepfather had had a bad stroke. They were staying in Iraan (pronounced *Ira-Ann*), a tiny town in West Texas where he had oil properties — modest ones that required his presence. Mama had also called my half sister, Patsy. She needed us to help her get Finch into a hospital in Midland, the largest city nearby.

Patsy was married and living in Rome, in upstate New York. Recently Mama and my stepfather had bought a house there, too, so they could be near Patsy and her family, husband Bill Bright, and daughters Julie and Melissa.

Patsy and I met at La Guardia and flew down to Dallas. Patsy was thirteen years younger than I. When I was living at home, we had never been especially close. By the time she was born, I was already in rebellion, angling to leave home. Now I was in my early forties, and this was the first time we had been alone together as adults.

When we got to Dallas, we had to take a puddle jumper, a single-engine propeller-driven plane, over to Midland. The weather was horrendous. Passengers coming off the plane as we awaited boarding said it was the worst flight they'd ever had. Patsy had piloted cargo planes during World War II and was unafraid. Not me. I needed alcohol, neat. Patsy, who had learned to fly in Texas, said, "This county is dry, Sister!" So we were going to crash sober. I think we flew upside down several times, certainly vertically more than once.

On that trip, Patsy and I got to know each other. We amused each other very much. Later, even though we would not see each other more than once or twice every two or three years, the instant we greeted each other, we'd begin to laugh.

Mama met us in Midland and drove us to Iraan. The three of us got Mr. Finch out of the motel room into an ambulance and to a hospital room back in Midland. Then Patsy had to return to Rome. Mama and I drove back to Iraan through a violent storm, requiring a fire engine and police escort to get cars through flooded roads. To their motel built entirely of concrete, ceiling to floor. No air-conditioning. Please! The heat was unpardonable!

There was an eight-stool diner close by, with a jukebox and a dispenser of cigarettes and chewing tobacco. The diner's owner/cook/gossip was a jolly lady. Her husband worked in an oil field. Over the next three weeks, Mama and I drank a lot of coffee and ate endless hamburgers, bacon and eggs, pork chops, pancakes. The only greenery I recall was turnip greens.

The other building in Iraan was a small one-room white-frame house. I put it in a painting years later, as I had first seen it perched on a knoll, a little boy with a hula hoop sitting on the step, its sign reading "VANITY BEAUTY CENTRE." It was silhouetted against the vast Texan emptiness, on a road going straight to the horizon.

Mama and I took turns soaking in the tub in tepid water. It was impossible to do anything but listen to country music (all there was on the radio), play double solitaire or checkers, read Midland's daily paper (a day late), or knit. To sleep, we soaked the sheets and lay on wet beds.

Mama had become even quieter than I remembered. She had never been "on" or strikingly animated but once she had been known as "Alice Vinegar." Bogey had named her that the first time he met her. He sassed her and she sassed him right back — "in spades!" as we say. She loved that nickname.

Now, the ready smile, her concern for others, were not in evidence.

As I watched her napping one day, I remembered that I had been thirty-two years old before I realized *who* and what my mother was. I can't remember what triggered my sudden emotional response, my desire to know these things. I do remember that I said to myself, "My God, Gloria, you've never really honored her!" From the time I was fourteen until that moment, I had fought my mother, taken her for granted. It had taken all those years to begin to think about what my mother had gone through to raise my brother and sister and me. And to consider where she had come from.

Mama never discussed her family, probably because she had a painful childhood. I do know this: When she was a young girl, she came down the stairs while her mother was entertaining a friend in the parlor, and she overheard her mother saying, "Well, of course, Alice was a mistake." That weighed heavily on her — Mama repeated it to me several times during her life — and she believed it! She felt she really was "a mistake"!

While his children were young, my grandfather, Thomas Deidrick, worked in his forge, inventing a machine he called the Deidrick Scraper. It was a simple tool, a rotating barrel that, pulled by one animal, could move large quantities of earth. He sold the patent for fifty thousand dollars to James Porteous, an inventor who lived in nearby Fresno. This foolishness (all signs pointed to its being invaluable), combined with my grandfather's sallies up to San Francisco to visit the theaters, saloons, and fancy ladies on the Barbary Coast, infuriated my grandmother. Finally, she left him — but not before she set fire to his forge. Burned it to the ground.

(I've read that Porteous took credit for my grandfather's invention, calling it the Fresno Scraper. During World War II, the machines, pulled by tractors, were used for dredging. And Mama told me that rice fields in southern Italy were created with her father's machine.)

When she divorced her husband — something unheard of in those days — my grandmother's settlement bought her an almond orchard in Paso Robles. But she lost it, probably to drought and amateur management. In "reduced circumstances" she brought her children to Los Angeles to live.

Then in 1899, when Mama was fifteen, her divorced mother and father both died on the same night — he in San Francisco and she in Los Angeles. Mama's sister, Nellie, moved Mama and their two brothers down to Ocean Park from Los Angeles. Brother Willie later drowned in the bay.

I think that Mama's youth and young womanhood had been so catch-as-catch-can, with very little opportunity to improve herself (certainly one of her major drives), that as her life rounded out into motherhood and becoming the wife of a successful lawyer, she put all the tag ends of her life away. My mother was very proud of the fact that her father had invented his Scraper. But her childhood in Selma and Paso Robles and her growing up in Los Angeles were never mentioned. Then, when the terrible disappointments came, the infantile paralysis of one of her babies, the death of another, the death of her young husband, she buried these memories.

After my father died, Mama rarely mentioned him. Once in a while I would get a sentence like, "Your father was very strict." Or "Your father was born in The Dalles in Oregon." Or "Your father took me to San Francisco on our honeymoon." Never any details, never any history. And of course I was so young, there would not have been any reason to ask about his parents or siblings. But he did have two brothers, Ernest and Jesse. Of whom Mama knew next to nothing.

There are no pictures. No family Bibles. So I don't know what any of my grandparents looked like. Regarding the Deidricks, Mama said everything was burned in the great San Francisco earthquake and fire of 1906. I don't know where Aunt Nellie is buried. I don't know where Uncle Willie, who drowned in the sea at Ocean Park before I was born, where he is. I don't know where my father is buried. Sylvia and I made a search for all these graves. Sylvia found my great-grandmother's grave in San Francisco and my infant brother's here in Los Angeles, but no others.

And even though I went to my Uncle Jesse's funeral, I couldn't tell you where he is buried. I only remember seeing him once when I was growing up and Mama only spoke of him once after that. He lived an hour north of Los Angeles, in Carpinteria. One day when I was in film, Mama called and said, "My brother Jesse died and he's a pauper and I have to bury him." I told her I would pay for the funeral. My reason was not pure. The publicity — "ACTRESS'S UNCLE BURIED IN PAUPER'S GRAVEYARD" — would not have been acceptable. Mama said to me, "Gloria, you owe nothing because of the accident of his birth."

I said, "Mama, you can't do it, so I will."

She said, "Family members are not other family members' responsibilities."

So I really have no more than a passing sense of family. But I can never get over the fact that I was thirty-two before I stopped to think about my mother at all.

And here we were together in this nothing town in West Texas, with Mama, once ambitious and celebratory, living in a concrete block motel, facing nothing in her life, nothing but doing her duty as a wife, devoid of marital affection or achievement, full of problems about her children, especially her son, an incipient alcoholic, and me, who had quit cold what she considered a promising career.

My stepfather recovered. And, although eager to leave for my home, I lingered a bit longer than needed to try and embrace — emotionally — my mother, and make up a little for those long years of neglect.

Early one morning a few years later when we were back in California, Mama phoned from Rome, sobbing, sobbing so pitifully, so unlike her.

"What's the problem, Mama?"

"Daddy has had another stroke. He's impossible. There isn't a nurse left in Rome that will work for us. I can't do it, Patsy can't do it, he's so angry and violent and it's going to kill me." I instantly knew I must go to her.

I called Dr. Kennamer, and asked him how to handle this. Rex said to "read the riot act" to my stepfather. In essence, scare the hell out of him.

Believe me, my pleasure!

Mama and I walked into Finch's room, a lovely sunporch in their home. Patsy wasn't there. Mama said she was too upset to come.

He looked up and away from the television set, paused, and said, "What the hell are *you* doing here, Sister?"

"I'm here because there's no one left to take care of you, and you're killing my mother, so I'm putting you in a nursing home. I ordered a ramp as I came into town, so that we can put you in a wheelchair, get you in a car, and take you to the home."

Instant explosion. "The hell you are, you bitch!" over and over again, all the foul words. Mama was crying.

I finally said, "You shape up, Daddy, you be good to Mama, she has to be able to keep a nurse, or we're going to ship you out! Tomorrow, or next week, or the next. That's what I'm here for. That's what I'm going to do."

Daddy went absolutely white and was suddenly quite silent. So then I said, "We're leaving you and I'm taking Mama out to lunch. We'll be back eventually. In the meantime you behave yourself, because you're all alone."

That night — old saying — butter wouldn't melt in his mouth.

The next day — soft-spoken, undemanding, a pussycat. Mama was able to keep a nurse again and have a life of her own, bridge with her friends, supper and breakfast with Patsy and her family, small excursions.

When I left, my farewell to him was, "Don't forget, Daddy. Next time you go into a nursing home. I mean it."

Yes, twenty years later, it was much the same with my Arthur. Physically as well as emotionally, things had grown too difficult for me to handle alone. We needed helpers. Big, strong women who could lift him up from the floor, the bathtub, his chair, ward off his angry swats, wrestle him onto the bed when he didn't want to go. He hated them, he hated me — or so it seemed.

Then Arthur began wandering out the front door, daytime,

nighttime, dressed or undressed, urinating anywhere, with no ac-
knowledgments or apologies. Often I would hear him talking to
someone — Darryl Zanuck, Nunnally Johnson, Sylvia, and no one
was there.

It was a nightmare. Night and day.

After two policemen brought Arthur home one early evening
completely bewildered — I guess when the helper was in the
shower and I was in the studio or something, he had unlocked the
locks I'd put on the door — I called Sylvia and Gene.

Finally the time had come when, for my own survival, I had to
send Arthur away. I would take him to the Motion Picture Country Home and Hospital in the San Fernando Valley.*

Sylvia and Gene and the current helper helped me get my husband into the car — he had fallen down several times without
warning — and away we went.

I felt a lot of relief that I no longer had to witness, and deal with,
this devastating illness. I had resigned myself to its existence, the
prognosis, the reality. And there, at last, were caregivers that could
manage a sullen, recalcitrant patient.

About a week later, I was horrified to greet Sylvia and Gene and
Arthur at the back door.

They had gone to visit him, and he had told them the place was
a "hellhole." Parentheses — needless to say, the Motion Picture
Country Home and its hospital were peerless, Arthur wasn't. Un-
parentheses. Not understanding the nature of his illness, they
panicked and packed him up and brought him back to me. Then
left.

I was hysterical that night. I hired another practical nurse the
next day, and tried to cope with Arthur's inconsistency, animosity,

---

*This is a fabulous retirement home/nursing home/hospital for people who have
worked in the motion picture industry. Everyone in the industry helps fund it — from
makeup artists to gaffers to directors to stars — because everyone is eligible to go
there, space permitting.

physical abuse of his new helper — who quit — without success. I phoned Sylvia to come out from Malibu and stay with me overnight! Which she did. After about one hour of witnessing this disaster, she agreed my duty was not to continue with my husband at home.

We found a good, caring place just a couple of miles away. Arthur seemed content there from the start. It was interesting and inexplicable to see his demeanor change over a period of a week or so. He became Laughing Boy — almost! He was charming to the nurses, the janitors, the other patients that were also non compos mentis. From time to time, the nurses even had to forcibly prevent him from climbing into protesting women's beds!

That's my boy!

19

By 1975, Arthur was utterly becalmed and withdrawn — almost completely unaware of anything happening in the world except what was a few feet outside his nursing home bedroom window, and rarely even that.

Since Arthur could no longer object, I decided to go back to work. Let's try and make a few bucks.

Here's what my "lines" were for *The Legend of Lizzie Borden*, starring Elizabeth Montgomery: "She took an ax." (Well, at least it was a crucial moment!) You know how many lines I had in *My Favorite Year* with Peter O'Toole. None. Oh, there were a few bright spots. I worked with Angela Lansbury twice, once in *Murder, She Wrote* and then in a film, *Shootdown*. What a lovely woman. She concerned herself with my wardrobe, my makeup, my hair. Was I happy with them? My role? Was there anything that bothered me? She made me feel important. In tiny parts. Such interest and support is rare and rewarding.

A few years later, one of the very few interesting and challenging roles given me in film came my way. That of an old flame of Rudolf Valentino's! The script, *Merlene of the Movies*, was by an accomplished young writer, Lisa Mitchell. Nancy Malone and Linda Hope were the producers par excellence, with Nancy Malone also directing. The distinguished camerawoman was Brie Murphy. Marvin Paige, then *General Hospital*'s casting director, suggested me, and my teenage grandchildren Benjamin and Amanda were extras in the movie.

Merlene was shown at several international film festivals and received many honors, among them at the Oklahoma Film Festival and the Houston Film Festival.

I rejoiced that I could work, would work, and possibly lightning would strike!

In all, I landed maybe a dozen roles in TV and film, all of them very small, barely warranting screen credit. But at this point in my life, I was no stranger to forgettable roles.

Besides, what else could I do? Up until then, the only time that I earned enough money to support myself was those seven years in the thirties when I was at Universal and Twentieth. After that, I was in the same boat as every other Hollywood wife.

Most Hollywood wives that I knew had been secretaries or actresses, or fresh out of school, and were not equipped to be VIPs in aerospace, electronics, steel. They had been raised to get married and have children. All their skills, and all their talents, and all their interest had been directed in one direction.

So when they married, they were totally economically dependent on their husbands. Very few wives worked. Those that did were either writers or actresses. Once in a while a wife would say, "You know I'm an interior decorator. I did Merry Mary's house for her. . . ."

I truly couldn't imagine what the future would hold. I was still willing to take a gamble — but on what? All I knew was this: As I told my oldest friend, Catherine Turney, "I refuse to end up at Sak's Fifth Avenue waiting on my friends."

I made visits to see my husband in the nursing home every day, wheeled him around, talked to him, stroked him, simply because I had promised to love, honor, and obey. It seemed the least I could do after forty-two years. At first, Arthur's men friends also went to visit him. But the distress they felt with him — no witticisms, no mordant remarks, no recognition of their presence — ultimately compelled me to ask them please not to come anymore. I think, I hope, they were grateful and relieved.

The only friend I didn't stop from coming was Groucho. He could afford the time, and Arthur still had moments of awareness. Arthur always lit up at the sight of his best friend, then murmured phrases, laughing and smiling. He was telling Grouch a couple of good jokes, no question.

Actually, in the early seventies, Groucho himself had been in sorry shape. Jack Benny and George Burns were still functioning, and although Groucho was doing an occasional guest shot, his radio-then-TV show, *You Bet Your Life,* was over, and he was despondent. His friends felt sorry for him. And he felt sorry for himself. One night, an old friend found him sitting alone in a room, lit only by one lightbulb.

Groucho and Arthur had been through a lifetime together, and now were facing the end of it.

Recently something, I don't know what, made me think of the day Groucho married Kay.

Groucho's second wife, Kay, had been the wife of one of the Dead End Kids, Leo Gorcey. She was also a sweet, young girl, madly in love with Grouch. They were married in our tiny Garden of Allah living room, with just us, the judge, and Harry Ruby playing "The Wedding March" on our spinet. Susan and Harpo invited all their mutual friends to their house afterward for a happy celebration.

Kay was an innocent abroad. Grouch finally gave in to her pleading that she be allowed to do the shopping for their household. Watching his pennies, *he* had always done it. Carefully and alone. It was wartime, there was rationing, and, of course, shortages of all kinds. Groucho gave Kay $100 — a lot in the forties to do the family marketing — and she came home that afternoon with a carton of toilet tissue and a cocker spaniel puppy.

Kay had Groucho's second daughter, Melinda, whom he also adored. But Kay was not up to the stresses and strains of wedlock with Groucho. They, too, were divorced.

Next, Grouch had an affair with a brilliant and beautiful actress, Virginia Schulberg, ex-wife of novelist/screenwriter Budd Schulberg. Groucho was in awe of her. Quick and literate, funny, and not too impressed or smitten with him. He finally gave up on her, confiding to Arthur she was just "too much" — probably in every department. After Groucho, she married and divorced novelist/screenwriter Peter Viertel. Later, she accidentally set herself on fire — cigarette plus flammable nightgown — and died of her burns.

At the time Arthur and I had left to live for a couple of years in Europe, Groucho was seeing a gorgeous model and artist, Eden Hartford. Her sister, Dee, was an actress married to the film director Howard Hawks. We had been living in Rapallo for a spell when Grouch wrote that he and Eden were marrying, and, together with a photographer/biographer (for some magazine), would be visiting us.

We made reservations at the Splendido, the best hotel in Portofino, met the Marxes at the train station, and drove up to the hotel. True to form, as we entered, Groucho assumed that famous crouched-over posture, swished up to the desk, and two very correct, monkey-suited hoteliers froze in their position as Groucho put his spread-out fingers under his chin, leaned over the mahogany ledge, and said, "*Voulez-vous couchez avec moi?*"

Speechless, they turned to each other, to us, looked down at this gross person, and I shrilled, "It's Groucho Marx! He's Groucho Marx! Groucho Marx, the American comedian!" several more times before the two dumbfoundeds got it!

Much later, when Eden and I were painting together in my studio, I asked her how she caught Groucho. She said that even though she had moved into his house and everything seemed fine, he had refused to marry her. So she had left for Egypt to join her sister, Dee, who was with Hawks while he was directing *Land of the Pharaohs*. Eden did not communicate with Grouch for several months. He finally wrote that he missed her, and offered marriage.

Eden and I were very fond of each other. She had been raised a Mormon, and as a child had an experience similar to one of mine. One Christmas, she and her sister busily filled baskets for the poor at their church. When they got home, she was stunned to find such a basket in the kitchen. Until then, she had not known they were poor.

Eden was very loving and simple. Not a reader, which was what Groucho wanted from a wife but never had. Eden once made a real faux pas — simply out of ignorance of Jewish history. We four were coming home from Vegas one weekend, discussing some disturbances in Israel, and I said, "But it was almost a pogrom, Grouch!"

He turned to Eden and questioned, "You know what a pogrom is?"

Pause. "Well, isn't it a sort of picnic?"

After she and Groucho divorced, Eden moved to Palm Springs to be near Dee, and died some years later, too young.

As he grew older, Groucho had one quality much to be admired. Whatever his age, he was always up on the talent of the times, and with great enthusiasm. It was from Groucho that we first heard the name of — then met at dinner — the brilliant new writer Woody Allen . . . the bright new interviewer Dick Cavett . . . the exciting new singing group the Mamas and the Papas . . . the arresting new performer Alice Cooper . . . the extraordinary new musical comedy actress Barbra Streisand . . . the wonderful new composer/pianist Marvin Hamlisch. . . .

It saddened me that my Arthur didn't have Groucho's vitality and forward thrust. Arthur felt no writers or entertainers could measure up to those he had loved in the past.

Groucho engaged in correspondence with many noted writers.

As a matter of fact, Arthur edited a collection, *The Groucho Letters,* at Knopf for the renowned editor Robert Gottlieb. The book was published in 1967.

One of his correspondents was T. S. Eliot. As I remember it, Groucho's daughter Miriam wrote Eliot that she was writing an essay about him in school, and asked about this or that. Eliot gave the answers, then said he wanted a picture of her father. So she went to her father, and said "T. S. Eliot would like a picture of you." Groucho gave her this nice studio portrait, it was mailed off, and it came back with a letter from Eliot saying, "Not that picture — one with a mustache."

So they mailed off another picture, and a note came back from Eliot saying thanks.

Eventually, Groucho was going to England, and he thought, Why don't I call on Tom Eliot? He sent a note, and the date he would be there. Nunnally Johnson, who had been to Eliot's house, advised. "Send for the car at ten P.M. No later."

Groucho asked, "Why?"

Nunnally replied, "You'll find out."

Groucho got there, and passed the dullest evening of his life. The great man had no interest in him, and by ten o'clock Groucho had no interest in Eliot. As he was showing them out, Groucho turned to him and said, "Tell me something. Why did you want my picture?"

Eliot replied, "For my butcher. I'm getting much better meat now."

It was around the time my Arthur started to decline that a young actress with auburn hair and features reminiscent of Vivien Leigh arrived on Groucho's scene. Erin Fleming cleaned Groucho up — manicured, pedicured, and barbered him, bought him new clothes, gave him lots of cuddling and compliments, a good cook, a clean, redecorated house. And appearances and honors. In 1972 alone, there was a solo concert at Carnegie Hall in New York, a medal of Honor at the Cannes Film Festival, and the *Commandeur des Arts et Lettres* presented by the French government. In 1974, a Special Academy Award in recognition of a lifetime's achievement. Then in 1977, The Boys were inducted into the Motion Picture Hall of Fame.

Despite his having rallied for a couple of years, age overtook Groucho and he, too, dwindled. An official entity decided Groucho needed someone who would be responsible for his well-being. A conservator — not of his money but of his person.

I was asked, but declined. I didn't need more to deal with! Bert Granet, veteran screenwriter/producer, his wife, Charlotte, and two other of Groucho's longtime close friends were approached, but in the end, Nat Perrin — Mr. Heart of Gold — took on the job. He took it seriously, even though he was still involved in teaching his university class in screenwriting. Nat never never discussed with friends the unseemly twists and turns of Groucho's life.

A painfully long way from *Duck Soup*.

One day, Groucho called and asked me to his birthday party at Hillcrest Country Club. I hadn't heard from him in months, and I said, "Gee, why thank you, Groucho, that's very nice."

He called back in about two hours. He said, "Gloria."

I said, "Hi."

He said, "You can't come to my birthday party."

Pause. "I can't? Why not?"

He said, "Erin doesn't want you. Erin says you treat Arthur very badly."

I said, "OK, Grouch." And that was the last time I talked to him. I took a deep breath. I didn't have to make nice anymore.

The only tender thing I ever heard Groucho say was to my husband on a visit the year before. Leaning down over Arthur's wheelchair he said, "Don't go before I go, Sheek."

Groucho died in the middle of August 1977.

In the middle of January 1978 the head nurse at the home called Sylvia. "Mrs. Thompson? Mr. Sheekman has expired." She made it sound like the time on his parking meter had run out.

Sylvia and Gene and the grandchildren and I had a brief ceremony under our beautiful old plum tree as we buried Arthur's ashes.

It had been a long twilight of seven years. Finally, mercifully, it was over.

Someone said all love affairs end unhappily.

But still I often think of those exhilarating years — full of love then, embroidered with his witticisms, my laughter, our marital love.

Addio to one life.

Avanti to the next.

20

I was happy.

When Arturo first showed signs of illness, cooped up in our Westwood apartment, surrounded by concrete walkways and uninspired flower beds, I suddenly realized I had better get the hell out of there into a house with a garden.

Where Himself — and I — would have some space and privacy.

Gene and I found a small bungalow in our old neighborhood, Brentwood. It was over fifty years old on a half acre of beautiful trees, classic rosebushes — space.

And the extra-large garage could be my studio.

It still is my pride and joy.

I continued my traveling. When Arthur had been safely ensconced at the nursing home, I took off for parts unknown. India, China — first tourist's voyage up the Yangtze — the Balkans, Egypt, Greece, barges on the historic French canals — Angor Wat ranks first in my memory, followed by swimming with dolphins off Key West, and Annapurna watching. I also was printing, painting, giving parties, and exhibiting my bonsai.

As you may have noticed, freedom is everything to me — in my art, in my life. The lovely circumstance of being on your own affords one freedom of choice. You don't have to be anywhere you don't want to be — at least for very long! You don't have to *do* anything you don't want to — at least for very long!

I've always loved my own company, and now I had lots of it. With all four children off to college, Gene and Sylvia had given up their Malibu establishment and moved to a chalet they'd built in the mountains a couple of hours away. But we talked on the phone every day and kept close.

Well! After all those years of pleasing my husbands, paying attention to their needs and tastes, being number two in their world, and having fits and/or spells and/or crises as a result, it was "paradise enow" to give those situations the finger. And to please myself. Only myself.

So my love life was nil.

After Arthur died, the time came when I said to my daughter, "I might take on a young man, but I never want an old man. I never want to have to take care of an old man again!"

Be that as it may, I did meet one or two men I thought might do, and so invited them to my house for dinner parties.

The first was a disaster. I have had a most engaging woman as a housekeeper and friend for over twenty-five years, Natalie Leavitt. She is Romanian, speaks several languages, is very knowledgeable about the theater, music, authors, foreign and domestic. She sent her beautiful daughter, Thaïs, to the Royal Ballet School in London, and has led a most cultivated, interesting life.

I gave a dinner party, and invited Bronislaw Kaper, the European composer-conductor. I seated him at my right. Natalie came in, served everybody, then stood there just for a moment, and I said, "What is it, Honey?"

She answered, "Nothing. Is there anything more you want?"

I said, "No no, that's fine."

She went back into the kitchen, and he turned to me and said, "Honey? To a servant?"

I said to him, "She's a friend of mine." I mean it was such a blow. "Honey? To a servant?" That was the last time he was invited.

The second man — I can't remember his name — kissed dirty.

Besides, I do not need a man. I am devoted to masturbation.

I think it's probably one of the most pleasurable things in my life.

As a child, I heard that terrible things would happen if you masturbated. I think the reason that I didn't believe it was that, when it got to the nitty-gritty of verboten things, I rebelled. And figured that some terrible, evil self-interested person had made up all these nonsensical things about what you should and shouldn't do. Because they themselves were doing them! And were full of guilt. I had, and have, no guilt whatsoever when it comes to pleasuring myself.

Then, out of the blue, in spring of '83, I received a lovely book of poems by Carlyle MacIntyre. It had been published by Ward Ritchie at his Laguna Imprenta press, with a note, "Dearest Gloria, do you remember him?"

Gordon, Ward, and Larry Powell had been best friends in college. Ward was to have been best man at my wedding to Gordon, but, at the last minute, he split and went to Paris, to study the book arts. He had become an internationally prestigious graphic designer/printer/bookman.

Carlyle MacIntyre was a professor of English literature at Occidental College and Gordon, Ritchie, and Powell took his classes. MacIntyre had evidently inspired them all to read, to write, to love literature, particularly poetry. In which he was very talented. Here's one of his more playful efforts, a limerick, in fact.*

> When Titian was using rose madder,
> His model was climbing the ladder.
> Her position, to Titian,
> Suggested coition.
> So he climbed up the ladder and 'ad her!

I called Ward at his home in Laguna. "Of course, I remember MacIntyre. Thank you so much, and how are you?" He was fine, and

---

*I've seen this attributed to Anonymous, but Mac's students are convinced *he* wrote it.

glad I remembered Mac. I asked if he ever came up to Los Angeles. Yes, he came up to Pasadena quite often — to the Huntington Library. Would he like to come for dinner and bring his wife, Marka?

Short pause. His answer, "Marka died last year."

It was a shock. But I hadn't been much in touch with them since Gordon's and my divorce. Once they came to a Beverly Hills vernissage of mine, and once to a dinner party the Thompsons gave for mutual friends in the food world. With very limited conversation beyond "How have you been? What are you doing now? Oh! That's nice. Very interesting."

Yes, he would like to come to dinner. When? We made a date for March 15.

I was seventy-two, and Ward was seventy-eight.

We had always been fond of each other. As a matter of fact, that first evening, gossiping, he reminded me we had gone to bed together after I'd left Gordon. I didn't and don't remember it, so it couldn't have been notable.

I think these two poems describe our first meeting quite accurately.

March 15, 1983
Gloria to Ward

Beware the Ides of March

And so it came to be, Himself walked up the path,
Spring-shaded with my elm's new leaves.
I watched behind the heavy silken knots
Masking my windowed door,
And opened it before he climbed the steps,
Making him welcome
As the bronzy bells tinkled on their long fringed knots
And we smiled uncertainly at each other,
And then so lightly clasped each other's hand.
He walked into my parlor,

Bright with lamps and flowers,
And then, into the bar,
Warmed with a burning open fire,
A mirrored crystal alcove full of all the alcoholic props.
He offered me a book,
A gift of his own making.
My cats then stalked around his feet,
Antennaed tails held high, and soon departed.
He mixed his vodka on the rocks, "with a lemon twist."
I poured my wine and we began to talk.
To laugh, to reminisce, with very few regrets,
About our friends and lovers (and with some surprises!).
Our own two sorrows, past now,
Not heard, or known about by either thee or me —
Not shared at any time.

I know I loved you instantly.
I know I felt your warmth and depth, your valor
And your love so very quickly,
There was no need for games.
There never has been.
That is what I treasure most.
My heart an open book upon your open hand.

March 19, 1984
Ward to Gloria

It was a year ago, you tell me,
When I walked up the path
And rang the bell a time or two before the door opened
With a warning there of a ferocious dog.

Our eyes met and you smiled
That smile I remembered from so many years past.

A yearning then caught my heart
To touch and hold the girl
I had known a half century ago.

And so I took her in my arms
As if it were yesterday
And we were in youth again.

We made love easily, often, and joyously. We laughed a lot. I was told our touchy-feely gestures and obvious delight in being together discombobulated many of his lady friends. Sorry!

Ward had lived for more than twenty years in the gated community of Emerald Bay. I had never thought about or realized what a "gated community" truly could be. Emerald Bay is beautifully situated on a tiny cliff-lined bay north of Laguna Beach — about an hour and a half south of Los Angeles. Very large homes dominate the scene. A mishmash architecturally, but with masses of flowering trees and plants, lots of Mercedes and Porsches, and until a few years ago, no You Know What, or, or, or — just WASPs.

Not my style.

But because I loved Ward, I forgave him, and made do.

Ward had an ongoing Monday afternoon bridge game. At the game, one friend-player was a California rancher/oilman millionaire, one a Pittsburgh family multimillionaire, one just a plain retired multimillionaire, and, once in a while, there was Ward's lawyer. When he and I first began keeping company, I went down to Emerald Bay to be with him for a weekend. We went to the home of one of the players, and Ward introduced me.

"How do you do?" Then the men sat down and started to play cards. Absolutely no interest, no polite inquiries. "You live here?" "Oh, where are you from?" No notice at all.

The host's ex-wife came in and said to me, "Hello, I'm so-and-so. What is your name?"

And I said, "Gloria Stuart."

And she said, "I'm in real estate. What do you do?"

I answered, "I'm an actress."

ACHTUNG! The three men playing cards with Ward looked up, and one of them said to me, "You're an actress?"

Ward said, "Yes, her name's Gloria Stuart. She used to be a movie star."

The other men put their cards down and asked me, "You're an actress? In movies? What movies?"

I said, "Well, two Shirley Temples, but I started on the stage and starred . . ."

It's a magic word, "actress." They treated me from then on with respect, made asides to me during the game, asked me if I would like to play with them. Suddenly, I was a person to be considered. It's incredible. And amusing.

Finally, I was to meet some of Ward's other friends at Mary and Mac Ropp's cocktail party.

I knew it was a momentous occasion for him. So I was careful to dress simply and look as beautiful as possible. We walked in to the patio, and Mary introduced me around. The women went back to talking among themselves. Ward and I stood with the men.

One of them, from a socialite family in Santa Monica, remembered me. He was very cordial. Then his wife came over and said snootily, "You knew Bob before?"

I answered, "Yes. He was ahead of me in school, but of course I knew the whole family." She sniffed, and split. I soon noticed that I was not approached by any of the other women. I said to Ward, "Don't leave me." And he didn't.

Finally I went into a large bath–dressing room. A woman joined me and said, "My name is so-and-so, and it's nice to meet you. I understand you live in Brentwood. It's good to see Ward with someone after so long a time." I thanked her.

Several years later I said to her, "You know you were the only woman who talked to me at that party." She answered — this was after *her* lover had married her — "Gloria, you and I were the only non-wives there. We were both coming from the same direction!"

Soon one of Ward's best lady friends came back into town, and *her* best friend told her that Ward had a girl. She asked who I was, and her friend told her.

She said, "You mean he went *outside* of the Bay?"

That's Emerald Bay, friends. Yes, he had gone outside of the Bay! It was pretty unacceptable and quite titillating for all the people there. Because Ward had resisted any liaison since his wife had died. Of course, I imagine when *that* happened, the casseroles and invitations to shack up came from innumerable widows and spinsters around him.

Larry Powell and his wife of many years, Fay, came to stay at Ward's. Fay said to me one afternoon, "Gloria, the women here are barracudas, and they will do anything to finish you off."

I replied, "You know, Fay, if he wants to be landed by someone else, that's fine with me. I am not a jealous woman. He has to be faithful, I don't want him cheating on me, but don't forget — he sought me out, not I him. I'm not going to fight for him if he wants to go into another net. If he ever wants to start over again with someone else, he's free to."

About a year after I started going down to Emerald Bay, one of the bridge-playing friends gave a lavish party in his home. About a hundred good friends gathered, and he came out on a balcony with the lovely woman who had been so kind to me at the Ropps'.

"Meet my wife," he announced, and everyone whooped and hollered in congratulations.

Then someone yelled, "Ritchie, you're next!"

Ward instantly yelled back, "Never! Never! Never!"

I looked up at him, and someone said, "Oh, come on — she's gorgeous!"

He shouted again even louder, smirking. "Never! Never! Never!"

I stood by his side and smiled (I hope with an "Isn't-he-a-card?"

expression). To be so publicly and loudly rejected was, to say the least, humiliating. However, it was the same smile that I used when I lost to Kim Basinger at the Academy Awards. A smile and a shrug. I never spoke of it to him. But I will never forget that moment.

Early in our romance, he joined me in London after I'd finished a trip with friends on the Orient Express. Ward and I had decided to tour England and Scotland together. I should have realized that he really meant it when he said we should "share the expenses." I was so enamored of him and my situation, I agreed. Well! I had never traveled with a lover before. I would prove to him how desirable, how adorable I was!

When we got home, he handed me a bill. I owed $1720.60. It was noted item by item. Even taxis and tips, candy and flowers for our hostesses.

His stepson, Dr. Mark Detrick, said his mother, Marka, called Ward as tight as the bark on a tree. Truer words were never said!

I've pondered and pondered my thirteen years of devotion to Wardela. Granted, the last few of those years, his fiscal stinginess was coloring his persona, and I was tiring of paying my own way on trips, our joint dinner parties, presents, flowers and plants for his Emerald Bay cottage, gas for the car (because I was driving him by then in my T-Bird), the groceries when we went marketing together.

Come to think of it, he did let loose a bottle of vodka every so often, and occasionally offered Korbel champagne.

But we were still physically attracted to each other, and conversationally he was amusing and in his field, erudite. I had long since despaired of a political conversion from right to left. He was basically so apolitical it didn't matter.

And, he admired me very much, often and openly — for the most part.

I felt stroked. Sort of.

And there was nobody else around.

*   *   *

It was after breakfast in Emerald Bay one morning, a few weeks after I began going down there, when Ward said he had to work, and started out the door onto the back deck. (There was no inside access from the upstairs to his studio downstairs.)

I had no intention of sitting around twiddling my thumbs while he was creating.

"Ward, I want to see your studio," I said.

He really didn't want any witnessing/kibitzing, but he couldn't refuse me.

So, down we both went. Into a series of ground floor rooms.

In the first room was a huge antique English iron press, an 1839 Albion, one of the all-time great hand presses. It was beautiful as an object of art as well as something functional. Against the walls and around the press were several chests with many thin drawers (they held various sets of type, I was to discover), trays of undistributed type in all sizes, a paper cutter, a book press, specimen pages of titles tacked to the walls, books books books, and, in one anteroom, shelves and shelves of virgin paper.

But that press!

I asked, "How does it work? Please, show me!"

He had type already set on the "bed." He inked it, hung the paper, and slowly turned the drum over the type.

Lifting the paper off the drum, voilà! A printed page.

I remember saying — and I wonder at my smart-aleckness — "I can do that!"

He replied, "Be my guest."

He helped me pin the next page up, roll the ink on the marble slab, then onto the type. He stepped back. I rolled the drum forward, over the type and back. I heard a sort of crushing sound. Ward winced, looked down at the type, and said, "You squashed it!" Then, he explained *he* had let the drum down too far, and the pressure as I rolled had smashed some type.

That was the end of my first lesson.

But from that moment on, I couldn't wait to have a press and Do

It Myself. At last. To make an immortal name. It was not going to be as an actress. It was going to be as a Printer of Books! The oldest records we have of man's intellect, his surfacing as a thinking organ, is in *print*. A performance is ephemeral, but the Book is forever.

In recent years, the challenges to me of painting as a primitive had been wearing a little thin, and I had become fascinated by the complex art form of serigraphy — silk screening. My dear friend, the artist and designer Ruth Albert, had discovered Evelyn Johnson, a brilliant serigrapher. Ever the mother hen, Ruth had urged me to sign up and take lessons with Evelyn. I did. Instantly, I plunged into the medium with the same intensity I'd brought to painting almost thirty years before.

My subjects for serigraphs ranged from large flower forms to the reflection of the château at Chenonceaux in its lake, a double image. I "pulled" images of kites flying against Mt. Fuji, and a series of serigraphs with my six-foot-tall harlequin doll and a beautiful nude redheaded model.

And now, all the free-spirited designing I had done in découpage, painting, and serigraphy — the fine cutting, precision measuring up to a ninety-sixth of an inch, neatness, and discipline — commingled in the art of printing.

I felt reborn!

My creative juices kept me awake nights. I couldn't think of anything else but making/printing a book. Dozens of projects filled my notebook, my conversations with Ward, my happy prospects!

I began to design broadsides* for several quotations I favored. Ward would choose the type and its placing, I would do the illustration, choose the colors, agree with him on the papers, inks, size. He would do the printing.

Then early in the new year, 1984, Ward helped me buy my own

---

*The broadside, I found out, was first used in Colonial days. The local printer would be given an announcement, notice, bit of news, print it on a single sheet, and tack it up on a pole in the front of his office. So, today, a broadside is a single printed sheet.

press — not a prestigious hand press like his, but a simple modern Vandercook SP15, the sort many book artists use today.

I signed up at the Women's Workshop in downtown Los Angeles to study typesetting with Susan King, and later with Kitty Maryatt, both consummate book artists.

I had not yet begun my first book — which I planned to be ready for Ward's birthday six months away — when, at a meeting of fellow artists (Serigraphs West), I saw, under a Lucite box on a black velvet stand, a most beautiful open book. Crystal book covers over stately herons, gold leaf, exquisite printed pages.

"What is that?" I asked my hostess.

"It's an artist's book."

"What's an artist's book?"

"Well, it's by Joseph D'Ambrosio. He designed it, did all the artwork — silk screens, collage, hand printing — and bound it. Everything."

Mind-boggling — such an astonishing, exquisite book!

I phoned Ward as soon as I got home. "Do you know a Joseph D'Ambrosio?" No, he didn't. "Well, you're going to! He's fabulous! You won't believe his work!"

Days later, we found D'Ambrosio in his San Fernando Valley studio and looked at his books. Both of us were overwhelmed by his inventiveness, techniques, skill, and warm personality.

I asked Joseph and his companion, Gary Moerke, over for dinner. After dinner, going out into the garden to smoke a cigarette, Joseph came back in. "What are all those little trees?"

"They're Japanese bonsais."

Joseph wrote a charming tale about an azalea bonsai that "wanted to be a movie star," hand made the paper embedded with flower petals, illustrated, printed, and bound the book in French black and gold leather. *The Small Garden of Gloria Stuart*. A masterpiece!

As are all of Joseph's artist's books.

I asked for his help in designing and assembling my first book,

Ward's birthday surprise, and he was more than helpful — enthusiastic and inventive. As he was with several other books I printed.

I was very lucky with my two tutors. Ward was the classicist, the graphic designer par excellence, each of his publications designed to illuminate and attest to its special subject. D'Ambrosio was the wild blue yonder boy, unfettered by custom (though trained in the classic forms and techniques of typography), with an awesome imagination and unique technical skills.

Ward had sent me a few dear poems that he thought were haiku. They weren't — this classic form of Japanese poetry is strict: three lines of five, seven, and five syllables. For example:

Haiku for Gloria

The butterflies carefully
Kiss her breasts.
I am in love.

So for his birthday I wrote several "ukiah"s and illustrated the pages with silk-screened golden butterflies hovering over a plump breast.

Ukiah for Ward

Withdraw thy net,
I am benet —
And thee is free.

I chose Ward's "house type" — Goudy 30 — as the type, Japanese papers in black and brick colors, gold foil for end papers, and sprinkled fireflies I'd drawn on the false title and colophon pages. The cover was bamboo bark imprinted with the Chinese character "Destined to be together" in black ink, sewn with a black silk twist as taught me by Joseph.

Upon its presentation, in Ward's words, he was "stunned!"

Me, too.

I would agree that most self-authored, self-printed books are vainglorious. An artist's book is a different breed of cat. Its raison d'être is not the writing but how the writing is presented.

I had written a poem about flying a kite on the beach. I was proud of it and I wanted to print it. To hell with vaingloriousness! I began designing my second book.

I chose an italic type called Eve — very structured and pressing forward, like a kite flying — designed by the genius Hermann Zapf. I used a deep sky blue Italian paper by Fabriano. For the title page, I cut out in silhouette a huge kite backed with silver tea-leaf paper, floating it free. It was bound in a flowing blue and white French hand-marbled paper.

What a ball I was having!

I couldn't wait to go on to my third project, printing the two poems Ward and I had written to each other about our first meeting, which I would title *Beware the Ides of March*. Here, I mixed two unlikely type styles, 60-point Columbus and 12- and 18-point Libra. Unheard of! Never done! said Ward.

I created designs for our astrological signs, Gemini and Cancer, and illustrated our poems with two hand-colored line drawings: a nude Gloria reclining on a branch regarding herself in a mirror, and a nude Ward stretched out on a limb reading a book. At the end of the poems was a silk-screened foldout drawing of the nude Gloria and Ward in a leafy vernal embrace.

The following year, Ward and I went up to Carmel with John Dreyfus, one of the world's most notable bookmen. He had come from his home in London to visit Ward and to speak at the Zamorano Club in Los Angeles, a venerable group of bibliophiles.

While we were visiting Tor House, Jeffers's beautiful stone cottage — which Ward and I had last seen in 1931 with Gordon — I noticed legends painted on the walls and furniture. In scarlet and sea blues. Robin's daughter-in-law, Lee (Donen's wife), explained they were quotations Una and Robin had gathered in Ireland years before. They were witty and poignant! Why couldn't I print them — design a book for them?

John volunteered to photograph the inscriptions — prone and supine! — and away I went.

With the photographs of Robin's script in their individual colors, I reproduced the legends, copying his calligraphy exactly. I also took lessons in paper sculpture so that the book's cover could be a three-dimensional reproduction of the cottage's stone walls and front door. Two learned ladies in Carmel's Jeffers Society furnished the quotations' origins, and Ward wrote the introduction to my book. D'Ambrosio bound the warm-straw-colored pages of German-made Nideggen paper in a heavy natural linen and encased the book in a clamshell box. It was the first book of mine that both the Victoria and Albert Museum and the Getty Museum purchased.

The last paintings and serigraphs I had done seem somehow to have been mostly female nudes — usually in meadows or lakes or forests — with lots of flora and fauna! Sappho had always interested me — her sexual orientation, fragments of song. And so had erotica, which I had collected when I was still in film with the help of *buchmeister* Jake Zeitlin, Ward's close friend.

I began to work on a book titled *Eve-Venus,* with the "Eve" on one plane and the "Venus" on the other, thus:

E V E
E
N
U
S

The book took me a full two years, working on the line drawings and collages of Eve, Leda and her swan, Venus and her child,

Cupid, Paris, gays as centaurs playing leapfrog, a daisy chain of amorous ladies, and a page from a thousand-year-old Chinese marriage book's instructions for the bride-to-be. I assembled the gold-dust-powdered pages and drawings of genitalia formed of various leaves from my garden, interleaved with phallic clouds cut from fragile Japanese transparent tissues sensuous to the touch. All the illustrations were printed on white English "satin" paper, serigraphed with a split fountain of colors — that is, pale verdant green blended into flesh tones.

Looking through them, I was reminded of the day I was pulling (that is, silk-screening) those pages, having a very frustrating time.

I called a dear friend of mine, much more talented in serigraphy than I, for help.

When she saw the two colors, she exclaimed, "You can't mix pink and green!"

I inquired, "Martha, where is that written?" She smiled, and we did it!

Deep bow in D'Ambrosio's direction. He bound my erotica with rods and silk — his own creation — and made a luminous slipcover of flesh tone and green tie-dyed Japanese paper in a Lucite case. Not content with this most skillful assembling, he impressed into the back cover a frame for a watercolor and ink collage I composed of "Sappho Ascending." Floating above a field, she holds a Greek lettered tablet, while one sister on high holds her harp, the other a laurel wreath.

Another lesson learned. Almost anything is possible and permissible in the arts.

Ward and I seldom agreed 100 percent on *my* designs, and he never asked my opinion on *his*. But he was generous to me privately in his approvals, and professed astonishment at times at my originality and/or exuberance!

I say "privately" because when books were discussed among friends and book people, he seemed unable to name or remember the collections I was in. In no time, they included the Getty Museum, the Victoria and Albert Museum, the UCLA Clark Library, Occidental College, the Library of Congress, and the Huntington Library. (And recently, Princeton University, and the Special Collections of the Los Angeles and New York City public libraries.)

By now my press, the Vandercook SP15, had become more than a press to me. It was a way of life, nirvana. Everything around it was in a constant state of flux — heaps and packages of papers, undistributed trays of type, half-filled drawers of still-packaged type, slugs and leads and metal and woodblocks in various sizes for placing type on the bed of the press, inks, solvents, rags, pinned-up notes, relevant articles, photos, drawings, proofs, sayings, answered and unanswered letters, filled and unfilled folders of bills, ideas, memorabilia, all piled pile on pile, in and out of trays, on tables, chairs, footstools. . . .

A trip Ward and I took to San Francisco was, to say the least, memorable. We were going to meetings of the Roxburghe Club and Book Club of California.

Ward was driving and I was reading to him from the *Oxford Book of English Verse*, mainly the Restoration poets. When I stopped reading for several minutes, out of the blue, Ward said, "You take things."

After a stunned moment or two, I said, "What do you mean, I 'take things'?" No answer. "What the hell kind of a nutty remark is that?" No answer. "What the hell do I take?" Again, no answer, just a small, secret smile. I tried once more. "What do you mean? What do I take? Where? When? Answer me, Ward!" No answer, just what I had come to know well, that silent, secret smirk.

That was the first inkling of his tortoising — which is a word I've just invented. To tortoise, i.e., to remain silent in one's shell, a non-presence.

So when we got back home, I wrote him a long poem. This is a small part of it:

> But if emotion
> Is a "thing" to steal,
> It has escaped my stealth.
>
> Take love, for instance.
>
> You say,
> "One cannot take from one who will not give.
> "It doesn't count —
> Your virtue here."
>
> My dear!
>
> I've seen love stolen
> Surreptitiously,
> Without the victim's ken,
> As smoothly, quietly,
> And with the grace
> Of practiced pocket pickers.
>
> Or stolen openly
> With flair and
> Heartlessness.
>
> I wouldn't.
> I couldn't.
>
> Just leave for me
> Debris.

I sent it to him. Never an acknowledgment, and, for me, never a clue to the remark.

On that trip, I brought along two of our broadsides. One to present to our host in San Francisco, Albert Sperisen — president emeritus of the Book Club of California, and the other for our old friend, M. F. K. Fisher. As I've mentioned, I gave MF up as a close friend many years before. But as she and Ward had been good friends since college, he always wanted to see her.

We went up to Glen Ellen and visited her at Last House several times. By the time Ward and I were together, I had made my peace with MF's meanness. However, she no longer held any charm or interest for me. There was total disaffection. She was ill. It was sad to see her failing.

A perfect example of tortoising: The last time we saw each other, I brought my Robinson Jeffers book to show her. After lunch, she wanted to nap, so we said we'd return to take her out for dinner. I showed her my book, took it out of its slipcase, opened it to a collaged page, weighted it down on a stool by the door, hugged her, and left.

We returned five hours later, and my book was still propped open as it had been. On the way out, MF picked it up, closed the book, and handed it to me without a word.

On MF's Death

Farewell a second time, old friend,
That was a dear friend
Till temper and a fine-tuned malice
Finished it.
No regrets for me.
For thee, I'll never know.

21

To WR — On Recording His Last Wishes

I may have my gifts,
   my loving gifts to you,
   returned when you are gone?
Surely you jest, old friend and lover,
   dying blind and joyless
While I sit here taking notes
   of your bequests,
   unregarded, passed on by!
O sweet revenge on you,
   now dead forever in my heart
   and yours.
Those loving gifts of mine,
   bequeathed so generously
   by you to me now
Are out of my life,
My sight, my mind.
Never, never, never
   to be seen or thought of,
   cossetted or desired.
No reminders ever
of those years you said you loved me
Gone, gone, gone.

                           9/16/96

*F*or all of us, Gene once remarked, fate has something surprising in store. It can be wonderful or terrible.

It can also be baffling.

For thirteen years, Ward Ritchie and I were lovers. He'd call every evening, promptly at 5 P.M. Every day we wrote one another.

Yes, he could be stingy and removed, yes, he had hurt me by not wanting to marry, but he could also be a good companion and inspiring teacher.

Oh, my. I knew the man for sixty-five years, but in the end, I had to wonder if I really knew him at all.

There were the little things. What was I to make of the fact that for the first year I went down there he kept his dead wife's clothes in the closet I was supposed to use — and that he kept her license plates on his car ("MARKA")? Or that, after many years, he turned in the little two-person settee in his study — where we sat and watched television together — for a huge one-man lounging chair? The room was so small, the only place left for me to sit was on a bridge chair jammed into a corner.

But *the big thing* was when I discovered one of his lady friends, a rich spinster entrepreneur in Newport Beach, was throwing a seventieth-birthday party for herself. I only found out about it because he said he couldn't come up and be with me that weekend, and told me why after I questioned him: I wasn't invited.

I asked, "You're going?" not believing he would in a million years! Ward said, "Yeah."

"It doesn't bother you that I'm not invited?" No answer. "It doesn't occur to you that after thirteen years of being together, I would *never* accept such an invitation?" No answer.

So I wrote him a really good letter. I mean I write *really* good letters. Scorchers!

The night of the party, I got high, called Gene (my son-in-law can also relish making mischief), and he and I had a ball on the phone, back and forth, inventing nasty things to say to the birthday girl. First we were going to send an airplane over her house, trailing a banner reading, "HAPPY BIRTHDAY! HAPPY 90TH!" Then a second one, "FUCK YOU, HENRIETTA!" Then we were going to send a funeral wreath, "With Sympathy." We also thought up some funky telephone calls.

I made one, and a female answered. I said, "This is Gloria. Is the Birthday Girl there?"

There was a long pause, and she said, "Yes."

I asked, "Who is this?" She answered with some unfamiliar name. "Oh," I said, "I want to congratulate her, if I may."

The phone was put down. Gene and I had planned a whole spaced-out dialogue, but she came back in a minute and said, "There are so many people — can't you hear them? — but she says thank you." I replied, "For what?" and hung up.

Then I thought, *now* I'm going to leave a message on Ward's machine, and tell him what I really think of him and his unacceptable behavior. So I dialed his phone, and I'm all ready to record, when I hear, "Hello?"

It was Ward. I thought, "Hmmm . . . he hasn't left for the party yet." So I hung up.

The dear Newport Beach Lady-in-Waiting-for-Ward Caper really gave me the shiv that weekend. Except I found out later that WR was too sick to go to her party. Pity! I thought

In the meantime he's got the letter.

The following Tuesday, I wrote in my diary, "WR called (1st time since last Sat!) 'Hi!' he said. He is not coming in for poker Sat. — He's 'lost 10 lbs.' and is more 'comfortable' there."

The ten pounds went by me, and I was rather relieved. I didn't feel like a big reconciliation jig.

The following Thursday, my grandson David drove me up to Idyllwild for our splendiferous family Thanksgiving with the Thompsons. Always in the past, Ward had joined us, but this year he said his stepson, Mark, and Mark's good-hearted Belgian wife, Laury, were going to be around, and he'd go over there. I talked to him after dinner, and he said he'd had a "little strenuous" Thanksgiving, but that he was feeling "better."

A week later, he said he'd be staying down at Emerald Bay instead of coming up for poker again as we had planned.

I was in the midst of printing one of my most important books. Christopher Isherwood and his lover, the portrait artist Don Bachardy, had been my friends for many years. Distinguished as a novelist (*Cabaret* was based on his *Berlin Stories*), playwright (in collaboration with W. H. Auden, then his lover), memoirist, and translator (the *Bhagavad-Gita,* with Swami Prabhavananda), I knew that, over the years, Chris had recorded hundreds of sayings, literary passages, observations, and poems. After Chris died, I asked Don if I could select about fifty of them and put them together in a book. The project — *Christopher Isherwood's Commonplace Book* — ultimately took two years to complete.

So! All right. Ward wasn't coming up. Fine. I was immersed in my work, and truly relished the lack of physical and spiritual interference!

The next day, the first of December, Ward called and told me he'd received two pints of blood the day before.

Sylvia called, too. She'd been talking with him. She said, "Ma, Ward is dying. You need to go down there."

I called Mark and Laury, and packed to go and stay for as long as Ward needed me. He was ninety and pancreatic cancer had overtaken him quickly.

When I arrived, Ward was very composed, quiet, and more or less housebound. He was really too weak to play cards, even double solitaire, but I read to him a bit, there was always TV, and he managed to dictate an article on his old friend Merle Armitage for *Matrix,* the Whittingdon's Press great annual book for bibliophiles.

So we kept occupied, but we both napped a lot. Ward very seldom complained, and as the weeks went by, he ate less and less, and indicated he wanted no visits from friends.

Twice I fell slightly apart, both times with huge hives from stress, and came home for shots and a day or two of healing solitude.

Early in December, I asked Ward to give Mark power of attorney. There were overdue bills and bank statements and business calls that concerned him. Ward agreed willingly. He dearly loved Mark and Laury. And should have. They were always wonderful to him.

We tried to gussie up Christmas for him — a little tree, stuffed stockings, a lovely dinner at the Detricks'. Lots of goodies — gingerbread men, Belgian chocolates, rum cakes, and we kept the carols singing. Ward's principal gift to Mark and Laury was a magnificent wood engraving by Paul Landacre, and to me, an exquisite miniature book designed and bound by Tini and Ewen Miura.

Just before Christmas, Mark said to me, "Gloria, does Ward have a will?"

I said, "I don't know."

He said, "Well, you know, there's a great deal of property there." *That* was a surprise! He'd been so miserly! "He should have a will. It's going to be really something, because of my mother's three boys, and his own two sons."

I said, "OK." So we went into Ward's study. I asked, "Ward, do you have a will?"

Ward said, "No."

I said, "Ward, you have to have a will. You can't leave all your properties in limbo. It'll be a mess for years."

He had Miró and Picasso graphics, some sculpture and rare pottery, lovely antique furniture — a magnificent desk, his valuable press.

No answer. I went on. "Ward, all those individual things you care about you should specially distribute, because your sons could have a hell of a fight. You don't want that."

After a moment, he said, "Well, write this down." So I got a pad and pencil and I'm sitting there, and he started.

"To my boys, I would like them to share equitably . . ." et cetera, et cetera . . . finishing with ". . . and Gloria Stuart can have back her paintings that she gave me."

He asked me to read it, I did, and he signed it. I gave it to Mark.

I called Sam Barnes, his lawyer and one of his best friends. Sam came over and they made an official will of Ward's properties and holdings.

In the meantime, I had said, "Ward, what are you going to do with your books? They should be in a collection. UC Berkeley, UCLA, Occidental College, wherever."

He hesitated. I think the finality of the end of his life — and the disposition of his library — had not truly been considered by Ritchie up till then. He said very slowly, "I'll sell them and give the money to the boys."

I answered, "You won't get a nickel for them, Ward. You have books worth ten to fifteen thousand dollars each. You've collected them all your life and you should leave them in toto to a college or library as the Ward Ritchie Collection."

Again, he very slowly answered, "Well, all right."

I called Larry Powell. I called Peter Reilly, the head of UCLA's Clark Library, and the head of the Huntington Library, David Zeidberg, and a lot more people. My message was, "Ward wants to sell his books. For God sakes, come down right away, have lunch, tell Ward he shouldn't — please come!"

Two days after Christmas, Larry Powell and the heads of all these libraries arrived. We had lunch, but Ward, on morphine, was too ill to join us. He agreed that his library should go to the Clark. OK, I did that, too, for the old boy.

Standing with me in Ward's bedroom, Larry cried on my shoulder. Ward and Larry had gone from grammar school through college together. "I love that guy. He's like my brother —" I was too distraught to flash back to the wonderful days when Gordon and I first came down from Carmel, and I was in film, and MF and Larry and Ward and I were together all the time, playing. But I sometimes think of them now. Regretfully.

A few days later, after lunch, just the two of us, WR said to me, "Would you like the paper in the basement?"

I said, "Yes, Ward, I really would." So the next day Mark helped me pick up the reams of paper from the basement floor — a lot of them water- and moisture-stained — odds and ends WR had bought and used and stored over forty years for his printing. We put them in my car.

Now to *l'affaire* T-Bird. Ward had the classic T-Bird with port-hole windows. It had been sitting in his garage since the early fifties. He'd only driven it, oh, maybe once a month to keep the battery going. I had said to him years before, "You're not using it, Ward, I would love it." In the fifties, I had had a T-Bird with port-hole windows, too, but I sold it because we were hard up, and Arthur wasn't a good driver anyway. Ward would always answer with some variation of "I'm using it" or "You can't afford it" or "It wouldn't last two minutes where you live." I'd always answer, "Ward, I told you. I'll build an extra garage for it. . . ." It got to be kind of a running gag! "Oh, sell me the T-Bird, I'll pay you for it . . . I'll give you twenty thousand dollars now . . . come on, Wardela, you've stopped driving it . . . please!" To any car buff, the classic T-Bird is a dream come true. Ward's was baby blue and needed a lot of work. I mean, a *lot* of work!

About two weeks into January, we're having dinner with Mark and Laury, and Mark said something to Ward about his other car, the red Camaro. Himself just shrugged.

I said, "Come on, Ward, sell me the T-Bird, it's not going to cost you a nickel. Please let me have the T-Bird now, and my twenty-thousand-dollar offer still holds."

He reached down into his pocket, took something out, and handed it to Laury. Keys for both cars.

That night I broke out in hives again. I couldn't sleep, I was so miserable and hurt. I had to come up to Los Angeles to see my dermatologist, then I went to bed for three days.

While I was home, I got a note from Ward. I kept it on the re-
frigerator (where I'd put up most of his daily notes) for a long time.

> You are an angel, and I love you.
>
> Ward

Do you get it? I don't.

Ward had two other stepsons and two natural sons. They loved
each other dearly. The phone calls! The letters! Ward was
swamped with loving messages over the holidays. And about the
twentieth of January, one of his stepsons came down for a day from
San Francisco, sat and held his hand and cried all afternoon. So
touching.

Ward was barely speaking by then, so occupied was he with the
realization that his good life was about over. Long ago he had written:

> The World began
> When I was born
> And will end
> When I am gone.
> The sun, the sky,
> The night, the day
> Will cease to be
> Along with me

At 10:15 P.M., January 24, 1996, Mark and Laury and I opened a
bottle of Mumm's and gave the dear boy a loving farewell. By the
time the Neptune Society* men arrived, it was dawn.

I was fully packed — I had taken down the ruby and crystal
stained-glass "LOVE" plaque that I had given Ward. It stands for
something in my life, I'm not sure what, but I'm working on it —

---

*Prearranges cremation and the scattering of one's ashes at sea.

and immediately drove out of Emerald Bay, never to go there again! Never.

Ward was revered. People thought he was just the most wonderful man. I have had letters from every book organization in this country and in England, France, Belgium, Czechoslovakia, saying what a wonderful man Ward was.

And I received a dear letter from his first wife, Janet.

Why did he trash me? Was it just because of the Birthday Party letter? Why did I stand still for his minginess all those years?

How could I have finished two loving poems about our affair as he lay dying?

Was it just momentum from the past years together, a sudden surge of emotion? — here I was adrift again at eighty-five — or just my tidying up so many hopes and disappointments?

This is why.

All those years Ward and I were together, he had shared with me his expertise in the printers' world. Given me a whole new life in art. Introduced me to many still dear and talented friends in that world, and in the all-embracing world of bibliophiles. I treasure them and thank Wardela for them!

So! I could write those poems and privately print them for our friends. I printed the poems for the traditional Zamorano-Roxburghe Literary Societies' annual conclave as keepsakes — with style and beauty.

And an emptiness of emotion.

I was home. After two days of a jillion phone calls, I began to straighten up my studio, throw out accumulated mail, stack drawings and mock-ups for my Isherwood/Bachardy book, have friends over for dinner, write a new haiku about spring, and really begin to look forward to my future, now beholden to no one. In time, I gave away or sold every book, broadside, memento, gift attached to Ritchie's and my relationship.

Back on track.

My track!

Out of my life, Ritchie!

Parentheses. A few weeks later, I received a small black leather book, Ward's handwritten copies of the poems we had exchanged over the years, from Larry Powell. Larry had asked Ward for it, thinking to publish some of the poems. There was an enclosure.

2-6-96

Dearest Gloria,

Poems herewith. Lovely suite of deep tenderness. You both were blessed. He will be in you for the rest of your life — and beyond in the world's heart. Do put them at the Clark which will ensure their survival. . . .

Love,
Larry

I quote two from the book:

Love is my life
And you are my love.
Down the long years
I have hoped
You'd come to me.
And that has come to be.
You are my love
And your love is my life.

WR, 6/21/83

My lover's left me tingling
My lover's left me mingling
In my dingling head
All my loving fantasies.
So, singling out their ecstasies,

Each and every one,
I shall the next time find
Neglected, no! Not one!

GS, 9/11/83

*   *   *

I carry on as best as I can. I turned *l'affaire* Ritchie into a positive lesson. That's how I operate. It's all about choices. I choose not to brood about Himself.

I have done the same thing with my breast cancer.

Just after New Year's in 1984 — less than a year after Ward had come into my life — my gynecologist found a lump in my breast. He aspirated it, the lab said it was "probably cancerous," so I went to see his surgeon. I didn't like the man — what he wanted to do seemed to be very complicated. I decided I'd better get a second opinion. Rex Kennamer recommended Mitchell Karlan, a brilliant surgeon with considerable breast cancer experience. I liked him instantly. He said in my case he could do either a lumpectomy or mastectomy, then added, "Let's do it simply to start with. Then if it reoccurs, we'll do a mastectomy." Fifteen years ago, a lumpectomy was not generally done, but he said he had had great success with it.

I went through the whole breast cancer episode with very little pain. Certainly with complete secrecy. Sylvia had a deadline on a book, and was frantic. Ward had had years of nursing Marka through lung cancer, our romance was still new, and I didn't want him to face the prospect of going through another cancer episode with *me*. So my grandson Benjamin, who took me to the hospital, was the only one in my confidence.

Of course Sylvia and Gene were very upset when I phoned them the day after the surgery. They wanted to come down immediately, but I made them promise not to come. Besides, I told them, there was nothing they could do.

I had the surgery on a Wednesday. The liver and bone scans were OK, so Benjy took me home that Saturday.

It was Super Bowl Sunday the next day, and Ward had told me he was planning to stay down in Emerald Bay to watch the game with friends. Fine! Perfect! As a matter of fact, for twelve years, he didn't know I'd had breast cancer — I only let him see me naked in the dark! And mostly, when draped in yards of diaphanous chiffon. Besides, the difference in size between breasts was negligible. I forget why I finally told him.

None of my friends guessed anything had happened to me until very many years later. One sharp lady asked me how much my surgery had cost, and when I told her, she said, "That wasn't just a small operation. That was either a mastectomy or a lumpectomy."

From the moment of diagnosis, I had complete faith I would be fine. And for that reason, it was never a big deal. But I know I was lucky. And thanks to Dr. Karlan's skill, the lumpectomy plus radiation worked.

But something happened about ten years after that that was a big deal and *did* upset me.

On a Sunday morning in June, I went out to pick up my paper.

Directly across the street were several police cars, a bunch of police, citizens, and cameramen.

"What's happened?" I asked my next-door neighbor, who was also kibitzing.

"It's a car-jacking, I think."

"In our neighborhood? Oh no, *please!*"

It wasn't. The bodies of O. J. Simpson's ex-wife and her friend, murdered earlier, had already been removed.

From that moment on, chaos!

Helicopters overhead, tourist buses, police reporters, TV trucks outside my door — all by the dozens for weeks and weeks and weeks.

When Judge Ito was to visit the site with the jurors, all of us neighbors were instructed — *ordered* — to stay indoors during their tour.

I came down my walk and two LAPD officers came up my steps and one said, "Go back in your house, Mrs. Sheekman."

Both were body to body with me.

I answered, "This is my property and you are trespassing and I will not go back in my house!"

"Go back in your house, Mrs. Sheekman."

"I'm going to get a lawyer and sue you!"

"You do that, Mrs. Sheekman. But in the meantime, go back in your house."

Suing would have cost me a fortune. Besides, I contribute to the police's fraternal fund, and I need, and generally admire, them.

But (expletive deleted) Judge Ito!

However, what really got to me — and it lasted almost three years — was the constant stream of families with little children enthusiastically pointing out where the bodies had lain. Day and night.

Incredible!

On a jollier note, I am a devout believer in fortune cookies. In my diary, February 12, 1996, two and a half weeks after Ritchie's death, one Chinese dinner later, three fortune cookie slips read:

The joy of a young person will be shared by you and you will make great gains in any project you undertake.

Have patience. It will benefit you.

You will spend old age in comfort and material wealth.

I will?
It's now, Stupid.

22

I never answer the phone when I'm printing in my studio. So early one spring evening — May Day, 1996 — I finished work, and, on my way into the house, checked the bonsais in the patio for dryness, dragged myself into the kitchen (hand printing is tedious, persnickety, and tiring work), and turned on my answering machine.

The first message was too fast and sounded garbled. A female voice said she was calling from Lightstorm Entertainment (what's that? I thought) about a movie to be shot on location, maybe Poland (I thought, why Poland? Why not Italy or France?), about the *Titanic,* directed by James Cameron (who is he?).

Was I interested?

Well, my agent had quit and decamped to Florida six years before, leaving me with no representation. I was very happy working as a book artist, but the word "location" hooked me. I had never been to Poland — maybe I could drop by London and Paris going and coming? And maybe the role was a good one!

The recording needed interpreting, so I called my best Hollywood resource, casting agent par excellence, Marvin Paige. He has encyclopedic knowledge of Hollywood, its ways and means, and where the bodies are buried. He came over immediately, listened to the message, and got very excited. He said Lightstorm was a first-rate company and James Cameron was one of the hottest directors in town — *The Terminator, Terminator 2, The Abyss, True Lies* — and that *Titanic* was going to be a big important movie.

Marvin said, "Call her back!"

So I did, and she introduced herself as Mali Finn, casting director. She said if I was interested, could she interview me the next day? Marvin nodded yes! So I agreed.

Early the next afternoon, Mali arrived with her assistant, Emily Schweber, who was carrying a video camera. I'd never seen one. We sat in my bar, and Mali and I talked while Emily filmed us. An hour or so later, having heard my past history of no work for six years and thirty-three years of intermittent acting, they thanked me and left.

The offices of Lightstorm Entertainment Studio are twenty minutes away, in Santa Monica. About an hour later — around four o'clock — Mali called. "Can I send a script over?" That meant to me that Mr. Cameron had seen the video. I agreed and half an hour later it arrived by messenger (the first of dozens of Mercurys that would eventually fly to my door as a result of that script).

Now actors read scripts — at least I did and do — first looking just for their speeches, without regard to the play itself — how many lines, scenes, how important, how interesting.

Old Rose in the *Titanic* script grabbed me instantly — her introduction, her voice-overs, her scenes. I knew that evening the role I had wanted and waited for all these many years had arrived!

As I was starting to read the script itself, Mali called and said the director, James Cameron, wanted to know if I would read for him the next day. By this time, I could *taste* the role of Old Rose!

It had been so many years.

I had put on my makeup and fussed with my hair (always a disaster area) when Mali had come, but she called back a second time and said, "Mr. Cameron wonders if you would read for him without makeup." I was told later he wondered if I could look 101, being not quite 86! I started to say, "I'll read for him without clothes on, if he wants me to," but I didn't know Mali that well, or James at all, so I just said, "Yes, of course."

I barely slept that night, reading and rereading Old Rose aloud, and digesting that wonderful script.

The next morning, I put on a little white cap that completely covered my blond hair, powdered my face a little, no lipstick, no mascara, had my usual breakfast — such control! only one cup of coffee! — and leafed through the *Titanic* script for the sixth time.

Mali and Cameron arrived at ten, and lo and behold, *he* was carrying a video camera. He was very soft-spoken, a man with grace and charm. I adored him instantly.

We sat down. Mali was to read with me while he recorded. I was not the least bit nervous. I knew I would read Old Rose with the sympathy and tenderness that Cameron had intended when he wrote the beautiful script.

I knew it I knew it I knew it.

We started to read, and Cameron never stopped me until I had finished the speech: "Fifteen hundred people went into the sea when *Titanic* sunk from under us. There were twenty boats floating nearby, and only one came back. One. Six were saved from the water, myself included, six out of fifteen hundred."

"You sound angry," he said.

I was so surprised. I thought the speech was to be read with indignation. "I'm sorry," I said. "The whole thing was awful, unacceptable."

He interrupted. "Well, if that's the way you feel — fine."

I replied, "How would you like me to read it? Without anger, just regret? How?"

"No! No!" he said. "That was fine."

We finished the reading, and, wanting to impress him (I wasn't just an *actress!*), I asked if they would like to see my studio. Seeing my paintings in the living room and bar, he had already commented on my being an artist, so I wanted him to see my books — my print shop.

He responded with generous words about my type collection, printing press, books. Noticed my bonsais. Thanked me. And left.

I immediately called Sylvia and Gene and, I think, crowed a lot. A *lot!* I was beside myself with a feeling of triumph — at long last! I had several glasses of champagne. Before noon!

I wanted my screenwriter friends to read the script and confirm my opinion of it — so I called Fay Kanin, Julie Epstein, and Nat Perrin and asked them to read it. I schlepped it around. When they called, all agreed it was a first-rate script, and their enthusiasm for me as Old Rose was overwhelming.

That enthusiasm spread like wildfire among my family and friends. The telephone never stopped ringing. I was dream-borne with hopes and doubts, and, often, slightly tearful.

Later, Mali told me that Cameron had said on the way out to their car that day, "Nice going, Mali." And, again, much later, "That was a fantastic reading." I also learned that he had seen the laser disc I recorded on James Whale's *The Old Dark House,* which received top-notch notices worldwide. I seemed to fit his casting idea of an actress from the thirties — not too recognizable under a 101-year-old's makeup (as, for example, Katharine Hepburn would be) — who could still remember lines, stand up straight, wasn't an alcoholic, hadn't had a facelift, and liked to travel!

Several days later, I left for London. I had planned to go to the Victoria and Albert Museum's celebration of the artist-printer William Morris's one hundreth birthday anniversary. John Dreyfus had managed an invitation to the opening for me, complete with Princess Alexandra's patronage (she's daughter of the Duke and Duchess of Kent). The museum has several of my artist's books in its special collections — one copy of Robinson Jeffers' *Inscriptions at Tor House,* two of *Christopher Isherwood's Commonplace Book,* and one of my erotica, *Eve-Venus.* I wanted to visit my books and talk to the librarian. Plus see my other dear friends in the printer's and artist's worlds.

After the initial shock of being asked to read for a film role, I now decided that I should touch base with the devoted fans of James Whale in England. He is a cult figure there, deservedly so (have you seen *Gods and Monsters?*). Arriving in London, I was not quite *besieged* with members of his fan club or BBC interviewers, but I was welcomed cordially by many of them. I certainly was happy to be back in motion picture mode.

Still, niggling questions pervaded my waking hours: Do I get the part or don't I? Why doesn't Mali call me? Or Marvin? Has it been announced? So, after a week, I called my dear friend Ann Epstein, who reads *Variety.* "No," she said, "it hasn't been." Several days later: "No, I haven't seen it."

I finally called the *Hollywood Reporter* and *Variety.* "Has it been announced?" Not that they knew. It wouldn't have been politic for me to call Mali or Cameron. I was walking barefoot on hot coals, and trying to smile.

I felt Old Rose was my last chance to finally prove I could be a first-rank actress. Why was he taking so long to announce his choice? What could I do to prove my worth? Go home, Gloria. Now! And find a way to reach him.

So, after the Morris celebration and tea at the Ritz with my dear friend Leda Lopez Kindersley, one of England's finest stonecutters and glass engravers, a dazzling week in Kent with Nina and Graham Williams, buying one of his mesmerizing mobiles, I finally cut the month's stay short and flew home.

In the weeks that followed, I worked on the design for Don Bachardy's book — the one I planned to do next — *The Portrait,* gave a dinner party for ten of my dear friends, celebrated Sylvia's and Gene's birthdays up the mountain in Idyllwild, and had my Fourth of July birthday weekend with a barbecue for twelve.

I wrote several poems full of bitterness and trenchant resolve. About Ward. About my future. Having read that Kate Winslet and Leonardo DiCaprio had been cast in *Titanic,* I checked out

Winslet's notices for *Hamlet* and *Jude* (excellent), and looked up DiCaprio's films and notices. But waking sleeping working playing I never stopped hoping for *Titanic* and Old Rose. Was it not going to happen? This one chance to prove myself?

Finally, Tuesday July 1, I wrote James Cameron.

Dear Mr. Cameron,

I just wanted you to know that I have aged fifteen years (eighty-six to one hundred one) since last we met. My wrinkles, my balding pate, my not quite fully opened eyes, the quavers in my voice — all — are looking very old.

I also feel, re: studying the wonderful script, that Old Rose should have been read feistery-er because Young Rose is just that!

Most truly and sincerely,

G. Stuart

I took it to my post office, this handwritten small note, and said to the clerk, "Priority — the big one." He tried to sell me the letter size, but I insisted. "Big — I don't want it to get lost on his desk."

July 2, 3, 4, 5, 6, 7, 8 went by. On the morning of Tuesday, the ninth, my astrological forecast said that I would become "a universal figure," that my dearest dream would come true "in dramatic fashion."

Mali called. "Gloria, how would you like to be Old Rose?"

I answered, "Really? Truly? He wants me? Really? Truly?"

"Really, truly, Gloria!"

I interrupted her. "Oh, my God, it's everything I ever wanted — it's everything I've ever dreamed about — oh, Mali —!" Then, the Scot in me took over. I thought a second, and asked, "How much?"

Instant reply was "Ten thousand dollars a week, three and a half weeks' guarantee."

My last salary at Twentieth Century–Fox had been fifteen hundred a week (twenty thousand or so in today's dollars). Somehow, without choking, I asked, "What about billing?" I had not been in a position even to *ask* that question for thirty-three years.

"You will get a separate card."

The truth is, at that moment, if she had said, "I don't know" or "We'll see," it wouldn't have made any difference. I had Old Rose and I was going to keep her!

I called everybody, my family, my friends, my housekeeper, my masseuse, my hairdresser, everyone! Friends called friends, flowers and baskets of champagne and all sorts of treats arrived. Love was everywhere! So I went to my beauty parlor (salon is a recent noun in my vocabulary) and had The Works.

Thursday morning at 8:45, July 11, my first limo arrived.

Now you have to understand I had never had the limousine treatment. Six years before, at the age of seventy-eight, I had driven myself to whatever studio I was shooting at, carried my own paraphernalia, sat in a canvas chair on the set — not in a trailer or mobile dressing room — had no production assistant to get me Cokes, a phone, a magazine, whatever. Of course, I had had a taste of stardom, long ago, back in the thirties, of having a maid when I filmed. (*I* had to hire her, not the stingy studios.) She lit my cigarettes, brought me coffee, lunch when I had lunch in my dressing room. She would call the wardrobe girl to get me pressed if I needed it, or needed mending. She called the hairdresser's attention, if the hairdresser wasn't paying attention. She checked my makeup. Ran errands for me. Came home with me if I needed her. Helped me there. But I drove myself. This personal verbal attention — was I comfortable, did I need, or want, anything? — was so welcome, so what I had dreamed of, tears were very frequent and equally frequently suppressed.

First, the limo took me to a doctor's office in Beverly Hills. The doctor had been hired by the studio to give me a physical checkup for insurance purposes. I passed.

Next I was driven to a studio out in the Valley to meet the film's costume designer, Deborah Scott, and have my measurements taken. She was charming, and seemed pleased with my old bod! At least it wasn't all over the landscape — a bit bulgy here and there, but still a size twelve!

I think women in Hollywood, *all* women, regardless of age and status, take care of themselves. Or maybe it's Southern California.

But, with the gorgeous girls flooding the landscape, it behooves us to Watch It!

In more ways than one!

I was introduced to the British wig maker Simon Thompson. He took measurements for my white wig, saying he would be leaving for London with them that night! I understand the wig he created cost a couple of thousand dollars. Real hair was used, woven strand by strand into what they call hair lace. The hair was down my back, about twelve inches long, done up into a bun for all my scenes but the last.

Friday morning, the twelfth, the limo arrived to take me out to Valencia in the San Fernando Valley, to Greg Cannom's studio. Greg's makeup credits included five Academy Award nominations and two awards — one for creating Mrs. Doubtfire, the other for Dracula. Greg is a big man, tall, strawberry blond, young-middle-aged. He put me in a barber's chair.

He barely responded to my cheery, "Just make me look one hundred and one. . . . I have no vanity about any of this. . . . Do your darnedest. . . ."

He worked quickly and quietly, using liquid latex, applied wet. He told me to screw up my face, and blew a warm hair dryer on me. I unscrewed my face, and lo and behold! Dozens of wrinkles, puffs, bags, lines. After painting on age spots and accentuating the wrinkles and lines with brown watercolor, Greg photographed me and sent me on my way. He was very solemn, withdrawn, uncommunicative — not at all the jolly, witty, generous companion I would later have in Halifax!

I had asked Mali if I could see Kate Winslet's screen test, to become familiar with her body language and line reading. And, as long as I was playing her later in life, it seemed important to me that we meet. She had arrived in town the day before.

That Friday afternoon, also wanting to meet me, Kate arrived for tea. Sylvia had sent me to the English bakery in Santa Monica for scones and I had set up an elaborate tea in my bar. As Kate started up my front path, I opened the door and met her halfway down the walk, arms wide open. We embraced with instant rapport. I said, "You must be tired. I have a wonderful tea for you."

I had put on a blouse and one of my loveliest long skirts, earrings, rings. Kate arrived in a studio limo, in very casual shirt and shorts.

I know this is the way the young women of her generation dress, simple, easy, inelegant. Most of them don't seem to care, and certainly don't know, the luxurious contented feeling of fineness in apparel.

Too bad.

I think.

She replied, "Oh, I'd love a *drink* —"

Don Bachardy had given me Cristal champagne for my Fourth of July birthday, it was in the fridge, so I said, "I have a bottle on ice."

We had just sat down in the bar and toasted each other when the doorbell rang. It was two men, one holding a video camera, the other a huge bouquet of long-stemmed red roses.

"Who is it you want to see?" Poor men. Garbled response. I exclaimed to them, "Oh, you must have the wrong house!" They just stood there. "Oh! All right! Come on in — I'm just kidding!" Groucho training.

Lightstorm had sent them over to record us. James Cameron wanted a complete record of EVERYTHING that occurred to EVERYBODY during the making of *Titanic*. They stood in a corner of my bar and Kate and I began to talk — of our families, our beginnings, where we were at the moment. Kate was very forthcoming. She said her family had been in the theater for several generations, that she had started very early on and was the only member to be so hugely successful. She was very modest, exceptionally so. We killed the bottle of champagne easily and happily, embraced each other, and said good-bye.

Saturday, I played poker with my friends. Gloria had finally landed a worthwhile role! "Well, it's about time," the group chimed. I lost $6.60 — a very big amount for our game. I chided the group, they should have let me win!

Monday, July 15, I had wardrobe fittings with Deborah Scott. She told me Cameron wanted Old Rose to have a Beatrice Wood look. Beatrice Wood was an extraordinary California potter — an original in every sense. She was now 104 and still working in her studio up in the Ojai Valley near Santa Barbara — where I had visited her in the sixties.

I had identified with Beato for many years even before then. In her teens, she left her comfortable New York home to study acting and drawing in Paris and live the bohemian life. When she returned as a young woman, she was drawn to the Dada movement — artists and writers celebrating nihilism, the spontaneous, and the shocking. Artist Marcel Duchamp and writer Henri-Pierre Roche became her lovers, and she was known as "The Mama of Dada." Like me, she loved rural California, and in 1948, moved her studio from Los Angles to Ojai.

Deborah showed me about two dozen caftans and djellabas and tons of silver and bronze jewelry — elaborate, heavy necklaces, rings, and earrings — she had collected in the Wood style, waiting for Cameron to approve them.

He was very late showing up. He put his hand out and said to me, "Welcome aboard," then turned to Deborah, "Let's see what you've got." He turned down everything not quite Beato. Eventually, I ended up in marvelously patterned, flowing embroidered robes and jackets, and lots of British Indian and American Indian jewelry.

Finally, it was time! At 6:30 A.M. Wednesday the seventeenth, the limo picked me up to take me to the airport.

Poland was out. The present-day story was to be filmed in Halifax, Nova Scotia, then the 1912 story would be shot in Baja California, Mexico.

The Russian scientific ship *Keldysh* we were to shoot on was in Canadian waters. It was one of only two Russian scientific ships equipped with those wondrous spheres able to descend so many hundreds of feet into the sea. James had taken half a dozen trips down to the *Titanic* in one, photographing, charting distances, exploring its remains, knowing that one pinprick, one tiny scrape, and the occupants were fish food. How brave can one be? Or reckless? Insouciant?

(I never did discover, and truly forgot to inquire, why there were three women on the *Keldysh*. They didn't wear uniforms — but then, neither did the crew.)

I flew to Toronto. There, James Cameron, the actor Bill Paxton, who played the fortune hunter, Mr. Lovett, and I boarded together to fly to Halifax. Bill and James are old friends. Bill has worked with Cameron on several classics — *The Terminator, Aliens, True Lies,* and *Apollo 13* (although uncredited, James was a visual consultant on the latter).

During the flight, Cameron moved out of his seat next to me, saying, "I'm so tired. I'm going to sleep. Bill! Come over here and talk to Miss Stuart."

Bill Paxton moved over, and, as my mother had always advised me on meeting a new man, I said, "Tell me about yourself." Bill is a charmer and a fun conversationalist, and so he went on and on very happily.

Finally, Jim woke up and leaned over the aisle, saying something like, "That's a lot of conversation."

Bill stopped quickly, asking me, "Am I boring you?"

"No! No!" I reassured Bill Paxton. "I *love* bores!"

Both men laughed.

It was an auspicious — wonderful! — beginning.

23

Arriving in Halifax, I was given a beautiful suite over-looking the bay at the Sheraton Hotel, although the bay view was not interesting — bordered by low-rise, colorless buildings against a bland, gray-blue sky. No ships, no seabirds, a few tugs and barges, maybe. I had visited Halifax years before in a whale-watching trip to the North Atlantic and had loved the lonely, rather desolate tiny Peggy's Cove north of there. (Unhappily, when the Swissair plane went down, Peggy's Cove was where the rescue operation began.) Its residents have a delightful and, I think, unique custom of hanging carved wooden butterflies above or on their front doors. I have one.

The next day, I sauntered a bit on the boardwalk, bought flowers for my room, studied my script, and napped a lot.

The next morning, my makeup artist, Greg Cannom, and English hairdresser, Ann Townsend, did me up. I put on my first wardrobe change — for arriving in the helicopter — and Mr. Cameron approved.

I didn't know, hadn't yet heard of, Cameron's reputation for explosive behavior on the set. Even if I had, this reserved, gallantly polite man belied it. Not possible. A flagrant falsehood. Spread by someone or somebodies vilely jealous, envious of an artistic genius.

An artistic genius who's also a perfectionist.

It took Deborah Scott three tries for just *my* small wardrobe — heavy patterned fabrics, loose tentlike dresses and jackets, clunky silver necklaces, rings, bracelets, pins, earrings — before Mr. Cameron saw what he wanted. Imagine her task for all the other principals!

And, it is true, on the *Titanic* set in Nova Scotia, as Mr. Cameron entered each day, I had the feeling he had four pairs of eyes — front, back, left, right. Our director would look around, carefully inspect all the photographs, dinner or tea settings, sofa pillows, paintings on the wall, bric-a-brac — whatever — and usually carefully rearrange things to suit *his* taste. Nothing seemed to escape him. Props, set colors, ambience, details, size, furnishings, actors.

We all — even Paxton and Lewis Abernathy, longtime pals — snapped to attention.

He is that kind of force.

That afternoon we had our first cast rehearsal, sitting around a long table. I met "my granddaughter," Suzy Amis, beautiful, soft-voiced, and very laid back; full-bearded, raucous, and adorable Lewis Abernathy; Nicholas Cascone, the Paxton character's backer; the captain of the Russian ship, *Keldysh;* even the yippy-yappy little Pomeranian dog playing my pet, Freddie. The last two characters had nothing to say.

I had *never* had this experience. I had always either received the script at the beginning of filming and only performed without prior rehearsals, or was handed my lines as I came on the set.

The reading went well. James seldom interrupted, smiled at the few light, bright character remarks, and seemed completely satisfied with our various readings.

The reading surprised me — so low key!

This rehearsal reminded me of the theater — where I wasn't, had always wanted to be, and probably never would be — but it was kudos enough, to be in His Presence, with His Company, and Old Rose. The difference with this reading and one for the theater is there was no need for voice or body projection.

The next night our director gave a lively dinner party for the cast, two Russian scientists, and the captain and his wife. Lots of vodka and toasts and wonderful Nova Scotia seafood.

You don't expect a director to play host, but I found James Cameron a host par excellence, and also a man of winning presence, with his soft voice and gentle manner — at least, with women. I sassed him a few times. He would react with a loud chortle, and then sass me back. (I really never heard anyone sass James. Maybe my age helped.) *Va bene.*

On the set, he only corrected me twice. Once, when my granddaughter wanted me to go back to the room, my "No!" wasn't strong enough for him, so we fixed that. The other time, during my dressing-down of the Lewis Abernathy character, James called out from his position behind the video monitor, "Gloria, you're being *grand.*" That fixed that!

James Cameron knows what he wants, and, unlike most directors, tells you *how* he wants it. There's none of this useless shilly-shallying — "We-ell, let's try it another way. . . ."

But he is also amenable to change, and surprisingly open to suggestions. Originally, Old Rose, on seeing once again the nude-with-diamond portrait, was to say: "Wasn't I a hot number?" But I felt that was not right — not in character, in period, in taste. I told Cameron so, and he instantly asked, "What would you like to say?" I said I'd need to think about it. "Be my guest" was his reply.

So many times I've been asked, "Is Cameron as tough as we've heard?" Or, "Is Cameron a loose cannon on the set?"

Titanic was the toughest technical test and achievement one could possibly imagine! And Cameron hires only the best technicians he can find. So, obviously, if something technical goes wrong, and seems insoluble, he may "flip."

He only did once while I was filming. In the scene where I go over to see the five moving videos of the sunken ship, I react with tears. The videos fell out of synchronization. Jim sat quietly for a while, then started pacing, then left the set.

Then, yes! There was a lot of brouhaha coming from way over backstage. Sounded like Himself. He/they finally got it right about two hours later.

I can't imagine the approach he would have with a recalcitrant or inept *actor*. On the other hand, thinking about it further, yes, I can!

I quickly realized that I was going to have a lot of close-ups, because I heard from Greg that James wanted my eyes left alone, not aged. He wanted to "morph" them into Kate's eyes. "What the hell is *that?*" I wondered. I learned that to "morph" is to do a dissolve — blend one shot into another.

I began to worry about my close-ups to come.

Would I blow it?

Would I be able to "connect" with the lens?

Lines during a close-up require such precision — not like a small, unnoticeable fluff in a group scene — that the prospect of BIG close-ups can be nervous-making, even harrowing. Being vain, I didn't worry about how I photographed, just how to be perfect — how to read a line and not blink, how to avoid a "stare" (static), how to project a lively presence *and* the appropriate emotion.

There is nothing so humiliating to an actor, certainly to me — proud of my infallible memory — as to forget one's lines during actual filming. The whole shebang stops cold. It involves the whole company — cast, director, assistants, camera, sound, props, crew, even, I suspect, the food mavens standing by! You feel like an idiot — apologetic — done in.

Well! The first time Jim said, "This is going to be a close-up, Gloria," I looked at the camera and it was "in my face" — six inches away. I'd never had a close-up like this in my whole professional life! I'd never had a close-up that filled the screen only with my eyes. I wished I'd had a chance to practice with the camera, but I told myself, Gloria, this is part of the technique you've learned. This is what you've always wanted. The ultimate exposure. The ultimate showcase of who you are, what you are.

And so I relaxed and welcomed it. With the camera in my face, I confirmed — at last! — that I'm an effective actress. That I can communicate to an audience what an author means, what he has hoped to communicate.

I was euphoric. It was so satisfying.

For so long I had beaten myself up — thought that, as far as the camera was concerned, I couldn't do this, couldn't do that. What Arthur had thrown at me — that I had no talent — had hardened inside as certainty. I had come to believe him, just as my mother had come to believe that she had been "a mistake."

But I COULD communicate with the camera!

And I knew my character — I knew Old Rose. In a flash one day, I knew what she would say for the "hot number" line: "Wasn't I a dish?"

Something else I knew: My first exterior scene was stepping out of a helicopter onto the deck of the *Keldysh*. But when Cameron told me I'd be in the helicopter when it landed on the ship way out at sea, I said I wouldn't do it. I believe that someday, they'll find out the whole flying principle is faulty and all the helicopters and planes will fall down! And I didn't want to be in one at that time. Of course, they said it couldn't happen, the craft was perfectly safe, I'd enjoy it, yatata yatata. I repeated, I wouldn't do it — land on a postage stamp–sized deck in the middle of the North Atlantic. No way!

The compromise was, I flew in a helicopter, all right — Cameron assured me it was the largest Sikorsky ever, with the most experienced pilot, very safe. I flew in the helicopter to and over the ship — being photographed from another helicopter flying tandem. But I didn't *land* on the ship. I returned to shore. Filming the next day, once the helicopter (without me in it) landed on the deck, filming stopped, I was hoisted into the helicopter from the ship's deck with all my paraphernalia. Then the camera rolled again, and I was unloaded with trunks, dog, fishbowl, and wheelchair. Diddleleedeeee! Who won? Who's counting?

The hours of filming were quixotic, to say the least. Not only did they have to depend on the camera and sound setups involving scientific shenanigans. But on the weather. We were blessed with truly almost perfect weather. No fogs, a few minutes of rain. The *Keldysh* always sailed twenty-odd miles out to sea in order to lose Halifax's silhouette against the daylight horizon, as well as its city lights when we shot on the open decks at night.

Some days I had breakfast in my room at 4 P.M., Malva, my production assistant (PA for short) picked me up at 5 P.M., off to the ship or the soundstage across the bay, makeup, my wig, and wardrobe, then on to the set. Sixteen hours later, back to the hotel. Some days I would start at 6:30 A.M. and finish by noon; next day on the set at 7 P.M., back in the hotel at 4 A.M.; no work for two days; the next day's call at 4:30 P.M., working until 8 A.M. the next morning, then sleeping all that day. . . .

Although the long shots of my walk across the dark deck were done at sea — on the *Keldysh* — close-ups were done on the soundstage in Halifax. No night breezes, rolling deck, or seabird cries to contend with.

Sunday, July 28, Cameron ran rushes for us of the few scenes we'd shot! My entrance *à l'hélicoptère,* the scenes watching the videos of the *Titanic* wreck — and a lot of the crew's deck action. We actors, production assistants, crew, all cheered — each scene seemed near perfect. At least, I felt that, especially about myself! Old Rose lived!

What a difference from my dailies at Universal and all the other studios in the thirties! Back then, watching my usually banal roles with mediocre production values from most of my directors and producers, my heart would sink, my dreams would shrivel. But up there in Nova Scotia, I was elated!

I've been asked many times: "Did you know *Titanic* was going to be the great success it is?" "Did you know you'd get an Academy Award nomination?" "Did you know the movie would gross over a billion dollars?"

Of course I didn't know all that. But I did know, for myself, I was giving a fine performance. And that *Titanic had* to be a classic — this Renaissance man, scientist, artist, author, director, editor, producer, had created it all.

You might think my saying this is a bit much. But since *The Birth of a Nation* (made in 1915 and considered the movies' first epic), when D. W. Griffith wrote the script and arranged the music as well as directed and created techniques of narrative and film editing that are still being used, how many directors have conceived the film's subject, written the script, devised and executed scientific bits and pieces, done original art, and produced a masterpiece?

Cameron did.

During a cast and crew party one Sunday evening, I noticed Cameron and Suzy Amis playing Ping-Pong. With an old lady's intuition, I sensed romance. A lovely, warm, happy happening. I watched them intently, applauding, moaning, whatever Ping-Pong reaction was appropriate. "Fine shot!" "Right on!" No doubt about it, they *liked* each other. What a beautiful couple! I thought.

(I had been told that Mr. Cameron had had several marriages, and a long love affair and adorable four-year-old daughter with the actress Linda Hamilton. She had been the leading lady in both *The Terminator* and *Terminator* 2 and is very talented and lovely.)

Gossip — familial relationships of others — really has never interested me. I don't care who sleeps with whom, or why, or where, or how. There are too many other wonderful, stimulating, amusing, impressive things/people to concern oneself with. Why bother with trivia?

By the way, among the questions I've been asked about making the film, one that often pops up is about amorous adventures. I realize most people think there is a great deal of hanky-panky going on on film sets. Well, there is and there isn't. I'm sure ours was an isn't.

Jim never seemed to rest/go to bed. The last to leave the set, the first to be there. Maybe even on Sundays?

Bill Paxton was celebrating the birth of his second child — a girl.

Jon Landau, James's coproducer, was hosting his wife and son.

Abernathy was in constant communication with his properties — restaurant and cattle — in Texas.

Suzy was showing her son, Jasper, around Halifax, and was almost invisible.

I was resting.

When I was visiting in Baja, I didn't follow any of the *Titanic* cast to an assignation or spy on anyone, or ask questions. Dear, dear. Dullsville, right? I don't think there was a great affair à la Taylor/Burton in *Cleopatra,* but you'll have to ask Kate and Leo. I wouldn't and I won't!

Knowing there would be a cast party, I had brought some of my fancy wigs and hats. So after the first round of drinks, I put on a shiny apricot pink Egyptian-blunt-cut wig over my own gray-blond hair (actually, I've been a more or less true blond all of my life — even today, Adela, my hairdresser, barely snuffs out the gray!). Ann, my set hairdresser, cried, "Is it really you? Unbelievable!"

Then I popped back into the ladies' room and pulled on my Fourth of July wig — masses of tinsel in reds, greens, blues, silver, and gold, long and sparkly. The ship's Russian crew — and their women — were entranced, coming up to feel it, grinning with approval. I also managed through the evening to wear several of my hats — Peruvian boater, sequined cloche, peacock-feathered skimmer.

I'm sure my friends, and certainly strangers, think I put on my wigs and hats to be amusing, to entertain them. Not at all! I put them on, and have been doing so since my late teens, because it amuses *me*. I love the way it changes *me*. I love looking in the mirror at chameleon *me!*

Everything was very special — except I'm afraid I thought the catered food was awful. Greg and Ann agreed. So every night we had a fabulous seafood restaurant in Halifax deliver our dinners to the makeup wagon.

One night while we were slurping lobster thermidor, an assistant threw open our door, anxiously asking were we all right? We were.

The rest of the *Titanic* company, Cameron, Paxton, Abernathy, first director Josh McLaglen, the whole crew, et cetera, were throwing up, falling down by the dozens, all around the chow wagon.

The tiny hospital nearby — one doctor, two nurses — was swamped by dozens of *very* sick people.

Eventually it was discovered that someone had sprinkled angel dust in the clam chowder! To this day the police have yet to find the culprit. Or a reason for this sabotage.

Toward the end of my three weeks' filming, I had a 5:30 P.M. call to get ready for my last close-ups. This is the scene when I walk across the deck — which I already had filmed — climb the railing at the ship's stern, and disclose the diamond.

So! Breakfast at 4 P.M., pickup at 4:30 P.M. Finishing makeup, hair, and wardrobe, the company not being ready for me, I retired to my trailer. (It was, by the way, complete with sofa and television, bathroom, and a small kitchen with microwave, fridge, and table settings.) I read for a while, napped for a while, nibbled at trays my PA brought in, made coffee, walked over to the set, kibitzed awhile, then went back to my trailer.

At three in the morning, my PA knocked on my door and announced in a stentorian voice, "They are ready for you! They want you on the set NOW! You must come NOW! You are going to do your final close-up. They want you NOW!" (I had inquired earlier about her parentage because she was something of a martinet with a slight Teutonic accent, albeit well-meaning and efficient. "I am half German and half Polish!" she said proudly.)

At three o'clock that morning, the prospect of having my final close-up in my final scene was unthinkable. I'd been up for twelve hours. The makeup had required one and a half hours. The costume a half hour, wig half hour, and for nine hours I'd been sitting in my trailer, or lying down in my trailer, or walking around the set schmoozing.

Now, I am completely addicted to expletives. I find them extremely useful for letting off steam. (Reading the dictionary — especially the English *Chambers* — is one of my greatest pleasures. As a matter of fact, I have a wonderful collection of very esoteric words that delight me. In Scrabble, for example, I think my favorite words describe a Himalayan cow, particularly when my opponent finds me using zo, zho, dso, and the female of the hybrid — zhomo!)

The most effective use of expletives that *ever* happened to me was that day. And you wouldn't need a dictionary to know what the words meant!

I hollered, "I won't do it! I can't do it! Shit! Shit! Shit! How the fuck do they think I can do it after eleven hours of sitting on my ass? You tell those motherfucking, cocksucking, asshole sons of bitches there is no way, no *way* I'm going to shoot my final close-ups now, and you may quote me!"

(When I was little and said a "bad" word, Mama washed my mouth out with soap. Fels-Naptha, bright hard rusty orange. Yech! But now I was desperate. And Mama wasn't around.)

The poor thing looked absolutely stricken. Malva had never heard anything from me except, "Please," "Thank you," and "All right, dear, I'm ready." She was silent. She let go the door, fell down the steps.

And I started to cry.

It seemed like only seconds before a voice at my screen door announced, "Asshole Number One coming in." Then I heard, "Asshole Number Two is here" and "Asshole Number Three!" Cameron came in first, Jon Landau next, Josh McLaglen next. James sat down and put his arms around me, so did Jon, who took my hand. Josh stood shyly by.

I wept, "I love Old Rose! I love this part! How can you want me to do close-ups of my most important scene after I've been sitting here hours and hours waiting to go on? Where is it written that female actresses' close-ups are shot at the end of the day, the actors' at the beginning? I won't do it! I can't do it! It isn't fair!"

By this time, Cameron and Landau are patting my hands and making reassuring noises, like "It's OK, you can go home, we'll do them tomorrow. Don't cry. We understand. . . ."

Evidently my explicit language reached the studios in Hollywood very quickly — like that morning. But no one ever blamed me for it. No one ever said, "How could you have?" Or "Oh, *Gloria!*" I was 100 percent right. And I don't think if I had said to Malva, "You tell those dear sweethearts, those darling men, those honey bunches that Gloria doesn't want to have her close-up nine hours after she's arrived on the set," they wouldn't have tried to go on into the dawn! My sags and bags and blotches and emotional and physical fatigue notwithstanding!

Why the hell didn't they let me go six hours ahead of that, when they knew they weren't going to get to me for another six hours? Why did they let me sit there? *Production schedules!*

So I hugged everyone and was driven back to the hotel, accompanied by my PA in silent shock. I SLEPT IN MY MAKEUP.

We did the close-ups the next night. After my reassuring James I was "fine," recovered from last night's tantrum, he called for a "waist and up" shot of my stepping up to the ship's stern railing. And instructed, "Be sure the face of the diamond is toward the camera. I like the way you're holding it, Gloria — with your pinkie out!"

The long and medium shots of the deck walk having been done long before, tonight it was mainly my puss — the emotion — expression of it, James said was up to me!

So! I truly felt regret at the tragedies surrounding the possession of this diamond, that such beauty should incite such venality, and recreated in my mind's eye the shameful scene, the frame-up of my lover, Jack — his nearly fatal arrest, my subsequent aloneness.

The small cry as I tossed the stone was completely instinctive.

Jim said he loved it.

When I got back to the hotel, I had a message waiting on my voice mail. "Hi, Gloria, this is Kate Winslet calling you at seven P.M. your time, eleven o'clock here at home, hoping everything is going well. I hear amazing things about you, how cheeky you are, making everybody laugh. Of course, that's the most important thing. I'd love to hear from you. I'll be back in LA on the sixteenth and we can get together. Meanwhile, I send you lots of love. Bye!"

For several days later, I heard from friends in the business — had I *really* said all that?

The day came when I finished shooting and Cameron called, "Cut! It's a wrap!" As I started toward the stage door, the whole cast and crew lined up and applauded me as I exited. Cameron called out to me, "I'll see you at the Academy."

I knew, when I first read Old Rose, the role was of Academy caliber. And, as the production progressed in Halifax, I also felt that not only was this film going to be a masterpiece, but some of the prestige would rub off on me. So the phrase "See you at the Academy" became a very present part of my persona.

At eighty-six, I was going to achieve my theatrical goal? How *nutty* can one's life be?

I returned to Los Angeles to learn I was to take pottery-throwing lessons immediately for my first scene in *Titanic* — à la Beatrice Wood. A limo arrived the next morning and carried me over to a pottery school, where I practiced all day throwing a pot on the wheel — bumpy, bumpy, gradually smooth and authentic enough to fool a camera not too close!

Fortunately, I am skillful with my hands — carpentry, plumbing, painting, gesturing. At 4:45 A.M. the next day, the limo carried me up Encinal Canyon into the Santa Monica Mountains, and Suzy and I shot our opening scene in *Titanic*.

By the end of the day, it was very evident to Old Rose that her "granddaughter," Suzy Amis, and her director were in love.

Their deportment was exemplary. No fond physical closeness, gestures, words. Just, and I speak truthfully, an electric sparkling field.

Loving them both, I felt kindled all over.

A few days later, early in the morning, carrying a heavy watering can toward a potted palm in my dining room, I caught my foot on the leg of a chair and sprawled full length on the floor. On the way down, with the massive pot and stand facing me, I tried and succeeded in breaking my fall with my left arm, so that I wouldn't hit my head.

A week later, I was invited to meet Kate and Leonardo DiCaprio at the Lightstorm Entertainment establishment in Santa Monica. I brought a large bouquet of red roses to Kate, and greeted Leonardo, who barely responded. He seemed shy, disengaged, uninterested in where he was — and with whom. "Be my guest," I thought. "I don't need a lot of togetherness either."

Days, weeks, went by, and I was invited to see rushes at the Lightstorm Studio. I quote from my diary: "The part is so abbreviated — Jim has cut 50 percent of my performance. In other words, not Academy nomination material. Too bad. It was still a wonderful experience."

The effects of my fall overtook me. According to my diary, I was feeling pain, depression, pain, pain.

So during these weeks of "I'm all right, it's nothing!" early in September, facing an MRI, my dear Mali Finn called and told me

Jim Cameron loved me. He had been thinking in terms of a Lillian Gish performance for Old Rose, and he got it!

I couldn't then, and I can't now, feel more flattered. That praise brought tears to my eyes. Still does!

Felt better.

The aches and pains from my fall persisted through September. Had the MRI — scary, but negative. So grateful, because so often I felt I was in a masquerade: a smiling face, but constant pain, an anxious heart.

An October 17 haiku.

> It is bitter to
> Unlove him so dearly loved.
> Bitter, bitter tea.

I have a page in my diary noting the gray November Friday that I called my new doctor and asked for a prescription for an anti-depressant — "I just feel awful" — and his nurse told me he said to call him back Monday. That was the end of my relationship with *him*.

During this rather bleak month, almost every diary entry noting pain, I received a residual for my role in Angela Lansbury's film *Shootdown* for $.05 "total gross."

I only wanted my own company. Not to share my misery with anyone.

Physical pain deep-sixes me. I am not used to it, have never had it over a period of time, a constant reminder every waking hour.

It immobilized me physically and creatively.

Another fortune slip from a home-delivered Chinese meal read, "Your mind is creative, original, and alert."

But what about my body? I called Nancy Malone for the name of a masseuse. She gave me Caty Van Sant — a miracle woman.

And my faith in Caty's healing hands and caring heart kept me going. I held the thought that soon the pain would go away.

I reluctantly had Thanksgiving dinner with Sylvia and Gene and grandson David in a much-admired restaurant. I am allergic to the new restaurants' compulsive brouhaha, crowded tables, cross conversations, bright lights, togetherness. How I miss long-lost Perino's! Subdued lighting, spacious booths, sound absorbers in the high ceilings, an air of elegance, gastronomical zest, contemplative appreciation. Increasingly, I prefer no holiday celebrations, rather a steady flow of quietness — contemplation — and, certainly, in a restaurant, soft lights and violins!

Aimless wandering in my garden, hand-feeding peanuts to Charlie, the blue jay — who keeps all the other birds at bay — or Shirley, the squirrel, pert and panicky, all of these, small comfort.

> Cruel, cruel life
> Cruel cruel end of it.
> Cruel cruel death.

And then, again, written-down phrases — unfinished poems, or finished ones and forlorn! A blank black curtain seemed to surround me. Oh, dear!

About December 5, Cynthia Scrima, wonderful assistant to Jon Landau, called to invite me down to visit the company in Baja California. I had to refuse. I was experimenting with various pain pills, homeopathic teas and herbs, therapists, and "How to Feel Good" videos. And getting ready for a torrential amount of family and friends arriving for Christmas.

For New Year's Eve, my cherished poker-playing friends and I decided to bring our own dinners to Ruthie Steiner's. We have always celebrated it together — always — for about forty years. I brought champagne. We dressed in party clothes and managed not to talk about the husbands and wives we'd loved and lost. We quit an hour before midnight, shared the champagne, smiled and embraced each other, and went our separate ways. No "lasting" power anymore — we used to stay and play till breakfast time, ham and eggs, bagels and Danish, on January 1, then, go to the Rose Bowl game. *Truly!*

I slept until 4:15 P.M. the next day, lay in bed, read a little, and ran across Montaigne's "What, have you not lived? That is not only the fundamental but the most illustrious of your occupations. To compose our character is our duty, not to compose books. Our great and glorious masterpiece is to live appropriately."

I resolved, once again, to "live appropriately."

I find it difficult to read these 1997 pages. "Feel terrible." "Feel terrible." "Full of pain." "Ditto." "Ditto." "Ditto." Today I am free and clear of pain and functioning with almost 100 percent energy and enthusiasm! See? If one just keeps up up up going going going hoping hoping hoping, IT HAPPENS, or, in the words of a cynic, It *can* happen!

One of the perquisites of being a film actress is keeping one's physical appearance up — or shall we say, keeping one's *youthful* appearance? So I had made, and canceled, and made an appointment again to have the bags under my eyes deflated. I had the lids lifted many years before. Both are simple, painless procedures. January 14, with my dear friend Nancy Lee Freed holding my hand, I had the procedure. Ice ice ice ice ice. I then stayed home alone, by preference, looking forward to no puffs.

An invitation to visit the *Titanic* set over St. Valentine's Day weekend sent me into the shops for presents for everyone. Feeling that Mr. Cameron was in love and also laboring under terrific pressures, I bought him a romantic book, *Love in Paris,* and a miniature tome, *58 Ways to Treat Stress.* Then fancy-wrapped boxes of chocolates and bottles of champagne for all the assistants, first and second assistant directors, all my friends there.

Mali Finn and I flew to San Diego, where a limo met us, drove us down the coast to Rosarito Beach, and delivered us to a beautiful suite overlooking the Pacific and the Coronado Islands.

We were driven to the set. The three-quarter life-size *Titanic* sat against the horizon, barely above the seawater, actually on the beach, staggering in size and authentic detail. One and a half million dollars' worth. And every dollar showed!

24

Onto the set. From the entrance a long flight of stairs led down to the subbasement flooded with water. Mr. Cameron ran up the stairs to meet us, we embraced, and he led us down to an enormous platform above the flooded corridor.

Unless you have been a frustrated actress, are in your eighties, feeling not very attractive (female competition in Hollywood is awesome), you cannot know what that special greeting, that embrace meant to me!

So, I will tell you.

It meant "Gloria, I am fond of you. I think you are a fine actress and have contributed to my film. I appreciate you, and I am your friend!"

Reward beyond recompense.

Kate Winslet and Leo DiCaprio were sitting in an enormous hot tub, and we hugged (Kate) and shook hands (Leo), were introduced to Leo's mother and grandmother. James was shooting the scene where Kate and Leo rescue the little abandoned boy, only to have him snatched away by his father, then the two of them are washed away.

All the camera crew and Cameron were in wet suits ten feet below. Ready! Kate and Leo climbed out of the tub, down the stairs into the waist-deep cold water. Lights! Camera! Action! We above watched on the remote control screen. Over and over again —

after each take, the action up the stairs — the two stars were wiped off and enveloped instantly in heavy white heated robes, helped over and dunked back into the hot tub, given Cokes, hot tea, cappuccinos, mineral water, cigarettes, anything the young pair asked for, they received.

That single episode took days. Not surprising when one considers how everything has to jibe. The movements back and forth of the camera, the sounds, the coordination of the crying child, his young rescuers, the father's entrance, the engulfing waters. Multiply this scene by hundreds of others, much more complicated, with many more actors, and no wonder the making of *Titanic* went over two hundred million dollars.

And I would guess the complaints one heard about the hours, conditions, disciplines, needs, and temperaments were not unexpected. But, in the end, most everyone involved seemed not only content but thrilled and fulfilled by their participation.

During one of our conversations in between takes, Kate complained that they had never asked her whether or not she could swim. My answer was "Kate! You read the script, didn't you?"

Later, her uncomplimentary remarks about James were in the papers, but Kate said she was misquoted, and, months later, joined us all at a togetherness party Sherry Lansing and Jonathan Dolger, CEOs of Paramount Pictures, gave for *Titanic* survivors.

By March, I was admiring my garden, working on exercising, dieting, preparing bonsais for the Californian Bonsai Association's annual show at the Huntington Library in San Marino — with excruciating arthritis pains in both legs necessitating heavy cortisone shots — congratulating Gordon Newell on his latest and, perhaps, last monumental sculpture, *The Fountain of Life,* carved from Sierra Nevada granite, and preparing for Easter with my family.

On April 7 the publicity blitz for *Titanic* kicked off with an *Esquire* interview with Cameron. From that point on, the deluge of publicity never stopped.

On April 10, my astrological forecast in the paper said something about "spectacular results" and that my wishes were coming true, an emotional jackpot.

The next day, a leading mention of me by *Variety*'s top columnist, Army Archerd: "Gloria Stuart, beautiful as ever at 86, plays Winslet's character today, visiting the site of the *Titanic*."

Late that month James Cameron called and asked if I would like to see "some film, mainly your scenes" in his home in Malibu. Would I ever? Could I bring friends? My Sylvia and Gene were stuck in Idyllwild so I brought Ruth Steiner and Julie and Ann Epstein. James ran three hours of film in his darkened dining room (altered so he could edit film at home). My friends were mightily impressed not only with the film but with James's courtesy, modesty. (I had brought him Julie Epstein's *Casablanca Remembered*, my second *and* international prizewinning miniature artist's book. He loved it.)

We left in a state of high excitement. Cameron's parting words were, "An Academy Award . . ."

I was emotionally exhausted the next day, and wrote him this letter:

Dear Jim!

It's enough already that I know you're charming, an accomplished auteur, a gentle man and a scholar, but do I have to listen to my friends, not only on the ride home, but also later during dinner, and then, all evening playing poker, praising you?

Really, sir, couldn't you try being a little monsterish, uncouth, stupid? I'm sick and tired of nodding "Yes," "Right on," "True!"

Let's try for a little churlishness, hmm?

G. Stuart

P.S. It was a wonderfully fulfilling afternoon, dear boy. I/we thank you so very much. Not a shadow, not a hint of negativism about *anything — incroyable!*"

Love,
Gloria

The next day, April 30, I took a taxi to Santa Monica Hospital. To spend two days and nights trying to find out why I was in so much pain all the time. My orthopod ordered a bone scan, X rays, ultrasound tests. I was truly frightened. Sylvia wanted to come down, but, again I told her I really didn't want her there. I need to get through these things *alone*. I *hate* hovering!

The next day, the doctor assured me, no life-threatening problems — just the aches and pains of *une ancienne! Moi? Etonnant!*

I was called that week to do some more looping — sound recording. Some of my lines spoken on the ship out at sea in Nova Scotia were imperfect because of the wind and ship sounds. To "loop," you sit with a script in your hands very quietly in front of a mike in a projection room, and, as the film is run, and that person up there, *you,* speaks, you speak, dubbing the sound, the lip movement timed perfectly. It is tedious.

The sound engineers were so complimentary about my performance. I heard the word "Oscar" again.

The tension was building.

But *Titanic*'s premiere was seven months away.

June 1, the first script offer after *Titanic* had wrapped was sent to me. It was for *Stargate,* the television series. I was to play a sixty-five-year-old scientist trying to meet her husband left behind in outer space many years before. I didn't find the role interesting, though, at eighty-six, I was certainly flattered to be considered.

On the ninth, the BBC called from London, wanting me to record an interview for a documentary on *The Old Dark House. Again?* But they refused any payment, so I refused.

June 14 my astrological forecast announced that I was on my way to a big hit, "possible stardom."

Moi?

On the day before my eighty-seventh birthday, *Titanic* friends Rae Sanchini and Jon Landau sent me eighty-seven roses. Jim Cameron sent a beautiful leather photo album, Suzy Amis brought over a foursome of Waterford champagne glasses (which we christened immediately with Cristal), and the dear assistants, Nancy Dobson, Cynthia Scrima, and Kim Troy, loving greetings. And my dear makeup artist Greg Cannom sent another of his extravagant bouquets of roses.

The Thompsons and my loving granddaughter, Amanda, and her Jim and Frannie made me a Mexican dinner.

I did not feel like celebrating. Celebrate what? My aches and pains? My disastrous printing? No acceptable offers of work — of acting, that is. My lethal fatigue twenty hours a day?

The only bright note was a birthday card a friend sent: "Think you should do something special to celebrate your first day? So get naked and have someone hold you upside down!"

I thought my work on *Titanic* was over. I was wrong. In the original climax scene we shot in Halifax, Bill Paxton, Lewis Abernathy, Nicholas Cascone, Suzy Amis, and the Russian captain discover me approaching the railing, the fabulous diamond in my hand, and rush me as I threaten, "Stay back or I'll throw it!" Then followed a scene where I admonish Paxton, let him hold the diamond, then retrieve it slowly and carefully, and drop it overboard.

But Cameron decided — wisely, I think I would agree — the scene would be more powerful were Old Rose to throw it into the sea without witnesses.

So months after the final wrap, Mr. Cameron rewrote the ending. What he produced was pure and simple.

On July 6, the limo pulled up at 7 A.M. and the Thompsons — who had never seen me work — and I headed off to a set of the ship's stern at Twentieth Century–Fox.

The scene required me to walk across the deserted deck of the ship, alone and at night, and fling the diamond overboard.

A large tank of water had been set up beneath the fake ship's stern. When the camera rolled, a prop boy standing in its middle swished the water back and forth with a paddle.

"Why?" I asked. James explained the lights from the ship on the *moving* sea reflected back on me and my surroundings.

Barefooted, arthritic with the damp air and wind machines gently blowing on me, I took a deep breath, resolved I would *not* have pain, and, at "Action!" walked slowly toward the railing.

After a few takes, "Cut and print," Cameron called out. He came over to me, helping me down from the stern, and said, "Love the red toenails."

"Oh, my God, I forgot to take the polish off!"

"You didn't put it on on purpose?"

"No, Jim, I didn't! I'm so sorry! Do you want me to take it off?"

"No! I love it! We'll keep it," he said.

And interestingly enough, many, many viewers have remarked about how much in character Old Rose's red toenails were!

He misses nothing!

James really is a Renaissance man. What actors call a "hands-on" director. His indescribable need for perfection that day and night really showed. We shot for fourteen hours, with lunch and dinner breaks — *one scene, no dialogue*. While I was relaxing in between takes, James went up the "ship's" stairs with a paint bucket and a brush and carefully painted out a large scratch on the railing! Then later my son-in-law found Jim in a corner of the set inking The Diamond's bottom with a deep blue marking pen, enhancing its color.

As we left that night, my director said to Gene, "I wish I had written more scenes for Gloria." Me, too! Or that half of my scenes and voice-overs hadn't been cut in the finished film . . .

I fantasized winning an Academy Award — I even wrote the speech one sleepless summer night.

"You see before you an actress who took a thirty-three year vacation because she was bitterly disappointed in her career but who has been given a forever place in theatrical history by James Cameron." (I imagined my holding up the Oscar.) "I owe all this to him."

Or, holding the Oscar, and quizzically asking, "Why this old broad?"

Adam and Eve.

Front view, The Watts Towers.

Les cerfs-volant a Les Tours Watts.

With my bonsais.

Découpage on 19th-century
papier-mâché globe on
black wrought-iron stand
(for M.F.K. Fisher).

Silk screening in my studio.

Binding by Allwyn
O'Mara for miniature
book *Boating with Bogart.*

G TO G   G TO G

Shall I adorn myself once more
for your delight?
Compose those witty bits
And - or
Accuse you of disregard?
Niggle on you good?
Or promise wildly naughty romps,
a seashore escapade -
The skinny - dipping kind?
Shall I play our special music
fraught with loving memories?
Oh, those days and nights
of wine and roses - spirits, too!
Or shall I sit quietly,
your hand in mine,
silently remembering
all those days and nights
those weeks and months
The years we've been as one?

Oh, pertinacious you!
Who? Me?
Yes, you!
Well, you too!
Hmm.... That's true....

I'm bringing you down, my girl,
You've lost your tail -
Those fluttering ribbons
and tantalizing bows
are gone!
Disappeared!
When? As the sun set?
Where?
Where did they finally
fall to Earth?
In the river -
Life's darkly running stream?
In the field? All blossoms,
leaves, and roots a'withering?
On the macadam highway?
No matter!
Now your fair form
rests quietly in my arms.
I shall always cherish you -
Steadfast, constant.
Night is upon us -
No windrift windswift humming sound -
But love abideth.

Gloria to Ward and Ward to Gloria. Written in 1996, as Ward Ritchie was
dying, and published—*Imprenta Glorias*—later as a keepsake for his family
and friends.

My beautiful family. (top row, left to right) David, Sylvia, Dinah, (front row) Benjamin, Gene, Amanda, Malibu, 1980. (*Gene Trindl*)

With Ward Ritchie. Together for a while, Brentwood, 1983.

Imagine, at my age, having to be made up to look older! Greg Cannom—a delight and an artist—won an Oscar for his work in *Titanic* and he deserved it!

The legendary sculptor Beatrice Wood was writer/director James Cameron's inspiration for the part of Old Rose. We all had lunch together at her Ojai Valley, California, studio just six days before she died. (left to right) Gloria, Beatrice, and James Cameron.

Paramount Pictures and Twentieth Century Fox
Thank the Screen Actors Guild and Proudly Congratulate

TITANIC

GLORIA
STUART

On Her Award For
Outstanding Performance
By A Female Actor
In A Supporting Role

(*Twentieth Century–Fox*)

Just a little ($20,000,000) bauble to perk up my Escada gown for the Academy Awards. I do think blue diamonds become me. . . . (*Reuters/Fred Prouser/Archive Photos*)

Still working at eighty-eight, playing a bag lady in *The Million Dollar Hotel* starring Mel Gibson, directed by Wim Wenders.

Or, "When I graduated from Santa Monica High in 1927, I was voted the girl most likely to succeed. I didn't realize it would take so long."

On the thirteenth, I made another documentary about James Whale for a tidy sum. On the eighteenth went to see a preview of *Titanic* that Cameron ran. Nearly four hours. The invitees were the cast (minus Leo and Kate, who were busy elsewhere), agents, other directors and producers, friends. I embraced Suzy when she whispered that she and James were engaged. She was a beamish lady and he a beamish boy!

Unlike any director I ever heard of, Jim asked for written or verbal comments from us all. I wrote him a very short appreciation — mentioning the length of the dining room chase, feeling it too drawn out. I was told later this was a consensus, and the dear boy cut it considerably.

July 25, I turned down a wrap party for the cast and crew of *Titanic,* to be held on the SS *Queen Mary,* now permanently anchored in Long Beach. To have to refuse such a celebration because of age is a real downer. I saw myself, limping slightly up the gangplank, or being helped so I wouldn't limp, wrapping myself up against the night air with a shawl while nubile and gazelle-like ladies cavorted about in tight black sheaths and tottery high heels, carrying champagne glasses while stroking and being stroked by their dates, and dancing up a storm. Then having to come home early alone.

During this period, I made chicken soup for ailing friends, kept the weekly poker game trysts, fussed with my bonsais, went through seemingly unending crises with printing and hand coloring Bachardy's *Portrait,* chatted for the first time in ages with Gene and Diane Crain — favorite friends who collect my books — experimented with amounts of pain pills, had a few checkups, kept printing, had an idea about a Garden of Allah documentary, and received a letter from Suzy that James was going back to Linda

Hamilton and their daughter, Josephine. She was composed, as always, a nonpareil of a woman.

In August, I recorded a cassette about James Whale (again!) for Tower Productions and continued every single day printing, setting type with my helper Amelia Frinier, and then going to bed at sundown, exhausted.

The end of August, I did some more looping and dubbing with James in the studio. James did not like my pronunciation of "Cherbourg"! I gave it the French lack of a "g" on the end, and he commented, "Keokuk won't know where you're describing. Give it the hard 'g' — burg!"

His company had started previews, and he was very up and excited. The ratings for *Titanic* were 70 percent "excellent," and for Old Rose, 70 percent "excellent" — top marks!

But age seemed suddenly to happen almost all at once to my nearest and dearest friends.

September 22, I had dinner with Julie and Ann Epstein, and actress/sculptress and actor/director Hazel and Don Taylor. Julie was leaving to be honored at his alma mater, Penn State. After that, he was meeting Stephen Sondheim in London to work on an idea they'd collaborated on in the fifties — the play was going into rehearsal. On the twenty-third, in the plane crossing the country, Julie suffered a massive stroke. He has been hospitalized ever since.

Meanwhile, Arthur's collaborator, Nat Perrin, our dear oldest friend, had gone into a nursing home, although he carried on alone for years after losing his darling Helen. Now Nat's gone. Ira. Mike.

Our Poker Group is down to ladies only, with Ray Evans, an occasional player. Ann, Ruth, Fay, Nancy, and I still hold Saturday night as the only place to be! Even on New Year's Eve. We have turned down, over the years, offers to be interviewed, photographed, documented in a video, but we maintain our privacy rigorously — although we are a fascinating assemblage! Or used to be.

About October 9, I received my second script offer since finishing *Titanic*. The role of a wealthy widow who discovers her husband was into kinky sex and grisly murders — all played out in the film. Thank you, but no thank you. Rapes, torture, murders, hardcore porno. Not my dish of tea — I had hoped it would never be made, but I couldn't bring myself to inquire. I didn't need to. I read a scathing review of it a year later.

I also tried (through various friendly channels) to get word to Cameron that I was dying for an invitation to the London Royal Gala. But he was honeymooning in Ireland with Linda Hamilton.

Finally, on the twenty-first, James's wonderful assistant Nancy Dobson called and said, "You're all set for London, November thirteenth!" I celebrated by ordering a cashmere coat from Bloomingdales in New York. Black and almost to the floor. A dinner skirt of solid black sequins, a black chiffon blouse of all-over black sequins and jet. Hand beaded, heavy! And luminous. Then I called Sylvia and Gino, then all my close English friends, and then all my close Hollywood friends. Hurrah! Hurrah! Hurrah!

When Arthur and I were living in London, we watched the royals and movie stars parade into the galas, the stars afterward greeted by the royals, limp handshakes and smiles all the way. I had always had a hankering to attend one of these.

The studio tour arranger called, did I want to go a few days early? Yes! Did I need a limo to tour around? Yes! I was to be at the Dorchester — one of the world's top ten hotels.

November 13, I left in the afternoon — flying first class — and arrived the next day. My suite was full of flowers, a brimming-over fruit and goodies basket, iced champagne. I began to feel like a movie star. Again.

Visiting the Royal Academy, shopping at Harrods and Fortnum and Mason, visiting my bookseller David Stephenson at the Rocket Press, dinner and tea at the Ritz with my English friends, and finally, on Tuesday, hairdresser, makeup artist, and my escort, John

Dreyfus, England's prestigious bookman, all arriving, then on to the gala, riding in a limo with Linda and James Cameron.

The fans and paparazzi were all heaped together, with the greatest cheers for Leonardo DiCaprio. Leo had brought his mother to London, and we sat together in a small anteroom waiting for the reception. The DiCaprios were sweet together. Then the *Titanic* cast members who were in town, and the producers (Cameron and Landau), all lined up in the lobby to receive Princess Alexandra and the Prince of Wales.

The men had been instructed to nod when the royals spoke to them, and the women to curtsy. On the way there, I said to Linda, "Are you going to curtsy?"

She said no, she wasn't.

I agreed. "What are you going to say to His Highness?" I asked.

She thought for a moment — it was three months after Princess Diana's death — and quipped, "How *could* you?" We all laughed a bit uneasily.

Going into the theater lobby, I was separated from my commoner friend, John Dreyfus, and placed in the line to be greeted by the royals. John was allowed to stand with the other "escorts, wives, lovers" behind a second red rope.

The lovely and stately Princess Alexandra came first, in a flowing beaded gown, pearls and diamonds and tiara, soft-spoken. And as HRH approached me, I noticed how beautifully groomed and tailored he was.

So, I did bob when HRH held out his hand and asked, "Did you get up at six-thirty every day to work?"

"No," I answered, "I got up to work every afternoon at four o'clock and worked all night!" He made a little moue, and moved on.

That evening was the first time I had seen *Titanic* in its final print. The audience — a charity one — was enthusiastic, and HRH seemed to enjoy it, standing at the finish to applaud.

Then on to a huge party at the Café Royale on Regent Street.

Arthur and I had dined there some thirty-odd years before. It is very Gay Nineties, lots of red velvet, gold leaf, fancy furniture.

So! The Royal Gala had been just that! Gala and royal. It was also the first time since leaving the *Titanic* set in Halifax that I heard (for sure!), "It's an Academy Award performance." And the first time I said, out loud, "All I want is a nomination." At least, that is all I *thought* I wanted.

(A small disappointment — I must say, I was surprised — was that not one person asked me for an autograph. To which Sylvia replied, "But, Ma, nobody could recognize you!")

The next evening our group — the Camerons, DiCaprio and his buddy and a bodyguard, Billy Zane and Jessica Murphy, Nancy Dobson, and I — boarded the Concorde for New York City.

On board, I celebrated the whole scene by giving each couple a present of my miniature book, *Boating with Bogart,* stuffed in, I thought, adorable hand puppets. Leo read it instantly. Billy Zane put it away as though it were a matchbook cover. I couldn't see what happened to it with the others. But no one ever mentioned it. Here I shall be venal. Common. Mercenary. *Boating with Bogart* sells for $175 and is not out of print.

The Concorde is more than thrilling. London Bridge, the Tower, The City, disappearedrightnow! Nothing but blue above and below. The food and wines are of four-star class, the freebies — portfolios, pens, stationery — are the finest, and the ambience is thrilling. On my first Concorde flight, from Paris to Washington several years before, after we had broken the sound barrier, I called my family on the phone. I felt like a sorceress! But this time I just sat back and mentally embraced myself, becalmed my mind, smiled and smiled and smiled. Ms. Fat Cat!

Another wish had come true.

The next day, the twentieth, after a luxurious, luxuriating night in the Righa Royal Hotel in New York City, Leo, Kate, Billy, James, and I went to work with the media. From ten to twelve I gave fifteen-minute interviews to the foreign press and television people, then a lunch break, then one-hour interviews with *Access America* and *USA Today.* From 3:30 to 5:30, I gave five-minute interviews for various television stations around the nation.

I counted seventy-two sound bites that day. In other words, I answered *Titanic* questions from at least seventy-two questioners.

The next day I did television interviews from 10 A.M. until 2:30 P.M. Nora Sayre interviewed me for the *New York Times.* Liz Frank and her daughter, Annie, also came over. Liz is the daughter of one of my dearest friends, Anne Frank, now deceased. Liz received the Pulitzer Prize for her biography of Louise Bogan. We schmoozed, dined at Le Bernardin, and dithered over my adventures.

The *next* morning I recorded more interviews with TV people, sponsored by Twentieth Century–Fox International (Europe, Asia, and the Middle East), and left at noon from JFK for LAX, exhilarated and exhausted. And again — and again and again, in response to "It's an Academy Award performance," I would respond that a nomination would be enough. It wasn't false modesty. I was trying to brace myself for what might happen — or not happen.

Home to a big Thanksgiving *chez moi.* I went to bed verrry early. The next night, Sylvia, Gene, and I hosted a gala wedding rehearsal dinner for my grandson David and his Jill Church, also *chez moi.* If you're into family, their wedding day was a doozer. I was immersed in grandchildren — David and Jill, Dinah and Gary, Amanda and Jim, and Benjamin (in a top hat). Benjamin's Ella had just popped Sarah-Leah, so she was home, as were their Jacob, Samuel, Deborah, and Tzipporah. But my other great-grandchildren — Dylan, Weston, Stuart, Jasen, Frannie, and Katie — were in tow.

And when she arrived, David and Jill's Maggie became my twelfth great-grandchild!

With Thanksgiving, the wedding, trying to finish decorative details on *The Portrait,* jillions of phone calls and notes from my loving friends and family, fan mail beginning to arrive in mind-boggling amounts, my avoidance of my bonsais' needs — and, I guess, anxiety over the upcoming performance awards — I began to feel swamped. My previously leisurely life, measured, rhythmic, and completely freewheeling, seemed, and was, far behind and unobtainable.

I hadn't realized that with my performance as Old Rose, and the dazzling success of *Titanic,* came twenty-four-hour-a-day almost mandatory devotion to being A Movie Star.

I was overwhelmed.

25

he Oscar race begins! L.A. Confidential wins the National Board of Reviews Best Picture Award. I read anxiously — what best supporting actress? Anne Heche for *Donnie Brasco* and also *Wag the Dog* — and sighed with relief. Up to then, Kim Basinger had been mentioned as a candidate by quite a few film critics. She was running in post position. I was disappointed *Titanic* was not the winner, and that *The Sweet Hereafter* won the best acting ensemble.

I was reminded of Lucretius: "It is pleasant when the sea runs high, to view from land the distress of another."

Now the press and TV pressure chez Hollywood began to gather. Army Archerd wrote about me in *Variety*. December 1, Leonard Maltin, my dear friend, came over for a morning interview for *Entertainment Tonight,* then that afternoon I was interviewed by *Venice* magazine. The next morning I was up at 5:45 for makeup and hair, and did interviews and TV sound bites at the Four Seasons Hotel from nine to four-thirty with a half-hour break for lunch.

With the exception of a harmonious and amusing interview for *Access Hollywood* on December 9, I began a retreat. Not answering the phone, or the mail, taking long naps after long hours of sleep from evening to morning, listening to music, walking the neighborhood alone.

Then, December 13, an invitation to the *Titanic* cast and crew party and showing of the film at Cineplex Century City. I took Nancy Malone and Lisa Mitchell — my director and scenarist on the long-ago *Merlene of the Movies*. Jim Cameron sent a limo for us. I confess that made me feel good.

This was followed the next night by another charity premiere at Grauman's Chinese. I invited Marvin Paige and my grandchildren, David and Jill Thompson, to go with me. Suzy Amis was hesitant about attending. She wasn't sure about meeting the Camerons there, but I promised to walk the paparazzi trot with her, and did. She is a beautifully composed lady, and managed a congratulatory greeting to Jim with grace.

The reception at the end of the film was a huge burst of applause, shouts, the clapping audience standing, all the approval one could wish for. At the party afterward, in the middle of all this hoopla, James put his arm around me and moved me away from a group. He cautioned me that, although I deserved an Oscar for my performance, the awards were very political and I shouldn't count on one. He finished by saying he knew, I knew, and all the other people knew I'd given a wonderful performance, and I should let it go at that.

"All I want is the nomination, Jim. Truly . . ."

Bullshit. I was so up I yessed him, hugged him, held his hand in mine, and almost kissed it. But later, I much appreciated his warning.

On December 17, the Golden Globe Award nominations were broadcast. Sylvia, Tim Menke — the bright darling young man assigned to me for the duration by the Paramount publicity department — and so many friends called to tell me that I was among the five best supporting actress nominees. Well, by now I had expected to be! Again, the phone didn't stop ringing! My family, most of my friends, quite a few strangers — it was a whirligig!

That day I had four interviews — CNN, E!, *Entertainment Tonight*, and *Access Hollywood* — and all were shown that night on television.

And that day extravagant flower arrangements started arriving — from Paramount executives Sherry Lansing and Jonathan Dolger (always so generous), Lightstorm executives Rae Sanchini and Jon Landau (ditto), old friends, new friends, unknown fans. There were more flowers, and more beautiful and luxurious arrangements of flowers, than I had ever received in my life. Deliveries kept up almost daily for the next three months.

In the midst of all this merriment, I received an invitation to the unveiling of Gordon Newell's masterpiece, *The Fountain of Life*, carved with his son from Sierra Nevada granite, to be held by his longtime friend and sponsor Gordon Zuckerman at Gordon's resort hotel in Scottsdale, Arizona. I immediately called Larry Powell. Larry told me that dear Gordon was a frail ninety-two, and on oxygen.

I fantasized about calling Gordon, and if he was dying, to say to him, Gordon, I love you and we had a wonderful marriage while it lasted, and I'm very proud to have been your wife. And bon voyage, blithe spirit.

But anyway, I made a reservation to attend in February.

December 20, the "Calendar" section of the *Los Angeles Times* gave me a front-page interview in depth plus three color pictures.

David called: "You're going to be famous forever, Gramma!"

On the twenty-third, I had a one-hour interview with the *San Francisco Chronicle*, the *New York Times* ran Nora Sayre's marvelous interview, and there were more TV interviews on local stations.

On the twenty-seventh, everyone said Sylvia and Gene's party for me was great. Most every one of my friends within shouting distance came — and many came from San Francisco. The Ts had a big tent and buffets of marvelous food — all my Sylvia's own delicious delicacies. It was a gathering of great love and sharing of my good fortune. I shall always remember it with astonishment and gratitude.

I didn't get dressed the next four days, staying in bed most of the time.

New Year's Eve Day brought memories of our Poker Group — its brilliance, the comradeship, the appreciation of ourselves, our accomplishments, the laughter and real affection for each other. We still celebrated and dealt the cards. In the afternoon, Nancy Lee took me to visit Julie Epstein at the nursing home. Ann was there and they both were smiling.

On the last page of my diary for 1997 is a lovely quote from W. H. Auden, "Poetry makes nothing happen." Just in the mind. I remembered another lovely fragment.

> Coolness.
> The sound of the bell
> As it leaves the bell.

As the word is used today, everything in my orbit was cool.

What would 1998 bring?

On the third I went with Suzy to the premiere of her new movie, *Firestorm*. It was an exciting film, and she was exciting in it. But Cameron was still on her mind. She truly loved him, and all I could do, literally and figuratively, was hold her hand.

I was named one of the fifty most beautiful people in the world by *People* magazine. It was rather unnerving, but what the hell! I accepted somewhat askance. I have exercised a minimal amount. I have been careful about the booze. I gave up smoking when it became apparent that it was a deadly habit. I have been in control. And that is the most important thing. It is very nourishing to the spirit, and it makes you feel grateful, or you are grateful that you have tried to take care of yourself and have loved yourself enough during all the years that you have not gotten out of shape very much or often.

On January 8, the magazine sent a photographer, makeup artist, wardrobe master, and helpers-out from New York City to photograph me. Again, the limo, the early early hour to a studio, the makeup, the hair, the terribly important choice of wardrobe (feather boas, scarves, shoes, jewelry, colors), the positions, props, lighting. Smiling gracefully and warmly and more or less continuously, surrounded by clutter, noise, multiple choices by staff members plus the photographer as to poses, moods, with rests in between, is hard work! However, I left at three-thirty with warm thanks.

By January 12, *Titanic* had grossed more than $197 million. It was the highest-grossing three-hour-and-fifteen-minute film ever made. By the next day, it smashed the $200 million mark. And all the dissing of this masterpiece — the time overrun, the cast costs, the "gross" extravagance of the director, who was "obviously" out of control — all these opinions went down the drain. All of us, and that included "a cast of thousands," were euphoric. After all, the classic Romeo and Juliet story had never failed, and now it had Leonardo DiCaprio. Mobbed in Japan, mobbed in London, New York, wherever, by *les jeunes filles* — and, too, the not-so-young ladies. *Titanic* had the New Heartthrob — for sure! I wasn't with Leo in Japan or New York — but I read the news reports and saw the brouhahas on television. Certainly in London, although the barricades were all-pervasive, the screaming and hollering blasted him — and us!

Full-page color portraits of Old Rose in *Variety* and the *Hollywood Reporter*, a shot of Suzy Amis and me at her premiere of *Firestorm*.

The *Variety* and *Reporter* ads, the constant news reports and interviews, building building building, began to give me the uneasy feeling of being oversold. But all this exposure was not my call, and, after all, I was in the hands of experts!

On the fourteenth I had an interview for Dan Rather's program *48 Hours*. The roses arrived, the camera and sound crew arrived, my makeup and hair artist Hayley Cecile arrived, then CBS's delightful Harry Smith arrived with several assistants, and I joined them in my garden.

I knew I hadn't truly "arrived," but I felt I was on my way! I know it sounds funny to hear an eighty-seven-year-old woman say that, but, Dahling, that's how it felt!

That same afternoon, the London *Daily Mirror* — very very popular English daily — people arrived for an interview. We all had some jolly juggling of spaces and settings. But we managed! Front and back and side gardens, patio, front porch, living room, bar!

Saturday, the seventeenth, the Ts came down from their mountain to escort me to the Golden Globes the next night.

The Golden Globes was the first of the ceremonies and awards for excellence in film. And it was my first experience on my home base with dozens of paparazzi, hundreds of applauding fans, shoulder to shoulder with the famous names and faces in filmdom, television and magazine and newspaper cameras — the whole scene. Exciting, but nervous making.

A small aside. When I did what I call the paparazzi trot down the red carpet — dear Tim Menke guiding me expertly — questions from the press, be they newspapers, magazines, or TV, were 80 percent, "Miss Stuart, what designer are you wearing tonight?" I couldn't believe it. Then, I shopped mostly by catalog, and in the beginning I'd say something like, "I got it in England" or "I had it made for me." Actually, my dressmaker is from Mexico, and once or twice it amused me to say, "It's a Maria Toledo of Guadalajara!" And that night I was wearing a brilliant blue satin sheath under a matching blue sequined jacket — a Maria Toledo!

Someday, I'm going to answer, "Catalog."

We sat at a *Titanic* table with Jim and Linda, Rae Sanchini and her husband, Bruce Tobey, and Jon Landau and his Julie. We all were nervous. The New York, Chicago, and Los Angeles film critics had already named *L.A. Confidential* as best picture, and Kim Basinger as best supporting actress, so I attended with faint hope.

And clairvoyance. The one hundred foreign correspondents

voted the same way. Jim did win for best director, and after his thank-yous, asked all cast members present to come up on the stage with him. I went up, and the rest is a blur.

But Wednesday revived my spirits. The Screen Actors Guild would make a documentary of my union activities, with James Cameron and me discussing "film" vis-à-vis *Titanic*. The guild would honor me especially for being a founding member (so few of us left!) at its annual awards.

The morning of the twenty-seventh I was nominated for a SAG Best Supporting Actress Award! That afternoon, I had a phone interview with Australian television.

On the twenty-eighth, I received a request from Gary Kurutz, librarian in charge of Special Collections at the California State Library in Sacramento, to see if I would please save everything to do with my role in *Titanic:* the videos, press, any personal props I used during the making, or relevant gifts. My archive there already contains all my printing work, early films and related material, and photos of my paintings. I am very proud of this and feel, perhaps, the archive is my way to everlasting fame! Well, at least until the Big Bang!

The SAG foundation interview with Cameron was the next day.

January 30. The English magazine *Hello* sent a whole shebang from London to photograph me for a documentary spread. Interviews, crew, makeup, production staff — a whole long long day of different sites, garden, studio, bar, living room, many hours of posing, relaxing, ditto ditto. It proved to be the most successful of all my magazine spreads. Real "movie star" stuff!

Around this time, Gene and Sylvia decided to come back to town — at least for a while. I invited them to stay with me. It's crowded, but we enjoy one another's company so much.

On the second of February, true to my word, I flew to Scottsdale for the unveiling of Gordon's beautiful sculpture. He was so warm and loving, as were all his friends. There with the eighty- and ninety-year-olds, I felt young and beautiful.

Back home on the fourth. On the sixth, an interview for French television. The eighth brought a Best Supporting Actress Award from the Academy of Family Films and Television.

On February 10 at 5 A.M., the Academy Awards nominations were announced on radio and television. Sylvia woke me up with screams and hugs and shouts of congratulation, the phone began to ring, and I happily thought, "Finally!"

That was a crazy day. *Twenty-two* interviews! There were so many film crews strung through my small house, at one point they reached gridlock! Flowers kept arriving and the phone kept ringing. Requests requests requests. Sylvia instantly became my manager!

Two days later, I received a telegram:

Gloria
   I am thrilled to be sharing not only this category but this rarest of honors with you.

Sincerely,
Kim Basinger

I sent one back to her, because I found this very unusual. Particularly among actresses who don't know each other, have never touched base or actually have any personal interest in each other.

Kim,
   In all my years, I have never received as gracious and generous a message as yours of the twelfth. Thank you so very much and good luck to both of us.

Gloria Stuart

That day, I gave a long-promised lecture to college theater students at Fullerton. On the thirteenth, had a telephone interview with *Newsweek*, and a young man from my old newspaper in Santa Monica, the *Santa Monica Outlook*, came for a long interview. His questions were unusually insightful, and I was sad to hear my paper folded about two months later, after so many years!

The eighteenth was a party of West Coast movers and shakers given by *The New Yorker*. Since I hadn't been given the option of bringing a guest, I went alone. Despite a lot of famous faces, I found the evening unexciting. On the nineteenth, Sylvia, Gene, and I had planned to go down to Palm Springs for Susan Marx's ninetieth — no! can't be! — birthday, but we had to cancel. I was too tired.

The next day, off at 9 A.M. for makeup to do an interview for the BBC and German television.

The best speech written for me for the many presentations I made was given to me the following night as a presenter at the Writers Guild of America Awards. The opening line was, "I'm very glad to be here tonight. As a matter of fact, I'm very glad to be *anywhere*." Big laugh. And I ended my speech with, "I've been asked over and over again — *why* did I throw the diamond into the sea? I threw the diamond into the sea, because the script said I did." Bigger laugh.

I think the reason I don't mind, and have never minded, telling my age is that from thirty on — this exactly pertains to my daughter as well — people would exclaim and say, "Oh, you look eighteen." And as my age advanced, people would say, "Oh, you look like thirty" — this at fifty. One of the most salutary things that happened to me after eighty-seven was when a casting director sent me a script where the woman was described as sixty-five. I phoned and I said, "Come on, there's no way I can play sixty-five," and he said, "We all know what you look like, Gloria, how you photograph. You can play sixty-five." So, evidently, there's no reason why I shouldn't tell, or why I should worry about public knowledge of my age.

The next day Sylvia and I packed for a round of interviews in New York City. I had asked Paramount to send Tim with us — by now I had come to depend on his always being one step ahead of me in terms of dealing with schedules, press, and crowd control. Besides, we love his company.

It was very exciting. A luxurious hotel suite with baskets of flowers, fruit, chocolates, champagne, limos, sumptuous dinners, seeing old friends — and especially with my most efficient, supportive, kindly Sylvia — but it was difficult to take a deep breath.

Not to mention having gentlemen from Escada come to our suite and create a dress for me to wear to the Oscars ("We're having the satin dyed in Germany to match your eyes . . ."). Then over to Harry Winston's to see their $22 million blue diamond that I would wear. One of three in the world. Tight security in a hideaway series of rooms reached through wrought-iron doors down an ill-lit concrete passageway. Meeting Winston's venerable designer who would set the stone in a necklace of diamonds just for my dress! I also met the gentleman who was to guard the necklace and me at the Academy Awards. Then a mini press conference for television and the press seated behind millions of dollars' worth of jewelry — featuring the ruby, my birthstone.

I may add here that if I ever could, I would adorn myself with hundreds of carats of rubies, emeralds, sapphires — and, maybe a canary diamond or two. I love color!

I was very hesitant about Charlie Rose. I'm asleep by nine o'clock (I didn't see Johnny Carson until the night he said farewell), and although everyone was elated — "He's the best," "You'll love him, he's so knowledgeable" — I had never done a talk show. Meeting right after his interview that day with Mike Wallace, he and I immediately jibed, and spent a lively, amusing half hour together.

The success of that half hour reassured me, and I stopped with the jittering.

Next day, Regis and Kathie Lee, then *The View* with a warm and welcoming Barbara Walters. And finally, a quiet one-on-one interview for the Saturday *Today* show.

Back to Los Angeles. Suddenly it was March. The Month.

Tuesday, the third, was the last date ballots could be mailed to the Academy. That night, I presented the winning Best Picture Award at the Screen Producers Guild. Very clever, I thought. Old Rose gets to give Mr. Cameron his reward award!

The next day, Nancy Lee and I went off to a breakfast for Women in Film. I gave a short inspirational (!) talk.

On the sixth, a trip to Ojai with James Cameron to meet Beatrice Wood.

The meeting we had with that incredible woman was part of the celebration of her 105th birthday — she gave James her Beatrice Wood Film Award of the Year, a beautiful simple mask in aquamarine glazes on a tall black pedestal, and a magnificent sailing ship perched on an amethystine stone, three figures against the sail, all in the most lustrous of her "luster" glazes, purple, green, blue, moonstone.

She was dressed in a lovely blue silk sari, adorned with her heavy silver and turquoise Indian jewelry, her gray hair a crown over her smiling face. I marveled at how closely Deborah and Cameron had come in capturing her style for me.

As I've said, I felt so much like Ms. "Dada" Wood in my mind. Even as to being "aged"! She had been an actress — off and on (!) — she had become an artist, associating herself with iconoclasts, and had stayed the course. She broke tradition's "usual" techniques and forms with her patterns. In the most modest way, when I started silk-screening and designing my artist's books, several gurus cautioned, "You shouldn't do that" or "That isn't acceptable," and I was able to say, "Where is that written?" and go ahead my way, with successful results.

As she had broken through the commonplace with her ceramics — so innovative, sensuous, and witty — I had, too, with my découpage. We shared many galleries, plus Neiman Marcus, Gump's, Bullock's Wilshire, and Lord & Taylor.

Saying good-bye, after a lively luncheon where our National Treasure ate only dessert and announced her lifelong addiction to "chocolate and handsome young men," I noticed a white needle-point pillow on a sofa that had her famous logo, a black stick figure kicking up its heels and thumbing its nose to the world. Marcel Duchamp had asked her to design it for a poster for his Blindman's Ball in Greenwich Village, in 1917.

Here was a woman who had achieved greatness. The afternoon was humbling, and I thought to myself, as I have so many times before, Gloria, you've always wanted lasting fame, why did you choose such an ephemeral medium as the theater? Can anyone hear and see Duse, Bernhardt, Henry Irving, Laurence Olivier as they really were? Painting is forever, so is sculpture, music, printing. Not a theatrical performance.

Beatrice Wood died six days after our visit. She had the naughtiest, most flirtatious smile I've ever seen. Saluto, Beato!

So back to printing, Gloria!

The first crucial night of awards arrived that Sunday, March 8, when my union, the Screen Actors Guild, held its event. I opted to wear a simple long black silk and wool skirt and white silk blouse — courtesy of Escada. I felt very strongly that in my role as a founder of the guild — a resolute, dedicated, tireless organizer — I should not be decked out in sequins and tulle! (Hence my splendid restraint the day before, when Sylvia and I slipped into Asprey of London at the Beverly Hills Hotel to select appropriate jewels for the SAG Awards. I chose a forty-thousand-dollar strand of South Sea black pearls.)

Besides, Elizabeth Taylor was slated to appear that night, and I was not going to try to compete with her in the glamour department. Sixty years earlier, I probably would've!

I was very nervous, but so grateful for the Special Award. The standing ovation my peers gave me was deeply appreciated. Brought on tears. The acting award truly took second place. To see players like Dustin Hoffman, Lauren Bacall, Shirley MacLaine, Robin Williams, and Gregory Peck applauding my efforts choked me up! Fortunately, the awards committee had asked me not to stand — so I just sat there at our table, nodded, and tried not to cry.

But when Billy Zane announced that the winner of the Best Supporting Actress Award was *a tie!* it was so unexpected, it took me several minutes — while Kim Basinger accepted her award — to compose an acceptable thank you. Evidently, I did, because I received another standing ovation.

I was bleeding, but I did manage, "This is the next best thing that's happened since the birth of my beautiful daughter!" But I was miserably disappointed. On my way to being a top star, a very famous person? No way, Gloria. Even your peers aren't quite sure about your talent.

On the drive home in the limo, something at the back of my head was niggling at me. By the time we got to Brentwood and the driver stopped, I got out of the car and through the side gate as fast as my legs would carry me. Unlocked the studio door. Went to my desk.

The moment I had received my ballot for the SAG Awards, I had filled it out. I voted unashamedly for *me.* I put the big envelope on my desk, front and center, so I wouldn't forget to mail it — didn't want to send it off in unseemly haste, and the deadline was January 9. But I had been so tired and things had been so crazy . . . I rustled around on my desk, frantically, but I knew what I would find. There it was. The stamped envelope. I couldn't believe I'd done that to myself.

Of course the guild isn't telling whether the vote was truly a tie or just close. And we'll never know!

Again, flowers and messages from all my loyal friends at Lightstorm and Paramount, and *finally* one crummy arrangement from

Twentieth Century–Fox, several days old, droopy hydrangeas in a plastic pot — was my former studio still dissing me?

Next day, a luncheon given by the Academy honoring all nominees. Kim Basinger was very cordial when we met.

Now! The interview with Jay Leno. I was feeling no anxiety at all on the way over to Leno's. But when I walked up the steps behind the screen and saw the audience, or part of it, I absolutely froze, my throat closed, I couldn't articulate, my mouth wasn't working, I wasn't breathing, I felt completely paralyzed. Which was not a feeling that I had had for many, many years, not since I used to do summer theater in the East. So I thought, well, I'm going to be terrible, I'm not going to be able to talk, I'm going to stutter and stammer, and not have an idea in my head, and it's going to be a complete bust. And then I heard "Gloria Stuart!" And I knew he was coming across the stage for me. I stepped out, and there was great big applause from the audience, he reached his hand out to help me across the stage, and by the time I got to my chair, with all the cheering, I had forgotten that I had dried up. I had a great time. Jay enthusiastically announced a film clip of Shirley Temple and me in *Poor Little Rich Girl*. And ran it. A hundred or so feet into the picture, I hollered, "That's Alice Faye, that's not me!" Sure enough, it was Alice singing to Shirley.

Consternation — and a Big Laugh.

I got a charming telegram from Alice the next day — she'd seen it, too!

The next night I talked with the engaging Tom Snyder. The day after that, a sensitive interview with Renee Montaigne for NPR. Talk talk talk talk.

On to St. Petersburg for a video promotion convention! At our layover in Paris, at the extraordinary four-star restaurant Carré des Feuillants, we were greeted with elegant flair, instant acknowledgment of *our* presence! It was exhilarating! Other diners nodding and smiling. My oh my! Even in Paris! And, of course, we ordered the specialty menu — umpteen courses, all with truffles! At Catherine's Palace in St. Petersburg, two elderly peasant women came up just to shake my hand, to be there with me.

Back to the real world — and real awards.

"You're a shoo-in." That's what everybody kept saying. "Don't worry about it." And I didn't worry about it. Much.

I think when Kim Basinger won the Golden Globes, and then when my own union, the Screen Actors Guild, tied Kim with me, I began to feel that circumstances were stacking up against me. Even though people patted me on the back, and wrapped their arms around me, and wrote me notes, telephoned me and assured me that "her role was not of great substance, and yours was. . . . You held the picture together," still . . .

I was being self-protective and trying to assure myself that it wasn't going to happen and that I wouldn't be unhappy or devastated. And I wasn't.

Instead, I was just surprised! My self-protective trick had worked.

Great, great surprise.

"Will I ever have a chance again at my age?" I thought. Probably not.

So, it didn't happen. In today's parlance, Big Deal.

Maybe subconsciously I'm putting down the award. It's not that important, not that prestigious. Not that interesting, not that desirable.

Perhaps. Losing gracefully helps a great deal. If you lose with anger, or lose with resentment, lose with a sense of being cheated and show it or you can allow yourself to feel it very deeply, you can do yourself in.

So when the call came that night, I had prepared myself that I would have a smile, and I did have a smile. I understand from many of my friends that the cameras segued back to me many more times than they did to anybody else. I don't know whether it's true. I have yet to see the Academy Awards video. When I finish this book, and it's on its way to the printers, I will open a bottle of champagne all by myself, pour some into one of Suzy's Waterford crystal glasses, click on the TV, and watch the awards ceremony, wishing so very much that it was Old Rose up there onstage.

An interesting note on Hollywood fame: My interview with Larry King the next night was canceled.

When I'd reread the script months after returning from Halifax, I realized that Old Rose was the glue of the story — Cameron had interspersed her actual scenes and her voice-overs throughout the film. Many times she interpreted and/or commented on what Young Rose and the other characters, over unspoken close-ups or silent long shots, were thinking. Very effectively.

I learned, to my sorrow, that one half of my performance — live and/or voice only — had to be cut in the final film. But the same was true of everyone's.

However, I do feel that if the whole body of my performance had remained — full strength — I not only might have but would have won the Academy Award. Not to take anything away from Kim Basinger. Just that the role itself was so strong.

But could you sit for five and a half hours if Cameron hadn't cut all of us a lot?

Well, now, I was free to go back to printing, to finishing my beautiful Bachardy book, hostessing dinner parties, playing cards, mollycoddling my bonsais, arising when I felt like it, breathing deeply in my yoga poses. . . .

BEING QUIET.

I have been lucky. Since *Titanic,* I've heard — in letters, by phone — from friends and acquaintances many years gone out of my life.

But I would say that the saddest thing in my life is that Mama doesn't know what has happened to her daughter. She was so ambitious for me. She sacrificed so much for me. She hoped so much for me. She was so disappointed in me. She was so frustrated at my various points of view, my various actions. I can't say that she ever said more than "Gloria, are you sure that you're making the right decisions?" "Gloria, you have so much ahead of you, why are you quitting now?" Yes, I think about her now a great deal.

Mama died in Rome, New York, October 24, 1959. Standing by her grave in the cold Northeast, the flaming colors of autumn gone, I embraced her, and remembered Alexandre Dumas:

All human wisdom is summed up in two words . . .
Wait and hope.

EPILOGUE

*H*allelujah!
It's just two years since my last throw-the-diamond-into-the-sea shot and I have two more wonderful films on my scroll.

Small roles, but choice.

Think of it! The frustration, envy, doubt, defeat of all those years, erased forever.

Hallelujah!

A charming comedy, *The Love Letter* — a DreamWorks production — produced by and starring Kate Capshaw, was directed by the brilliant Peter Ho-sun Chan.

A fascinating film noir, *The Million Dollar Hotel*, starring Mel Gibson, was directed and produced by the wondrous Wim Wenders. With music by Bono, too!

How lucky can I be?

Just keep unrolling my scroll, dear angel. There's a lot left, I'm sure.

And I don't have to keep hoping anymore!

ACKNOWLEDGMENTS

To Gene Thompson, Dinah Sapia, Sarah Crichton, Dan Strone, Judy Ross, Judy Crichton, Michael Kaye, Nicole Marcks, Jill Church Thompson, RoseMarie London, Mike Mattil, Marvin Paige, Miriam Allen, and all our other family, friends, and colleagues who held our hands, urged us on, and rejoiced, our loving gratitude.

GLORIA STUART'S FILMOGRAPHY

Listed by release date. * *Includes character's name, production company, and film's genre (three dots = unknown).*

1932   *Street of Women,* Doris Baldwin, Warner Brothers, Drama
        The All-American, Ellen Steffens, Universal, Football
        The Old Dark House, Margaret Waverton, Universal, Horror
        Air Mail, Ruth Barnes, Universal, Adventure
1933   *Sweepings,* Phoebe Pardway Gilitziv, R.K.O., Drama
        The Invisible Man, Flora Cranley, Universal, Science Fiction
        Hollywood on Parade No. 9, Herself, Paramount, All-Star Entertainment Short
        The Girl in 419, Mary Dolan, Paramount, Crime
        The Kiss Before the Mirror, Frau Lucie Bernsdorf, Universal, Mystery
        Secret of the Blue Room, Irene Von Helldorf, Universal, Mystery Thriller
        Private Jones, Mary Gregg, Universal, War
        Laughter in Hell, Lorraine, Universal, Crime
        It's Great to Be Alive, Dorothy Wilton, Twentieth, Science Fiction Musical

---

*Films in a given year are correct, but order of release may be arbitrary.

Roman Scandals, Princess Sylvia, United Artists, Comedy
    Musical

1934   *Beloved,* Lucy Hausmann, Universal, Dramatic Musical
    The Love Captive, Alice Trask, Universal, Drama
    I'll Tell the World, Jane Hamilton, Universal, Comedy Ro-
        mance
    Here Comes the Navy, Dorothy Martin, Warner Brothers,
        Comedy Romance
    Gift of Gab, Barbara Kelton, Universal, Musical
    I Like It That Way, Anne Rogers, Universal, Musical

1935   *Laddie,* Pamela Pryor, R.K.O., Drama
    Gold Diggers of 1935, Ann Prentiss, Warner Brothers, Musical
    Maybe It's Love, Bobby Halevy, Warner Brothers, Comedy

1936   *Professional Soldier,* Countess Sonia, Twentieth, Adventure
    The Prisoner of Shark Island, Mrs. Peggy Mudd, Twentieth,
        Biography
    Poor Little Rich Girl, Margaret Allen, Twentieth, Comedy
        Drama Musical
    Girl Overboard, Mary Chesbrooke, Universal, Mystery
    The Girl on the Front Page, Joan Langford, Universal, Comedy
        Drama
    36 Hours to Kill, Anne Marvis, Twentieth, Drama
    Wanted: Jane Turner, Doris Martin, R.K.O., Crime Drama
    The Crime of Dr. Forbes, Ellen Godfrey, Twentieth, Crime
        Drama

1937   *Life Begins in College,* Janet O'Hara, Twentieth, Comedy
    The Lady Escapes, Linda Ryan, Twentieth, Comedy

1938   *Keep Smiling,* Carol Walters, Twentieth, Comedy
    The Lady Objects, Ann Adams, Columbia Pictures, Drama
    Island in the Sky, Julie Hayes, Twentieth, Crime
    Change of Heart, Carol Murdock, Twentieth, Golfing Romance
    Rebecca of Sunnybrook Farm, Gwen Warren, Twentieth,
        Comedy Drama Musical

Time Out for Murder, Margie Ross, Twentieth, Mystery

1939   *It Could Happen to You,* Doris Winslow, Twentieth, Comedy
Mystery

Winner Take All, Julie Harrison, Twentieth, Drama

The Three Musketeers, Queen Anne, Twentieth, Action Adventure Comedy

1943   *Here Comes Elmer,* Glenda Forbes, Republic, Comedy

1944   *The Whistler,* Alice Walker, Columbia, Mystery Thiller

Enemy of Women, Bertha, Monogram, War Drama

1946   *She Wrote the Book,* Phyllis Fowler, Universal, Comedy

1975   *The Legend of Lizzie Borden* (TV), Store Customer, Paramount Television, Drama

Adventures of the Queen (TV), . . . , Irwin Allen/Twentieth, Action

Barbary Coast (TV), . . . , Paramount Television, . . .

1976   *Flood* (TV), . . . , Irwin Allen/Warners Television, Adventure

Gibbsville (TV), . . . , Columbia Pictures Television, Drama

1977   *In the Glitter Palace* (TV), Mrs. Bowman, Columbia Pictures Television, Crime Drama

1978   *The Two Worlds of Jennie Logan* (TV), Roberta, CBS Television, Romance

1979   *The Incredible Journey of Doctor Meg Laurel* (TV), Rose Hooper, Columbia Pictures Television, Adventure Drama

The Best Place to Be, . . . , . . . , Drama

1981   *Merlene of the Movies* (TV), Evangeline Eaton, Lilac Productions, Drama

1982   *My Favorite Year,* Mrs. Horn, Brooksfilms, Comedy

1984   *Mass Appeal,* Mrs. Curry, Operation Cork, Religious

Second Sight: A Love Story (TV), . . .

1986   *Wildcats,* Mrs. Connoly, Warner Brothers, Comedy

1988   *Shootdown* (TV), Gertrude, . . . , Drama

1997   *Titanic,* Old Rose, Lightstorm Entertainment, Twentieth, Paramount, Historical Disaster

1999   *The Love Letter,* Eleanor, DreamWorks SKG, Comedy
   The Million Dollar Hotel, Jessica, Icon Entertainment
    International/Road Movies Filmproduktion, Black Comedy

DETAILS UNKNOWN
   Pursuit of Truth
   Second Sight
   Jailbreak
   The Waltons (TV episode), Lorimar Television, Drama
   Murder, She Wrote (TV episode), Universal Television, Mystery

INDEX